George Orwell and the Origins of *1984*

George Orwell and the Origins of *1984*

WILLIAM STEINHOFF

ANN ARBOR

THE UNIVERSITY OF MICHIGAN PRESS

To my wife Rosannah Steinhoff

ACKNOWLEDGMENTS

THIS BOOK owes much to my association with the University of Michigan. Throughout the writing I have benefited from the encouragement and patience of colleagues. Among those in the Department of English Language and Literature, I am particularly grateful for specific counsel from Professors John Arthos, Arno Bader, William Coles, Russell Fraser, and Warner Rice. Professor James H. Meisel of the Department of Political Science also read the manuscript and offered useful advice. The help of Miss Mary E. Rollman of the University Graduate Library was invaluable. Research for the project was accomplished in part through the support of the Rackham Endowment Fund of the Horace A. Rackham School of Graduate Studies. Farther afield, Professor Josephine Miles of the University of California at Berkeley and Dr. Robert Coles of Harvard University were unstinting in their comments at a time when friendly reassurance was most needed.

All scholars of the period in which Orwell wrote must be grateful for the existence of the Orwell Archive in the library of University College, London. Its curator, Ian Angus, Deputy Librarian, gave me free use of the materials there and was generous with his help on many occasions, as were members of his staff. The late John D. Gordan, curator of the Berg Collection at the New York Public Library, was likewise helpful.

Special thanks are also due Mrs. Sonia Orwell for permission to quote from her husband's writings, including *The Collected Essays, Journalism and Letters of George Orwell*, which she edited with Ian Angus. Permission to quote from the writings of James Burnham was kindly granted by Mr. Burnham and the John Day Company.

CONTENTS

PART ONE

Literary Forerunners of *1984*

I

UTOPIAS AND OTHER FICTION

GEORGE ORWELL told Richard Rees that in Burma he once read an article in a "mildly avant-garde magazine" and disapproved of it so much that he "set the magazine up at the end of his verandah and used it for target practice."[1] Several years later, having given up that kind of literary criticism, Orwell began appearing before the public as a left-wing writer with a mind of his own. The target practice had by then turned into something like guerrilla warfare, not merely against the abuses of the time but also against those we have now learned, rather self-consciously, to call "the intellectuals." Even if one does not accept as finally just V. S. Pritchett's characterization of Orwell as "the wintry conscience of his generation," we must acknowledge that one of the principal features of his career is his persistent criticism, even nagging, of those who, like himself, made it their life's work to present, analyze, and advocate ideas.

One can go further. In 1949, when controversy arose over the meaning of *1984*, Orwell made a statement about his purpose in writing that book in which he said, among other important things, "I believe that totalitarian ideas have taken root in the minds of intellectuals everywhere, and I have tried to draw these ideas out to their logical consequences."[2] The view taken in this book is that Orwell's development as a writer coincided with his growing knowledge and hatred of totalitarianism and of the mentality that espoused and practiced it.

Orwell was singularly constant in his adherence to the code or criteria by which he judged conduct, and to a considerable extent ideas, for the two lay close together in his mind. This code—which, as more than one critic has agreed, may be summarized in the word "decency"—must have been formulated early in his life and hardly amended as he grew older. Its implications appear more than once in the following pages when it is a matter of explaining why Orwell accepted or rejected an idea or a program. But his rejection of left- and right-wing totalitarianism was not based only on a temperamental repugnance hardened into habit. It was grounded also in detailed

3

knowledge gained from reading and personal experience. Throughout his adult life he was preoccupied with certain questions: What is and ought to be the relation between the individual and other individuals, particularly when the power of others manifests itself in the form of the state? Why did people permit a society to develop which they knew might enslave them? What were the forms such a society might take? What were the motives of those who shaped the system? How did they obtain and keep their power? What were the relations between fascism, socialism, and totalitarianism? Was a totalitarian structure of society inevitable?

In the course of trying to enlarge our knowledge about Orwell's answers to such vast questions I have come to believe, and it is the thesis of this book, that the best way to approach them—and to understand both the comprehensiveness and richly significant detail of *1984*—is to regard that novel as a culminating work which expresses, almost epitomizes, a lifetime's ideas, attitudes, events, and reading. The history of the atmosphere, details, insights, and judgments in *1984* is embedded in Orwell's life and earlier work. Parts of this background can be isolated and studied, though only incompletely and uncertainly, for no full account of his adult life has been published.[3] We know something about the books Orwell read, and the contents and significance of some of them are examined in detail in the following pages, but beyond these there must be others now undetectable. *Homage to Catalonia,* in addition to its other merits, is an invaluable personal record of a collision between idea and reality and of beliefs abandoned, altered, and adopted because of that collision, but for all the similar collisions which must have occurred the record is sketchy or missing. Nevertheless, in what we know of Orwell's life and work, especially his reading and what he wrote about his reading, there is a considerable body of unexploited evidence which can be used to deepen our understanding of *1984*.

The following three chapters survey the more important works which appear to have contributed in some way to Orwell's last novel. The survey is not comprehensive. Nothing is said, for example, about Samuel Butler's *Erewhon,* though Butler was a favorite of Orwell's and *Erewhon* a utopia he praised, for there is only the most general connection between it and what he wrote. The same is true of such books as W. H. Hudson's *A Crystal Age* and Ernest Bramah's *The Secret of the League.* On the other hand, some writings are so full of suggestion when considered in the context of *1984* that they merit comment even when one cannot be certain of a direct connection.

The intention in these chapters is to convey a sense of the solid base of Orwell's reading on which, in part, *1984* rests. Some of the relations between this body of writing and *1984* are inferred as each work is considered, but other inferences about them are postponed until later chapters. The first important aim is thus to call the reader's attention to books known to Orwell which touch on the themes in *1984*. The second is to make readers aware of the cumulative force of the material exposed here and brought to bear on the argument in the latter part of the book.

Many of Orwell's fears and hopes about the shape of the future were responses to what he read. All his life he was interested in what he once called "utopia books,"[4] and he wrote about them frequently. The most important contemporary writer of such works was, of course, H. G. Wells, and he was one of the favorite authors of Orwell's boyhood:

> Back in the nineteen-hundreds it was a wonderful experience for a boy to discover H. G. Wells. There you were, in a world of pedants, clergymen and golfers, with your future employers exhorting you to "get on or get out," your parents systematically warping your sexual life, and your dull-witted schoolmasters sniggering over their Latin tags; and here was this wonderful man who could tell you about the inhabitants of the planets and the bottom of the sea, and who *knew* that the future was not going to be what respectable people imagined.[5]

Writing on another occasion about Wells's knowledge of things to come, Orwell suggested that his novels were more than just interesting visions of the future; they contributed to shaping it:

> How far any novelist really influences contemporary events is doubtful, but Mr. Wells has certainly been the most influential novelist of our time, at any rate in the English-speaking world. If, up to the year 1930, any mere writer could look about him and say, "This is my work. I did this," that writer was H. G. Wells.[6]

When Emmanuel Goldstein, the author of the Book in *1984*, says, "In the early twentieth century, the vision of a future society unbelievably rich, leisured, orderly and efficient—a glittering antiseptic world of glass and steel and snow-white concrete—was part of the consciousness of nearly every literate person,"[7] that vision epitomized Wells's utopias.

Not everyone will agree with this estimate of Wells's importance, but his influence on Orwell himself is unmistakable. *Coming Up for Air* is a comic novel in the manner of *Mr. Britling Sees It Through* or *The History of Mr. Polly,* in which Orwell, like Wells, depicts an apparently insignificant, ordinary man trying to discover a personal meaning in the great events and institutions of his time. Orwell said that it suggested "Wells watered down." George Bowling's excursion into the past and Winston Smith's dream of the Golden Country have something of Wells's gift for making readers feel what life was like in the "golden years between 1890 and 1914,"[8] a talent for which Orwell professed his admiration. Even the pseudonym under which Orwell chose to write echoes the names of the earlier author.

More important to this study are Wells's ideas foreshadowing the image of the future, since Orwell's work contains scarcely a topic related to politics and social systems which cannot be found in Wells's books, especially *The New Machiavelli, The Shape of Things to Come, When the Sleeper Wakes,* and *The Island of Dr. Moreau.* One such topic is the crucial position of intellectuals in the struggle for power that will take place in the World State. Others are the importance of a simplified world language; the constraints that oblige a successful ruling class to be austere and fanatical; the need to conquer the human will if one is to rule the world; and the resort to "mental reconstruction," or what Wells calls "psychic surgery" in *When the Sleeper Wakes,* in order to keep the future inhabitants of the world tractable. This novel suggests also a device we encounter in *1984:* the dictatorship perpetually reenacting the drama of crushing its enemy. It contains as well the germ of the idea, used to such good effect in *1984,* that a ruling class seeking to control the future must begin by making sure of its grip on the past, for the eruption of the past into the present and the inability of the aristocrats to control the past in the person of the Sleeper, "the coveted man out of the past,"[9] cause the revolution that Wells describes.

There is a considerable likeness between Wells's view of the masses and Orwell's representation of the Proles, Orwell's view being foreshadowed of course by his reading of Jack London and the experiences narrated in *Down and Out in Paris and London.* Wells, like Orwell, denied the usual Socialist claim that the future would produce, in Wells's words, a "splendid Working Man cheated out of his innate glorious possibilities," who would "arise and dash this scoundrelly and scandalous system of private ownership to fragments."[10] Both writers thought that the poor and weak were more likely to become tools and victims of an intellectual elite than to have any part in governing themselves. Wells says, in *The New Machiavelli:*

> Even the tragic and inspiring idea of Marx, that the poor were near-ing a limit of painful experience, and awakening to a sense of intoler-able wrongs, began to develop into the more appalling conception that the poor were simply in a witless uncomfortable inconclusive way—"muddling along"; that they wanted nothing very definitely nor very urgently, that mean fears enslaved them and mean satisfactions decoyed them.[11]

In this book Orwell also met, perhaps for the first time, the idea that an important reason for the intellectuals' attraction to socialism was "a hypertrophied sense of order," the same motive that caused Wells in such novels as *Tono-Bungay* to rage at the inefficiency and muddle of the ill-organized world of the twentieth century. Wells himself was at least occasionally aware of the dangers implicit in his high regard for orderliness and system, and it was partly this realiza-tion that led him to caricature the Webbs and their intention of creating a new ruling class of experts. Like the *maires du palais*, they would attain power at last because they had made everyone else de-pendent on them. Wells has Altiora Bailey, who was modeled on Beatrice Webb, say:

> We want to suggest to you . . . that from the mere necessities of convenience elected bodies *must* avail themselves more and more of the services of expert officials. . . . The more complicated and techni-cal affairs become, the less confidence the elected official will have in himself. We want to suggest that these expert officials must neces-sarily develop into a new class and a very powerful class in the community. We want to organize that. It may be *the* power of the future.[12]

But Wells also approved this development. As he saw it, only three or four thousand persons in the whole English-speaking com-munity were responsible for "all the thought, all the art, all the in-crements of knowledge,"[13] and this aristocracy of understanding and purpose—supplemented by the expert officials—would create the new society. What disembodied experts like the Baileys lacked was the vitality which was to come from sexual energy released from its in-hibitions, and one point stressed by Wells is that sex is becoming "collectively portentous"; the liberation of women will culminate in "a justifiable vision of the ordered world."[14]

Wells's constant themes are progress through science and the eternal struggle between progress and the status quo, ending usually in a victory for progress and, in Orwell's words, a "vision of humanity, 'liberated' by the machine, as a race of enlightened sunbathers whose sole topic of conversation is their own superiority to their ancestors."[15] One of the exceptions to this optimistic formula, however, is *When the Sleeper Wakes,* perhaps the Wellsian utopia that interested Orwell the most:

> He draws a picture of a glittering, strangely sinister world in which the privileged classes live a life of shallow gutless hedonism, and the workers, reduced to a state of utter slavery and sub-human ignorance, toil like troglodytes in caverns underground.[16]

On another occasion, discussing literary prophecies of fascism, Orwell wrote that "everyone who has ever read *The Sleeper Wakes* remembers it."[17]

This hedonistic utopia has gone wrong because the morale of the ruling class has been destroyed through self-indulgence. "In the old days," says one of the characters, "man was armed against Pain, now he is eager for Pleasure."[18] The highest achievement in this society, except for the unrestrained use of power, is the creation of "pleasure cities" for the use of the plutocracy. Wells also supposes the existence of "black belt territories" which are not part of the "cosmopolitan social organization." These are exploited by the ruling class, especially for the purpose of securing mercenary troops. Sport and gambling have been immensely expanded as a means of controlling the slaves in the Labor Companies. The street corners are equipped with loudspeakers which broadcast "the world-wide falsehoods of the news-tellers."[19] These and other details of the novel are interesting to readers of *1984.*

Orwell called this work a "pessimistic Utopia"; but, as he says, Wells's pessimism stems merely from his supposing that progress has taken a wrong turning. The only evil Wells imagines is inequality, which he believed could be removed by overthrowing the privileged class and creating a world socialism instead of a world capitalism.

Orwell believed that the trouble with Wells's outlook was his "confusion of mechanical progress with justice, liberty and common decency."[20] Wells identified the scientist with progress, and science with common sense; but for Orwell the equation does not hold good. Both Wells's pessimism and his optimism were shallow, he thought, and Wells himself was "too sane to understand the modern world. . . . He was, and still is, quite incapable of understanding that nationalism, religious bigotry and feudal loyalty are far more powerful forces than what he himself would describe as sanity."[21] In a word, Wells did not give sufficient weight to the irrational element in human motives and interests.

Another of Wells's stories, *The Island of Dr. Moreau*, is important to us for its connections with both *1984* and *Animal Farm*. The world of Dr. Moreau's island is, in effect, a state in which an elite rules a group of slaves. What makes the society extraordinary is that the slaves are animals who have been given certain human characteristics through Dr. Moreau's skill as a surgeon; by his experiments in vivisection Dr. Moreau aims to create a human being, presumably in his own image. The primary means of controlling the slaves is, of course, his surgical procedures, but he has also devised a set of commandments known as the Law, which is impressed on the flickering humanity of the beasts, first through surgery and then through repetition:

> Not to go on all-fours; that is the Law.
> Are we not Men?
> Not to suck up Drink; that is the Law.
> Are we not Men?
> Not to eat Fish or Flesh; that is the Law.
> Are we not Men?
> Not to claw the Bark of Trees; *that* is the Law.
> Are we not Men?
> Not to chase other Men; that is the Law.
> Are we not Men?

The Law has another formula, of which the following is a sample:

> *His* is the House of Pain.
> *His* is the Hand that makes.
> *His* is the Hand that wounds.
> *His* is the Hand that heals.[22]

This Law is supposedly inviolable, but in the inevitable revolt against Dr. Moreau's dictatorship the Law is progressively disregarded. We note, too, that some of Moreau's more successful experiments are known as the swine people, and there is especially a fierce swine-hyena.

Dr. Moreau is, of course, the epitome of the mad scientist who seeks to satisfy his curiosity at whatever cost. The emphasis he puts on the usefulness of pain is, however, remarkable: "But I will conquer yet! Each time I dip a living creature into the bath of burning pain,

I say, 'This time I will burn out all the animal; this time I will make a rational creature of my own!' After all, what is ten years? Men have been a hundred thousand in the making."[23] With such melodramatic statements as this we are not far from O'Brien and Winston Smith.

It would be difficult to exaggerate the influence Wells exerted on Orwell, who called him "this wonderful man." There is the direct influence evidenced by specific ideas that appear both in his work and Orwell's. There is the negative effect of Orwell's reaction against Wells's principal themes, a reaction brought on by Wells's neglect of human issues in favor of abstract theories. Not only was Orwell markedly receptive to Wells's vision of what the future might be like, down to the specific details of his prophecies, but he responded also to something more pervasive, Wells's sense of what was important—the organization of society and its leadership, the relation of sex to politics, the relation of the past to the present and the future —the whole bias of the writer's mind which leads him to work in one direction rather than another.

These are matters to which we will return when we consider *1984* more closely. For the moment it will be enough to quote Orwell's tribute to Wells in order to emphasize his own sense of indebtedness: "More than any other writer, perhaps, he has altered the landscape of the contemporary mind. Because of him the moon seems nearer and the Stone Age more imaginable, and for that we are immeasurably in his debt."[24]

For a long time Wells thought that socialism and the World State would be the rational outcome of efforts by scientists and revolutionaries to alter capitalist society. A second writer whose work interested Orwell and in important ways foreshadowed *1984* had no such confidence. Jack London is credited by Orwell with having the insight to realize "that the transition to Socialism was not going to be automatic or even easy."[25] As London put it, "Out of the decay of self-seeking capitalism, it was held, would arise that flower of the ages, the Brotherhood of Man. Instead of which, appalling alike to us who look back and to those that lived at the time, capitalism, rotten-ripe, sent forth that monstrous offshoot, the Oligarchy."[26] Orwell detected a streak of savagery in London's nature enabling him to understand more readily than Wells could how the Socialist dream might turn into a nightmare, and in any event that a society ministering solely to hedonistic aims could not last.[27]

Orwell's friend Rayner Heppenstall thought he shared this streak of brutality with London. Whether or not we agree, it is certainly true that the emphasis on force and pitiless fanaticism is what Orwell found psychologically persuasive in *The Iron Heel*. London's book is a far from subtle demonstration that the brute exercise of unrestrained power is necessary and pleasing to fanatics, and Orwell thought this to be a better explanation of why some men act as they do than Wells's imputation to them of a sane desire for a better world. In fact, Orwell said about London's analysis of the rulers' mentality in *The Iron Heel:* "It's one of the best statements of the outlook of a ruling class—of the outlook that a ruling class must have if it's to survive—that has ever been written."[28] London emphasizes the utter confidence of his Plutocrats, their self-satisfied conception of their own righteousness, and he is certain that they will be overcome only by those who are equally fanatical.

The "Iron Heel" of London's novel is the ruling Oligarchy, served by mercenaries whom Orwell compared to the Nazi SS.[29] They are pitiless tyrants who maintain themselves in power for some three hundred years, crushing the group London also calls the Proles and justifying their brutality by their claim to be saving civilization. London's certainty that force (and pleasure in the use of force) will characterize the way the Plutocrats coerce the masses is amply recorded through the medium of an old-fashioned rhetoric. Challenged by Everhard, an early leader of the Revolution, one of the Oligarchs responds: "Our reply shall be couched in terms of lead. We are in power. Nobody will deny it. By virtue of that power we shall remain in power."[30] And further:

> We will grind you revolutionists down under our heel, and we shall walk upon your faces. The world is ours, we are its lords, and ours it shall remain. As for the host of labor, it has been in the dirt since history began, and I read history aright. And in the dirt it shall remain so long as I and mine and those that come after us have the power. There is the word. It is the king of words—Power. Not God, not Mammon, but Power. Pour it over your tongue till it tingles with it. Power.[31]

But Everhard, the revolutionary, is identical in temperament and ambition to the Oligarchs he opposes. His reply to this speech is its echo:

> Power will be the arbiter, as it always has been the arbiter. It is a struggle of classes. . . . It does not matter whether it is one year, ten, or a thousand—your class shall be dragged down. And it shall be done by power. We of the labor hosts have conned that word over till our minds are all atingle with it. Power. It is a kingly word.[32]

The psychological truth Orwell found at the heart of *The Iron Heel*, which he encountered again in the writings of James Burnham and which reappears in modified form in *1984*, is augmented by a number of other resemblances worthy of notice. London's book, for example, begins with a long philosophical discussion about the nature of the real world, an essential analysis which Orwell with better judgment dramatized as the Book and located about two-thirds of the way through *1984*, where it impedes the action less. London, like Orwell, was fascinated by language and its effect on man's ability to think:

> The people of that age were phrase slaves. The abjectness of their servitude is incomprehensible to us. There was a magic in words greater than the conjuror's art. So befuddled and chaotic were their minds that the utterance of a single word could negative the generalizations of a lifetime of serious research and thought. Such a word was the adjective *Utopian*. The mere utterance of it could damn any scheme, no matter how sanely conceived, of economic amelioration or regeneration. Vast populations grew frenzied over such phrases as "an honest dollar" and "a full dinner pail." The coinage of such phrases was considered strokes of genius.[33]

Orwell claimed that London had regained a certain popularity during the war because he had foreseen something of the quality of life that characterized Nazi Germany; for example, "that peculiar horror of totalitarian society, the way in which suspected enemies of the régime *simply disappear*."[34] Orwell had reason to commend London's prescience, since the *Nacht und Nebel Erlass* was a recognized Nazi terror tactic, one which Orwell himself used in authenticating the atmosphere of *1984*.[35] It is not so remarkable that London's three classes—Plutocrats, Middle Class, Proletariat—are duplicated by Orwell's High, Middle, and Low, or that Orwell and London both think it necessary to explain that the surplus of goods has to be disposed of somehow, in *1984* by warfare and in *The Iron Heel* by vast expenditures on "wonder-cities," an idea that London got from H. G. Wells. It is, however, notable that the construction of one of these cities, marking the consolidation of the regime, is to be completed in the year 1984. London puts it this way:

> Ardis was completed in 1942 A.D., while Asgard was not completed until 1984 A.D. It was fifty-two years in the building, during which time a permanent army of half a million serfs was employed. At times these numbers swelled to over a million—without any account being taken of the hundreds of thousands of the labor castes and the artists.[36]

Two other recollections of London's work were probably in Orwell's mind when he came to write *1984*. Discussing the proletariat, London explains in a footnote the origin of the term and its relation to the Latin word *proles*. Orwell, commenting in 1944 on London's use of the word, observed that few readers knew it had originally meant people who were valuable to the state only as the rearers of offspring.[37] Finally, the title of London's novel vividly recalls O'Brien's remark: "If you want a picture of the future, imagine a boot stamping on a human face—forever."[38]

But if neither London nor Orwell was able to believe in Wells's brand of rationality as a guide to the future, and if their work and their characters exhibit certain other likenesses, there is nevertheless a profound difference between the two men's interpretation of the totalitarianism they both envisioned. Orwell summed it up when he praised London for his understanding of the ruling class but strongly doubted his sympathy for the weak. "London was a Socialist," he wrote, "with the instincts of a buccaneer and the education of a nineteenth-century materialist."[39] A comparison of *The Iron Heel* and *1984* brings out significant resemblances between the two authors. The differences are equally evident in *Animal Farm* and *The Call of the Wild* or *White Fang*.

Orwell did not regard Aldous Huxley as one who, like Wells, had helped create the modern mind, but he believed that *Brave New World* marked an advance on the eager Wellsian acceptance of machine civilization and faith in scientific progress. *Brave New World* was a "brilliant caricature of the present," though it "casts no light on the future" because the hedonism of Huxley's imagined society, especially the interest in having a good time exhibited by its ruling class, would destroy it within two generations.[40]

Even so, Orwell found Huxley's outlook superior to Wells's. The difference lay in the contrast the two writers present between the "over-confident and the deflated, between the man who believes innocently in Progress and the man who happens to have been born later and has therefore lived to see that Progress, as it was conceived in the early days of the aeroplane, is just as much of a swindle as reaction."[41] As a "memorable assault on the more fat-bellied type of perfectionism," he said that Huxley's book "probably expresses what a majority of thinking people feel about machine civilization."[42]

Despite the parallels one finds between *Brave New World* and *1984*—the caricature of certain features of modern life like increased drug-taking, the tendency toward the development of a new sort of hierarchical society, the intellectuals as rulers, the aggressive, liberated young woman—Huxley's book was most useful to Orwell because it provoked him to objections. Geoffrey Ashe has cited some of the deliberate contradictions introduced by Orwell in his own novel of the future: the shoddiness and inefficiency of things in 1984 are denials of the cleanliness and efficiency of Huxley's world; compared to soma, Victory Gin is unpalatable and violent; the Two-Minutes' Hate is a debased form of the cult meetings in honor of Our Ford; the distortion of sex into war hysteria contrasts with the casual simplicity of sex in *Brave New World*.[43]

On the surface at least, a closer parallel to 1984 than any so far mentioned is Cyril Connolly's story "Year Nine," which Irving Howe called "a capsule anticipation of Orwell's book."[44] Seemingly Orwell never commented on this remarkable attack against the totalitarian state, but there can be little doubt that he read it. It was first published in the *New Statesman*,[45] which Orwell habitually read, and it was reprinted in *The Condemned Playground*, which Orwell reviewed for the *Observer*, calling it "an intelligent and amusing book."[46] Orwell's long association with Connolly, which began in school, makes his acquaintance with the story even more likely.

Despite its brevity, "Year Nine" has a surprisingly large number of resemblances to 1984. "Our Leader" is a ruthless, omnipresent dictator. Intellectual freedom is denied the ordinary citizen; no one is allowed to express feelings or opinions about works of art that are contrary to those held officially. The man and woman in the story are under constant surveillance by party officials and by machines, and all mail is censored. Like Winston Smith, Connolly's principal character keeps a diary. He records there the hostility of his fellow citizens and their efforts to do "everything to attract attention to me by causing me to fail in my work." According to official doctrine, private love and personal friendships are vestiges of a degenerate past when women wore gaudy clothes and painted their lips. In this society sexual life is regulated by the state, and the community is organized into a strict hierarchy. Workers are "inspired by a true party horror of bad work," highest priority going to work in preparation for war. Accused persons in "Year Nine" are first tortured, then interrogated and criticized if they do not confess, and at last cruelly executed. Before his death, the condemned character in the story acknowledges his "crime" and admits that he has been treated with great kindness.

As far as details are concerned, *1984* resembles *Gulliver's Travels* less than it does "Year Nine," but from the point of view of the subjects that interested their authors, to say nothing of their tone, the two books are profoundly related. Some critics have even seen a temperamental and ideological likeness between Swift and Orwell and have applied to Orwell himself, though I believe mistakenly, the phrase "Tory anarchist," which he used to characterize Swift.

Orwell wrote that *Gulliver's Travels* had been presented to him on his eighth birthday and that "its fascination seems inexhaustible."[47] It is not surprising that evidence of this lifelong interest should appear in *1984*, and in Orwell's use of animals in his own satire, quite apart from any stylistic resemblances arising from Orwell's admiration of Swift's gift for clear, powerful prose.[48]

The relation of the individual to the state is one of the principal themes of *Gulliver's Travels*, and Orwell considered Swift's attack on totalitarianism, especially in Part III, to be his most telling contribution to political theory. Swift had, he said, an "extraordinarily clear pre-vision of the spy-haunted 'police State,' with its endless heresy-hunts and treason trials, all really designed to neutralize popular discontent by changing it into war hysteria."[49] In fact, the passage about the Kingdom of Tribnia, with its multiplicity of informers, plots, and suspected persons, came so close to twentieth-century reality that he felt "positively in the middle of the Russian purges."[50]

Besides these ideas, the dictators of Laputa have a school for Political Projectors which might almost be found in Oceania, for the professors "invent simplified languages, write books by machinery, educate their pupils by inscribing the lesson on a wafer and causing them to swallow it, or propose to abolish individuality altogether by cutting off part of the brain of one man and grafting it on the head of another." In calling attention to this passage, Orwell remarked that Swift showed "a perception that one of the aims of totalitarianism is not merely to make sure that people will think the right thoughts, but actually to make them *less conscious*."[51]

Part IV of *Gulliver's Travels* describes a less conventional totalitarianism than those of the earlier sections, one which Swift pretends to approve because it was governed by reason, though reason of a peculiar sort. As Orwell says:

> The "Reason" which he so admires in the Houyhnhnms does not primarily mean the power of drawing logical inferences from observed

facts. Although he never defines it, it appears in most contexts to mean either common sense—i.e. acceptance of the obvious and contempt for quibbles and abstractions—or absence of passion and superstition. In general he assumes that we know all that we need to know already, and merely use our knowledge incorrectly.[52]

The Houyhnhnms are governed by this sort of reason, whose commands are conveyed through advice or exhortation. Paradoxically the result of such a permissive system is a form of totalitarianism:

> In a Society in which there is no law, and in theory no compulsion, the only arbiter of behavior is public opinion. But public opinion, because of the tremendous urge to conformity in gregarious animals, is less tolerant than any system of law. When human beings are governed by "thou shalt not," the individual can practice a certain amount of eccentricity: when they are supposedly governed by "love" or "reason," he is under continuous pressure to make him behave and think in exactly the same way as everyone else.[53]

This is the same idea that led Orwell to establish a Ministry of Love in Oceania, whose function it was to make citizens like Winston Smith think the right thoughts. In the effectiveness of this feature of their society, the Houyhnhnms even surpassed Oceania, for "they had reached, in fact, the highest stage of totalitarian organization, the stage when conformity has become so general that there is no need for a police force."[54] Furthermore, the Houyhnhnms' "reason," like a decision made by the Inner Party or the Pope speaking *ex cathedra*, is infallible: "In other words," Orwell wrote, "we know everything already, so why should dissident opinions be tolerated? The totalitarian Society of the Houyhnhnms, where there can be no freedom and no development, follows naturally from this."[55]

Another of Orwell's favorite writers who had something to do with *1984* is G. K. Chesterton, and although one cannot be certain that Orwell read *The Napoleon of Notting Hill* his extensive knowledge of Chesterton makes it seem likely. One can perhaps find only coincidence in the fact that this story is concerned with events happening in London in the year 1984, but two features in it would have engaged Orwell's interest. The first is Chesterton's scorn for people like H. G. Wells, Cecil Rhodes, and Sidney Webb, because in their role as prophets "they took something or other that was certainly going on in their time, and then said that it would go on more and more until something extraordinary happened."[56] The fault attributed to these latter-day prophets was a habit of mind that Orwell was particularly severe about when he came to discuss James Burnham in that role. The other feature of this book is that 1984 is represented as a time when a world-wide truce exists. Chesterton called it "the compromise or deadlock which had made foreign wars impossible," and it is this truce that in his story permits a local war to occur.[57] Orwell, of course, drew a more sinister inference from the idea of deadlock.

We can be certain that Orwell had read *The Man Who Was Thursday* because he compared it to C. S. Lewis's *That Hideous Strength* in a review of the Lewis book published in 1945.[58] Chesterton's ideas about the future, like those of Wells and Hilaire Belloc, stayed in Orwell's mind. In one of his essays on James Burnham, he remarked, "Chesterton, in a less methodical way [than Hilaire Belloc] predicted the disappearance of democracy and private property, and the rise of a slave society which might be called either capitalist or Communist."[59]

The evidence to be found in *The Man Who Was Thursday* is more particular than this. The novel's action concerns a vast conspiracy of radicals whose aim is to conquer and destroy humanity. The conspiratorial network is composed of intellectuals—philosophers, artists, scientists—who hate the institutions human beings have created, such as the family and the state. The intellectuals also hate ordinary men and intend to annihilate them after seizing power. The conspirators are arranged in two groups: the inner and outer rings, or the priesthood and the laity. The members of the outer ring are said to speak of "the paradise of the future." So do the members of the inner ring, but as one of the characters says:

> In their mouths these happy phrases have a horrible meaning. They are under no illusions; they are too intellectual to think that man upon this earth can ever be quite free of original sin and the struggle. And they mean death. When they say that mankind shall be free at last, they mean that mankind shall commit suicide. When they talk of a paradise without right or wrong, they mean the grave. They have but two objects, to destroy first humanity and then themselves.[60]

A number of policemen have infiltrated the conspiracy, and to help them a man named Gabriel Syme has been drawn in. Unlike the Syme of *1984*, who is a philologist, Chesterton's character is a poet. He is said to be a rebel against rebellion, a rebel for "sanity." That was the only direction left to him, since all his family were extremists who had preempted the usual possibilities. It is Syme who becomes the "Thursday" of the inner ring and who helps wreck the conspiracy.

In addition to the similarity of theme, several details are worth mentioning for their possible bearing on *1984*. As Syme confronts a crisis having to do with opposition to the leader of the inner ring and the threat of discovery, he, like Winston Smith, hears some popular music:

> A barrel-organ in the street suddenly sprang with a jerk into a jovial tune. . . . That jingling music seemed full of the vivacity, the vulgarity, and the irrational valour of the poor, who in all those unclean streets were all clinging to the decencies and the charities of Christendom. . . . But he did feel himself as the ambassador of all these common and kindly people in the street, who every day marched into battle to the music of the barrel-organ. And this high pride in being human had lifted him unaccountably to an infinite height above the monstrous men around him. For an instant, at least, he looked down upon all their sprawling eccentricities from the starry pinnacle of the commonplace.[61]

We have in this passage, obviously, a number of relevant details placed in a context remarkably like that in *1984*.

Furthermore, "the starry pinnacle of the commonplace" is also symbolized here—as we shall see it is in *1984*—by the equation $2 + 2 = 4$. Syme, like Winston Smith, is haunted by his own loneliness:

> Through all this ordeal his root horror had been isolation, and there are no words to express the abyss between isolation and having one ally. It may be conceded to the mathematicians that four is twice two. But two is not twice one; two is two thousand times one. That is why, in spite of a hundred disadvantages, the world will always return to monogamy.[62]

In *1984*, the commonplace equation is consoling for a different reason, for there it is evidence of the existence of objective reality. Winston Smith realizes the significance of the Inner Party's attack on this concept, and so, in Chesterton's novel, does Gabriel Syme:

> Was there anything apart from what it seemed? The Marquis had taken off his nose and turned out to be a detective. Might he not just as well take off his head and turn out to be a hobgoblin? Was not everything, after all, like this bewildering woodland, this dance of dark and light? Everything only a glimpse, the glimpse always unforeseen, and always forgotten. For Gabriel Syme had found in the heart of the sun-splashed wood what many modern painters had

found there. He had found the thing which the modern people call Impressionism, which is another name for that final skepticism which can find no floor to the universe.

As a man in an evil dream strains himself to scream and wake, Syme strove with a sudden effort to fling off this last and worst of his fancies.[63]

Thus Chesterton describes what was to become one of the major themes of *1984*, the fear that by some means O'Brien's organized skepticism would corrode all possibility of believing in the reality of the external world and the trustworthiness of common sense.

Still another of Orwell's favorites, Rudyard Kipling, wrote at least three stories that may be related to Orwell's work: "The Walking Delegate," "As Easy as A.B.C.," and "With the Night Mail." "The Walking Delegate" is interesting principally, of course, in relation to *Animal Farm*, since it is about a projected revolt of farm animals —in this story horses—against man. It reminds us that the idea for *Animal Farm* came to Orwell when he saw a child leading a draft horse along a country lane and was struck by the contrast between the horse's strength and the fragility of the child, whom it nevertheless obeyed.

The other two Kipling stories resemble the sort of thing that Wells was so good at. Each presents a world ruled by a dictatorship, the "Aerial Board of Control," and each shows how the Board performs its duties, in the one instance carrying the mail by air across the Atlantic under hazardous conditions, and in the other subduing a rebellion. "As Easy as A.B.C." depicts a population which, except for a dwindling group called the "Serviles," has repudiated democracy and learned to love dictatorship. The few remaining Serviles revolt; but the A.B.C., with the help of the majority of people, subdues them and carries them off to London where—like the savage in *Brave New World*—they will appear on the stage as amusing relics of the past. Like the Inner Party in *1984*, this dictatorship uses slogans which epitomize its principles: "Transportation is Civilization" and "Democracy is Disease." The story ends with a poem containing a constellation of themes familiar to readers of *1984*:

McDonough's Song

Whether the State can loose and bind
  In Heaven as well as on Earth:
If it be wiser to kill mankind
  Before or after birth—

These are matters of high concern
  Where State-kept schoolmen are;
But Holy State (we have lived to learn)
  Endeth in Holy War.
Whether The People be led by the Lord,
  Or lured by the loudest throat:
If it be quicker to die by the sword
  Or cheaper to die by vote—
These are the things we have dealt with once,
  (And they will not rise from their grave)
For Holy People, however it runs,
  Endeth in wholly Slave.
Whatsoever, for any cause,
  Seeketh to take or give,
Power above or beyond the Laws,
  Suffer it not to live!
Holy State or Holy King—
  Or Holy People's will—
Have no truck with the senseless thing.
  Order the guns and kill!
Saying—after—me:—
Once there was The People—Terror gave it birth;
Once there was The People and it made a Hell of Earth.
Earth rose and crushed it. Listen, O ye slain!
Once there was The People—it shall never be again![64]

Among these fictional forerunners of *1984*, two other, quite obscure, works need to be noted: the first a pamphlet by Robin Maugham called *The 1946 MS.*, and the second a novel by John Mair, *Never Come Back*. The pamphlet was in Orwell's collection; and he recommended it to his readers in *Tribune*, because it represented the "average middle-class man's conception of what Fascism would be like, and more important, of the reasons why Fascism might succeed."[65] The pamphlet's narrative is thin: a coup d'état by a general supported by the state bureaucracy, then an abortive rebellion carried out by Secret Freedom Troops. One detail is striking —the narrator calls the attention of the authorities to himself by approaching one of them with information about a plot to subvert the state. The narrator's concern for what might occur is so intense that he falls sick and is cured only after a number of operations on his brain, just as Winston Smith is cured of his aberrations by O'Brien's attacks on his reason. But more important than this likeness is the tone of the pamphlet, which is dominated by the loneliness and uncertainty that mark Winston Smith's state of mind, as though the big questions—How can the dictatorship maintain itself in power? How can ordinary people keep their sanity under the incessant barrage of propaganda? How can seemingly isolated individuals unite to overthrow the oppressor?—could only be asked again and again and never answered. It is this tone of pathos and doubt that one remembers.

Orwell said of John Mair's novel, *Never Come Back*, which he commented on in the context of his review of *Darkness at Noon*, that it really dealt with the same world as Koestler's but "in a spirit of burlesque."[66] To suppose that Orwell remembered this left-wing thriller in much detail is almost absurd, even though it may have become associated in his mind with Koestler's novel. Nevertheless some things in the book are worth glancing at if only because they tend to confirm the generalization to be made later that when Orwell wrote *1984* he was saturated with ideas, impressions, and details about totalitarianism derived from many sources.

The plot hinges on the struggle between the hero—an unscrupulous writer-journalist, defiant of authority—and a secret society, the International Opposition, a temporary alliance of revolutionary and disaffected organizations, which seeks to overthrow all existing governments. The hero murders his mistress, one of the Opposition's agents, and steals from her a diary in code which contains information which the I.O. tries to recover and destroy. The action occurs in an atmosphere of war and almost universal treachery and suspicion:

> Who sat on the "Central Committee" so often respectfully mentioned? Desmond had a terrifying vision of treachery everywhere, sitting invisible at Cabinet meetings and Trade Union Councils, on the boards of great companies and in the workshops of key technicians. But today, as never since the Renaissance, was the great age of treachery, and traitors of one colour or another—men too weak to be rulers, too strong to be ruled—gnawed and burrowed under every power in the world. All over the earth the great gleaming structures of the absolute states were secretly rotten; beneath the facade of the powerful governments lurked, under any of a dozen labels, eating rust and the death-watch beetle. Even I.O. itself was no doubt in dread of its own internal enemies. No-one was safe any longer, no-one at all.[67]

The narrator is, of course, betrayed and captured. He is placed in the care of an agent of the Opposition, a "heavy, fair-haired man"

named O'Brien, who is later killed. There begins for the narrator a
painful time of imprisonment and interrogation under torture:

> So began a queer half-life that continued for days until Desmond lost
> all count of time. The light burnt for stretches of what must have
> been twelve or sixteen hours; then went out, presumably for the
> night. . . . It was as if he was buried, or in the deepest cell of an
> asylum for the incurably insane, and once, waking in the thick dark-
> ness, he began to believe he was dead and had to bite his hand till
> it bled to stop himself screaming.[68]

Thane, the hero, is contemptuous of his interrogators and torturers
because they are as anachronistic as the Inquisition, but the pain
they inflict is so terrifying that he almost succumbs. He manages,
however, to persuade them that their own agent, O'Brien, is the
traitor they seek. He has, in fact, the assignment to spy on the others.
In the confusion provoked by the suspicion which Thane has awakened he escapes, is recaptured, pretends to suffer a loss of memory,
and at last escapes for good into the anonymity of the army.

Three other items in the novel are of further interest. The first
is that Thane, like Winston Smith, is a talented parodist and ghost-
writer who works in what Mair calls a "ten-storied intellectual fac-
tory." In order to obtain his release he is obliged by the I.O. to forge
a series of twelve letters recounting events which supposedly occurred in the past and incriminating himself in such a way that the
letters, though they are quite false, will seem to be true. The
second is Thane's wife, who has something in common with
Katherine, Winston Smith's wife, as the following suggests:

> . . . he had quite misjudged Vera's character, and had imagined that
> because she was weak-willed and emotional she would be very easily
> influenced. In this, as he soon found, he was dreadfully mistaken.
> Her ideas, like those of most stupid people, were absolutely un-
> shakable because they were part of her feelings and so beyond the
> reach of reason; and after yielding readily to his storms of angry
> argument, her former attitudes, as resilient as bell-buoys, would pop
> up again directly the pressure was relaxed.[69]

When Thane is released from captivity and before he at last
finds a place to hide, he shelters in his club, the Radical Club,
which he imagines is his only refuge; his mood reminds one of
Winston Smith's when he revisits the Chestnut Tree:

> Although, like Lazarus, he had marvelously returned to his own
> familiar world, he remained oppressively aware that he dwelt there
> only on sufferance; at any moment, in the height of any felicity, he

might be pulled back to the dark and pitiless underworld. . . . The porters cleaning the steps had the faces of spies, the spacious streets were a prison, the houses traps. Whatever happened, something was wholly lost; he would never, he knew, feel quite the same again.[70]

In this state of mind he discovers and attacks his chief persecutor, the head of the International Opposition. This man is interesting in connection with *1984* chiefly because he is the author of an empty and ill-written book called *The Path of the Philosopher King*:

> Half-digested Plato, misunderstood Hobbes, a vulgarisation of Nietzsche and a misreading of the minor Freudians were applied to a sketchy outline of anthropology and world-history to prove that enlightened autocracy was the aim of all society, and that human progress was about to culminate in the sudden apotheosis of the rational tyrant.[71]

Although Thane is ready at first to dismiss this work altogether, it occurs to him that he may be mistaken in his judgment of it, just as men misjudged *Mein Kampf* and its author without sufficiently realizing how fatally easy it is to underestimate the power of a fanatical bully and his doctrines. The greatest difference between *Never Come Back* and *1984* is that Mair's book sets out to be, and is, an amusing thriller. But in some ways it is so close to *1984* that it might almost be said to parody it in the manner of someone with the same talent for the absurd as Kingsley Amis.

Many writers on Orwell agree with the view being developed here that *1984* distills the reading, writing, and experience of an observant and sensitive artist in an age dominated by wars and politics. But several assert more narrowly that much in the novel originates in Eugene Zamyatin's *We*. The most notable among these was Sir Isaac Deutscher, biographer of Stalin and Trotsky, whose statement of Orwell's debt to the exiled Russian writer is sweeping:

> The lack of originality is illustrated by the fact that Orwell borrowed the idea of *1984*, the plot, the chief characters, the symbols, and the whole climate of his story from a Russian writer who has remained almost unknown in the West. That writer is Evgenii Zamyatin, and the title of the book which served Orwell as the model is *We*. Like *1984*, *We* is an "anti-Utopia," a nightmare vision of the shape of things to come, and a Cassandra cry. Orwell's work is a thoroughly English variation on Zamyatin's theme; and it is perhaps only the thoroughness of Orwell's English approach that gives to his work the originality it possesses.[72]

George Woodcock, who implies that the reading of *We* may have stimulated Orwell to begin his own novel, writes extensively about the resemblances and differences between the two, but his discussion does not mention this attack by Deutscher,[73] whose charges are worth examining because his influence has been great, especially among the intelligentsia whom Orwell attacked so freely.

Two points in his statement need not detain us long. First, the "perhaps" in his last sentence can be disregarded, for it is merely a conventional disclaimer of omniscience; in the context he does not mean "perhaps," he means "certainly." Second, Zamyatin's book, though not a popular success, has become well known largely because Orwell, and certain specialists like Gleb Struve, repeatedly called attention to its merits. After he had read *We* in a French translation Orwell told his readers in *Tribune*, "This is a book to look out for when an English version appears."[74]

When an English version was announced for publication in England—a translation into English had been published in the United States in 1925—Orwell once more reminded his readers that it was worth their attention.[75] A year later Orwell wrote to Gleb Struve that he was arranging to review *We* for the *Times Literary Supplement* and making inquiries about Zamyatin's widow with the idea of promoting the publication of Zamyatin's other books.[76] The plans to publish *We* fell through, but as late as March 1949 Orwell wrote to Warburg, "It is disgraceful that a book of this kind with its curious history as well as its intrinsic interest should stay out of print when so much rubbish is published every day."[77]

If Orwell had borrowed as much from *We* as Deutscher says he did—in effect plagiarizing it—he would not have been likely to give it so much publicity and to persist in trying to get it into print. One might argue that he could unconsciously have borrowed certain details from *We*, but unconscious borrowing on a large scale seems improbable, especially when one recalls Orwell's excellent memory and his sharp eye for literary influences. In any event, we can best determine the extent of Orwell's debt to Zamyatin by considering the five items of alleged borrowing Deutscher mentions.

Orwell said of *We*, "It has a rather weak and episodic plot which is too complicated to summarize"; nevertheless, he gives a sketch of the action with some comment on the characters:

> The teller of the story, D-503, who, though a gifted engineer, a poor conventional creature, a sort of Utopian Billy Brown of London Town, is constantly horrified by the atavistic impulses which seize

upon him. He falls in love (this is a crime, of course) with a certain I-330 who is a member of an underground resistance movement and succeeds for a while in leading him into rebellion. When the rebellion breaks out it appears that the enemies of The Benefactor are in fact fairly numerous, and these people, apart from plotting the overthrow of the State, even indulge, at the moment when their curtains are down, in such vices as smoking cigarettes and drinking alcohol. D-503 is ultimately saved from the consequences of his own folly. The authorities announce that they have discovered the cause of the recent disorders: it is that some human beings suffer from a disease called imagination. The nerve-centre responsible for imagination has now been located, and the disease can be cured by X-ray treatment. D-503 undergoes the operation, after which it is easy for him to do what he has known all along he ought to do—that is, betray his confederates to the police.[78]

Among the complications to which Orwell alludes are an attempt to take over D-503's space ship during its trial flight, two chases in subterranean passages, and two love affairs. The book's aura of mystery, even confusion, has several causes. First, D-503 is torn between his genuine loyalty to the state and his determination to spend his life with I-330, with whom he has fallen in love. These opposing desires produce in him states of mind which sometimes alternate so rapidly that they are not always comprehensible. Second, the story is told in a notebook kept by D-503, whose style—spasmodic, disconnected, sometimes deliberately allusive and vague—is intended to reflect the division in his mind. Third, D-503 does not really understand the aims and motives of those who try to subvert his loyalty, nor is he aware of all the things being done by the leaders of the rebellion. The result is that he (and the reader) must try to fill in not only the gaps in the plot but also the details of how it is to be carried out.

In contrast, the plot of *1984* is simple—some say it has no plot—and the clarity and solidity with which the world of *1984* is represented is quite unlike the mist which seems to envelop *We*. Perhaps this is what is meant by the "thoroughness of Orwell's English approach."

In *We* there is an actual conspiracy which develops into open revolt, momentarily threatening the security of the state and causing damage to the city where it happens. Preparation is necessary before the rebellion; and there is a considerable amount of unexplained coming and going before the plot reaches a climax. The conspiracy in *1984*, on the contrary, is invented by the Inner Party. The rebel, the Brotherhood's leader Emmanuel Goldstein, is a fiction, deliberately impressed on the minds of the populace and kept prominent as a focus for their hatred. These inventions have the further use of trapping dissidents like Winston Smith, and some of the pathos of his defeat lies in the realization that he had neither leader nor comrades in his attempted revolt.

The major characters in the two books could scarcely be more different. D-503 is a mathematician and the builder of a space ship, the "Integral," destined to carry the social doctrines—founded on mathematics—to the other inhabitants of the universe. He is loyal to the United State because he is content with his place in it and full of admiration for the mathematically certain way it functions. Only the attractions of the mysterious female with whom he falls in love seduce him from his duty. But Winston Smith, the typical Orwell "anti-hero," is a dissatisfied writer, rebellious from the beginning, full of hatred for the state and all its works. It is he who persuades his sweetheart Julia, who is only "a rebel from the waist downwards," to join the nonexistent subversive group with him. There is in 1984 another major personage, O'Brien, the interrogator and torturer of Winston and Julia, the embodiment of the Inner Party, and the spokesman for the methods and objectives of Ingsoc. We presents no corresponding figure, though D-503 does have a "guardian angel," S-4711, a state employee who seeks to prevent the conspiracy and to save D-503 from his worst follies.

The principal symbol these books have in common is the deified leader of the state. In We this is a living person called the Benefactor or the Well-Doer. He has no supernatural gifts, but his role is God-like. On great ceremonial occasions he is the central figure, descending from the sky and controlling the machine that destroys the victims, whose ritual death enacts the triumph of the many over the one. D-503 twice confronts the Benefactor in person: once to be persuaded that he has been naive in trusting I-330, and on a second occasion to witness her execution under the Glass Bell. But in 1984 Big Brother is a fiction, like Emmanuel Goldstein; he neither interrogates nor kills. In any case, this coincidence of symbols is not remarkable. When the Sleeper Wakes has a similar figure called the Master; "Our Ford" is the deity of Brave New World. Historical parallels are also plentiful: in the Soviet Union, Stalin—like the Tsars—was called the Father of the People, Father of the Nation, Leader of the People, Savior of the People, Leader of the Blind, and Sun of the Revolution.

Other symbols in We include the Hour Tables, schedules (on the analogy of railway timetables) which determine every action in the daily lives of the citizens. Based on the pure reason of mathematics, these tables epitomize the control the rational faculty exerts over the emotions. Similarly, the Green Wall surrounding the city prevents the incursion of the barbarians who live outside it and isolates "the perfect world" of the select ones from "the formless, unreasonable world of trees, birds, animals," thus symbolizing the desired separation of the artificial and civilized from the natural and savage. These ideas and symbols do not appear in 1984. On the other hand, and despite the presence in We of an Ancient House, there is nothing in We corresponding to the nursery rhymes of 1984, or, more important, to the crystal paperweight. Nor is this surprising, since Zamyatin makes little of the theme that Orwell found so significant, that is, the meaning for human beings of history, memory, and the past.

Deutscher declares that the whole climate of 1984 was taken from We. If he means what is conveyed by the term atmosphere, his remark is a puzzling one, for here the two novels are quite different. This feature of Zamyatin's work interested Orwell, who compared We to Brave New World: "The atmosphere of the two books is similar, and it is roughly speaking the same kind of society that is being described," he wrote. The cleanliness, order, glitter, and avoidance of strife in We help define the hedonistic ideal of happiness which the Benefactor reproaches D-503 for having endangered. In contrast, the shabbiness, discomfort, violence, and induced hysteria of Oceania are logical consequences of the unrestrained exercise of power for its own sake. In Woodcock's opinion this feature is Orwell's most striking departure not only from Zamyatin but from others writing on the same theme:

> But what distinguishes it [1984] even more strikingly from previous Utopias and even anti-Utopias is that the pretense of providing happiness as a compensation for the loss of freedom is not maintained. Even the synthetic pleasures and comforts promised by Zamiatin and Huxley no longer exist.[79]

There is a further difference in the atmosphere of the two works: whereas in We the order and machinelike beauty are deliberately kept general, the quality of life in 1984, owing to the detail with which it is evoked, is one of the most solid features of the book.

In the context of Deutscher's article, the idea which he thinks Orwell also borrowed from We seems to mean the body of beliefs it represents, not simply the impetus to write a similar parable. The idea, in that sense, was explained by Orwell in his Tribune article.

He pointed out that *We* is a fantasy dealing with the distant future. The book has, as all such books must, political implications, but "it is not about Russia and has no direct connection with contemporary politics":

> Writing at the time of Lenin's death, he cannot have had the Stalin dictatorship in mind, and conditions in Russia in 1923 were not such that anyone would revolt against them on the ground that life was becoming too safe and comfortable. . . . What Zamyatin seems to be aiming at is not any particular country but the implied aims of industrial civilization. . . . It is evident from *We* that he had a strong leaning towards primitivism. . . . His book is in effect a study of the Machine.[80]

Evidence in *We* which supports Orwell's opinion includes comments about F. W. Taylor, the American engineer and economist, whose pioneer work in time and motion studies and in the rationalization of production attracted world-wide attention, not all of it favorable. In *We* he is referred to as "undoubtedly the greatest genius of the ancients . . . this prophet who saw ten centuries ahead."[81] Orwell clearly considered *We* to be first of all an attack on Taylorism, like René Clair's film *A Nous la Liberté* and Chaplin's *Modern Times*.

The Road to Wigan Pier analyzed the deadening effect of machine civilization on human beings but argued nevertheless that it was useless to think of returning to a preindustrial age. Again in 1944, writing about Eric Gill's condemnation of machine culture, Orwell observed that at best Gill was advocating a half-truth; he had no idea of what a society without machines would really be like. Most people in such a system would, ironically, be slaves, dependent on the invention and perfecting of machines for any improvement in their lives.[82] Insofar then as Zamyatin repudiated machine culture and recommended a return to nature, Orwell, although sympathetic, disagreed with him.

On the other hand, just as he had commended Jack London for a similar insight, so Orwell is full of praise for Zamyatin's "intuitive grasp of the irrational side of totalitarianism," manifested in his book by the cruel ritual of human sacrifice.[83] But here too, the distinction noted by Woodcock is important. In the United State created by Zamyatin men choose happiness instead of freedom, and the Benefactor is represented as being necessarily cruel if the one can be guaranteed only at the expense of the other. Such a detached, even virtuous, motive is expressly denied by O'Brien and the Inner

Party. Winston Smith, indeed, when he is questioned on this point, foolishly thinks that "the Party was the eternal guardian of the weak, a dedicated sect doing evil that good might come, sacrificing its own happiness to that of others."[84] And for a moment he supposes that O'Brien believes this too, but only for a moment. O'Brien quickly puts him right, telling him that the good of others does not interest the Party, which seeks power entirely for its own sake. But in any event the motive for cruelty is not the major theme in *We* that it is in *1984*, and there is little to suggest that Zamyatin was writing about totalitarianism in anything like Orwell's sense of the term.

There is too much in *1984* that does not appear in *We*—the superstates, the direct attack on totalitarianism, permanent warfare, the dreary squalor, such novelties as doublethink and Newspeak, the disappearance of belief in objective reality, the substitution of "love" for law, the disaffected and defeated intellectual, the importance of history, tradition, and memory, and the ruling intellectuals of the Inner Party—to leave much ground for the claim that Orwell took *We* as his model.

To sharpen the contrast, one might say that *We* exhibits in the Hour Tables the mathematical perfection of human reason and conduct—objectivity carried to its utmost limits—and it is against the dominance of rationality that Zamyatin, like Dostoevsky, protests. But in *1984* human reason has turned into its opposite—pure subjectivity.[85] What the Inner Party wants to create is a "collective solipsism" which destroys objective reality, including the reality of mathematics and the reality of common sense. Zamyatin revolts against the ideal of the machine; Orwell revolts against the ideal of ideology.[86] In both books humanity is victimized, for in *We* the crime is to turn human beings into machines, and in *1984* the crime is to turn human beings into lunatics.

II

WRITINGS ON TOTALITARIANISM

ORWELL had a prolonged interest in several other writers more directly concerned with social developments and political structures in the actual world than the writers of fiction considered in the preceding chapter. Reflections of their ideas in *1984* as well as what he said about them in his critical writings make it almost certain that their work helped to shape the image of the totalitarian state he was to portray. These are not utopia books, even in the ironic sense that the phrase may be applied to *Brave New World* or *We*. Of those considered here, two describe contemporary events in Stalinist Russia: Arthur Koestler's *Darkness at Noon* and Boris Souvarine's *Cauchemar en U.R.S.S.*[1] The setting of Koestler's novel is in all important particulars the actual world described by Souvarine in his pamphlet. The other writers, Hilaire Belloc in *The Servile State* and James Burnham in *The Managerial Revolution, The Machiavellians,* and *The Struggle for the World* did look to the future; but Orwell perceived no utopian promise in what they saw.

Two developments explored in *The Servile State* were frequently on Orwell's mind when he considered the future. One was the possibility that most men would be made slaves, and the other was that socialism might take an oligarchical instead of a democratic form. His first encounter with the second idea—at least the first time he saw it worked out with some care at the theoretical level—was apparently in reading Belloc's book, published in 1912.

We do not know when he first read this book, but in 1940 he wrote that "it must be thirty years since Mr. Hilaire Belloc, in his book *The Servile State*, foretold with astonishing accuracy the things that are happening now."[2] He repeated his observation in an essay on James Burnham[3] and made another allusion to the book when he criticized Harold Laski for not recognizing that communism and fascism were twins. "A hierarchical version of Socialism (Hilaire Belloc's 'Servile State') is probably just as workable as the other [i.e., democratic version], and at this moment is much likelier to arrive."[4]

Orwell's own hierarchical version of socialism, Ingsoc, appeared only a few years later in *1984*.

The idea that civilization might revert to a long period of slavery haunted Orwell for years. As early as 1933, he had a personal impression of what that might mean, for in *Down and Out in Paris and London*, after describing how he came to be a dishwasher, he writes:

> I think one should start by saying that a *plongeur* is one of the slaves of the modern world. Not that there is any need to whine over him, for he is better off than many manual workers, but still, he is no freer than if he were bought and sold. His work is servile and without art; he is paid just enough to keep him alive; his only holiday is the sack. . . . If *plongeurs* thought at all, they would long ago have formed a union and gone on strike for better treatment. But they do not think, because they have no leisure for it; their life has made slaves of them.[5]

Enslavement of one kind or another is a recurring theme in Orwell's fiction, and it stemmed from a fear that the *plongeur's* lot might become universal except for the few controlling the system. In a review appearing in the *New Statesman*, Orwell wrote that "slavery, which seemed as remote as cannibalism in 1932, is visibly returning in 1942."[6] Two years later, in a review of a book by H. G. Wells, he said, "The danger seemingly ahead of us is *not* extinction: it is a slave civilisation which, so far from being chaotic, might be horribly stable."[7]

The Servile State was written, according to the author's introduction, "to maintain the thesis that industrial society as we know it will tend toward the reestablishment of slavery." Belloc's argument is this: the notorious instability of capitalism is caused by the continuing insecurity of the mass of people, which is in its turn caused by the heavy concentration of capital in the hands of the few; most people have neither land nor capital and hence cannot be secure. To combat this insecurity people will gradually enter into legal contracts for the sale of their services to the owners of capital; and these contracts, though obviously unfair, will be enforced by the power of the state. Thus the mass of people will exchange their theoretical freedom for economic security, and a slave society will in effect arise—the Servile State.

Belloc foresaw three possibilities in the political future: distributivism, slavery, and socialism. Though he would have preferred the distributivist scheme—a plan for small-scale, widespread peasant ownership—he rejected it on the grounds of its impracticality. Orwell agreed with Belloc on this latter point, for he included this statement in the Book, probably alluding to Belloc or Chesterton: "In the long run, a hierarchical society was only possible on a basis of poverty and ignorance. To return to the agricultural past, as some thinkers about the beginning of the twentieth century dreamed of doing, was not a practicable solution."[8] Belloc also rejected the possibility that the pagan system of open slavery would be re-established, because of "the distaste which the remains of our long Christian tradition has [sic] bred in us for directly advocating slavery."[9] The remaining alternative is collectivism or socialism, whose cause is advanced consciously by Socialists and unconsciously by those whom Belloc calls "Practical Men." The efforts of both groups will lead society to adopt formally the concept of status or caste, and men will thus relinquish their supposed political independence for actual economic security: "The Capitalist State breeds a Collectivist Theory which *in action* produces something utterly different from Collectivism: to wit, the Servile State."[10]

It would be incorrect to say that Orwell accepted Belloc's analysis in detail, but he judged *The Servile State* to be a "very prescient book,"[11] and it presented to his mind in a memorable way a coherent and persuasive explanation of how a modern slave state could emerge. It also showed how slavery was compatible with socialism or capitalism, and in the 1940s Orwell had become quite sensitive to this possibility. In 1944, reviewing books by Konni Zilliacus and Friedrich Hayek, the one attacking and the other defending capitalism, he noted that according to each author the policy favored by his opponents would lead to slavery; then he added, "And the alarming thing is that they may both be right."[12]

A slave society was being brought nearer to actuality, though through more old-fashioned methods than Belloc had conceived, by developments in the Soviet Union. Orwell learned about these through his personal experience in Spain and his association with left-wing politics in England. He learned also from books written by his contemporaries something of what was happening in the Soviet Union. Arthur Koestler's *Darkness at Noon* was one of these. It seemed to Orwell "rather like an expanded imaginative version of Souvarine's pamphlet, *Cauchemar en U.R.S.S.*"[13] In fact, *1984* also expands and elaborates ideas from the same source.

Boris Souvarine, a naturalized Frenchman, had been one of the founders of the Parti Communiste Français, a member of the Executive Committee of the Comintern, and editor of *L'Humanité*. By 1935, however, when he published a study called *Staline—aperçu historique du Bolchévisme*, he had become deeply critical of developments in Russia; and his pamphlet *Cauchemar en U.R.S.S.* asserts by its title the nightmare quality he then perceived in events taking place in his former homeland. The appearance of this short work in July 1937 almost coincided with Orwell's return from his personal adventure with the Stalinist terror in Spain. Coming just at this time, it must have helped him formulate more objectively and with a deeper sense of their significance his ideas about the form of totalitarianism developing in the U.S.S.R. The magnitude of the human perversions Orwell was now beginning to confront was well indicated by the quotation from Georges Duhamel which Souvarine chose as the epigraph of his pamphlet: "Formerly Galileo had to confess on his knees, under the threat of torture, that the earth did not revolve. The prisoners of Moscow confess things no less outrageous."[14]

Orwell found in Souvarine several things he might have stored in his mind for later use. The pamphlet gave detailed evidence about the purge trials, including a brief history of the trials, estimates of the number of persons affected by the purges, and indications of why the purges began and how the trials were used for "public education." He found in it also ideas about the exaltation of Stalin and the denigration of Trotsky which were to have important counterparts in *1984*. The following quotations from Souvarine, for example, could serve to describe Orwell's view of Big Brother and Emmanuel Goldstein: "No one is concerned about truth, neither the judges, the accusers, the defendants, nor the press; but everyone busies himself in glorifying a certain Stalin and heaping opprobrium on a gentleman called Trotsky."[15] Souvarine describes Trotsky as forever being accused, "the eternal offender."[16] Those who accept the myth of Trotsky's magnetic and sinister power, exercised in all corners of the earth and over everybody—even his enemies—are succumbing, he says, to a belief in "black magic."[17]

Because of its multiple relations to *1984* this statement is particularly revealing:

> Spiritual tortures eliminate the need for physical tortures. In this respect the G.P.U. has acquired a refined knowledge whose effects are tangible. It equals or surpasses the Inquisition to which it has been freely compared by many commentators . . . . During the "trial of the Mencheviks" Leon Blum wrote a masterful account of the

"exhibitionism of confession," showing "how the Stalinist terror adds a sort of mental decomposition to the spiritual perversion." Another eminent Socialist leader, F. Adler, has justly compared the Zinoviev trial to the sorcery trials of the Middle Ages. Here Trotsky replaces the Devil.[18]

In this paragraph Souvarine has set forth the principle underlying the tortures applied to Winston Smith and the moral and mental breakdown that follows. In addition to these important ideas, one finds certain details in this pamphlet which would have impressed Orwell. For example, Souvarine lists some thirty-five epithets used by the Soviet press to characterize the enemies of the regime—gangster, spy, bandit, Fascist, paid assassins—the same abusive language Orwell commented on in "Politics and the English Language."

There appears also this instance of the Soviet disregard for objective truth:

A defendant confesses to having gone from Berlin to Copenhagen in the company of Sédov to meet the exile [Trotsky] at the Hotel Bristol there. It is asserted and proved that the hotel has not existed for the last twenty years, that Sédov has never set foot in Copenhagen, that the interview is a complete fiction.[19]

Compared with some of the big lies told during the trials, the incident is not in itself important. The big lies were functional, usually discrediting some person or doctrine. This, however, is a clear-cut example of lying almost divorced from personalities and motives, and it is therefore also an example of the link between totalitarianism and habitual lying, a connection elaborated into a philosophy in *1984.*

Orwell and Koestler were friends, and Orwell thought highly of *Darkness at Noon,* whose subject is the motives which inspired the purge trials and the confessions of the accused. This novel was the first work of art in English to present coherently and dramatically the disaster for humanity brought on by the intellectual and moral collapse of the Communist party and hence of the Soviet leadership. In his review Orwell called attention to one of the consequences of this disaster. "Nowadays, over increasing areas of the earth, one is imprisoned not for what one *does* but for what one *is,* or, more exactly, for what one is suspected of being."[20] No doubt Orwell was remembering what had happened to him in Barcelona because of his association with the workers' Marxist party known as the P.O.U.M. (Partido Obrero de Unificacion Marxista):

> It did not matter what I had done or not done. This was not a round-up of criminals; it was merely a reign of terror. I was not guilty of any definite act, but I was guilty of "Trotskyism." The fact that I had served in the P.O.U.M. militia was quite enough to get me into prison. It was no use hanging on to the English notion that you are safe so long as you keep the law. Practically the law was what the police chose to make it. The only thing to do was to lie low and conceal the fact that I had anything to do with the P.O.U.M.[21]

This same review is also noteworthy for the way it touches upon several of the major themes that were to appear in *1984*. When he wrote of Gletkin as belonging to "the new generation that has grown up since the Revolution, in complete isolation both from the outside world and from the past," Orwell is describing men perverted by Ingsoc.[22] And his own novel illustrates the principle he remarked on in Koestler's: Gletkin was strong because he was completely cut off from the past and thus left unburdened by pity, imagination, or "inconvenient knowledge."[23]

Like Orwell, Koestler made such ignorance of the past not only a feature of his character's personality and a cause of other traits— like his toughness—but also a characteristic of the system that bred him. Rejecting tradition and placing no value on anything antedating the revolution, the leaders made sure that the new race—Orwell called it the "new race of monsters"—would have no ties to an older era and no other demands on their loyalties. As Rubashov describes Gletkin's generation, "It had no traditions, and no memories to bind it to the old, vanished world" and what he called its "vain conceptions of honour" and its "hypocritical decencies."[24] Ivanov, the older interrogator, was still hampered by his past, but "the Gletkins had nothing to erase; they need not deny their past, because they had none."[25]

Orwell also observed that Rubashov had forfeited "any right to protest against torture, secret prisons, and organised lying" because he had been corrupted by his own deeds, these in turn having followed directly from his acceptance of the party's philosophy.[26] Koestler makes the point explicit when he quotes from Rubashov's diary, which tells how No. 1 kept Machiavelli's *The Prince* by his bedside. The diary records also the belief that the revolutionary ethics of this century have rightly replaced the older liberal ethics based on fair play, and that the turning points of history call for action whose only rule is the old one—the end justifies the means. The extract from the diary concludes with these words: "We were neo-Machiavellians in the name of universal reason—that was our greatness."27

Koestler saw this neo-Machiavellianism also as the conflict between cleverness and decency. In one of the most moving passages in the novel, Rubashov taps out a message to a former Czarist officer in the next cell, telling him that he is finally capitulating to Gletkin. The officer replies:

"I WAS INCLINED TO CONSIDER YOU AN EXCEPTION. HAVE YOU NO SPARK OF HONOUR LEFT?"
"OUR IDEAS OF HONOUR DIFFER."
"HONOUR IS TO LIVE AND DIE FOR ONE'S BELIEF."
"HONOUR IS TO BE USEFUL WITHOUT VANITY."
"HONOUR IS DECENCY—NOT USEFULNESS."
"WHAT IS DECENCY?"
"SOMETHING YOUR KIND WILL NEVER UNDERSTAND."
"WE HAVE REPLACED DECENCY BY REASON."28

Since "decency" was the key word in Orwell's ethical code and the nature of reason a constant preoccupation, this passage, with its unusual contrast of "decency" with "reason," must have given him much to think about. Questions about the role of the neo-Machiavellians and of the significance of "reason" will arise again when we consider James Burnham.

The themes in *Darkness at Noon* which I have touched on as being important for *1984* are surrounded by details and ideas which reinforce both their message and the similarities between Koestler's and Orwell's thinking about totalitarianism. Koestler's title is taken from Milton and was suggested to him by his translator, Daphne Hardy. The metaphor stands for the contrast, as Koestler evokes it, between the hopes once felt by millions of human beings that socialism would succeed and the destruction of those hopes by the Communist party and the Soviet Union just when they seemed capable of being fulfilled. Orwell expressed the same contrast on several occasions. Writing for *Tribune* in 1946, he said:

And yet exactly at the moment when there is, or could be, plenty of everything for everybody, nearly our whole energies have to be taken up in trying to grab territories, markets and raw materials from one another. Exactly at the moment when wealth might be so generally diffused that no government need fear serious opposition, political liberty is declared to be impossible and half the world is ruled by secret police forces. Exactly at the moment when superstition crumbles and a rational attitude toward the universe becomes feasible, the right to think one's own thoughts is denied as never before.[29]

This perverse turn of events must have stayed in Orwell's mind, and it lies behind the question "Why?" that so puzzled Winston Smith.

Several times in *Darkness at Noon* we find Koestler marking the parallel between the aims and methods of the Roman Catholic church and those of the Communist party. These passages too must have caught Orwell's attention, for he had a pronounced bias against the Roman Catholic church, and even more elaborate parallels than Koestler drew are to be found in *1984*. In Koestler's novel, for example, Rubashov declares the party to be infallible and excuses its acts by citing its special relationship to history, just as the church's acts are explained by its special relationship to the Divine. The party, like the church, is unique in the authority of its interpretation because it alone has access to history's revelation. Like the church also, the party is licensed by its uniqueness to disregard the laws of conventional morality. In this context, Koestler quotes a striking sentence from the work of a fifteenth-century Roman Catholic bishop:

> When the existence of the Church is threatened, she is released from the commandments of morality. With unity as the end, the use of every means is sanctified, even cunning, treachery, violence, simony, prison, death. For all order is for the sake of the community, and the individual must be sacrificed to the common good.[30]

This freedom in the exercise of power leads to the creation of "thoughtcrime" as well as its punishment. Rubashov says in his diary:

> Therefore we have to punish wrong ideas as others punish crimes: with death. We are held for madmen because we followed every thought down to its final consequence and acted accordingly. We were compared to the Inquisition because, like them, we constantly felt in ourselves the whole weight of responsibility for the super-individual life to come. We resembled the great Inquisitors in that we persecuted the seeds of evil not only in men's deeds, but in their thoughts. We admitted no private sphere, not even inside a man's skull.[31]

Finally, Koestler says that the party's ideology had become rigid. Like Wells's "puritan tyranny," it had entered a period of "wholesome sterility," and Koestler's description of this state again involves the comparison with the Church:

> Revolutionary theory had frozen to a dogmatic cult, with a simplified, easily graspable catechism, and with No. 1. as the high priest celebrating the Mass. His speeches and articles had, even in their style, the character of an infallible catechism; they were divided into question and answer, with a marvellous consistency in the gross simplification of the actual problems and facts. . . . The dilettantes in tyranny had forced their subjects to act at command; No. 1. had taught them to think at command.[32]

Another aspect of the totalitarian mentality that appears in *Darkness at Noon* is elaborated in *1984* as "doublethink." This is the induced schizophrenia which Koestler recognized as an important means by which the party controlled its members. It is the hopelessness of finding ordinary logic in what has happened to him that finally leads to Rubashov's confession. As he analyzes the matter:

> The Party denied the free will of the individual—and at the same time it exacted his willing self-sacrifice. It denied his capacity to choose between two alternatives—and at the same time it demanded that he should constantly choose the right one. It denied his powers to distinguish good and evil—and at the same time it spoke pathetically of guilt and treachery. The individual stood under the sign of economic fatality, a wheel in the clockwork which had been wound up for all eternity and could not be stopped or influenced—and the Party demanded that the wheel should revolt against the clockwork and change its course. There was somewhere an error in the calculation; the equation did not work out.[33]

This is the equation which, with O'Brien's help, Winston Smith finally masters.

There remains a word to say, before we leave this novel, about some of its narrative details, which are echoed in *1984*. Rubashov notices propaganda posters of two sorts: one is the color print of No. 1., "which hung over his bed on the wall of his room and on the walls of all the rooms next to, above or under his; on all the walls of the house, of the town, of the enormous country for which he had fought and suffered."[34] There are the other posters also "on which youth was always represented with a laughing face"[35] in contrast to the ugly reality of the brutal youth who comes to summon Rubashov.

Winston Smith makes the same comparison; and Orwell remarked on the same contrast between the posters in wartime England and the reality he knew.

Also worth pointing out is the part that a photograph plays in *Darkness at Noon;* Rubashov has a daydream in which this photograph figures:

> A picture appeared in his mind's eye, a big photograph in a wooden frame: the delegates to the first congress of the Party. They sat at a long wooden table, some with their elbows propped on it, others with their hands on their knees; bearded and earnest, they gazed into the photographer's lens. Above each head was a small circle, enclosing a number corresponding to a name printed underneath.[36]

When Rubashov is first interrogated in Ivanov's office, his eye "was caught by a square patch on the wall lighter than the rest of the wall paper. He knew at once that the picture with the bearded heads and the numbered names had hung there—Ivanov followed his glance without changing his expression."[37] Later on, the same photograph is mentioned as one in which a prominent Party member, now liquidated, "sat to the leader's left."[38] Thus disappears a bit of objective evidence that could prove something about the past of the Party and its practice of killing its former leaders. In *1984,* a similar photograph of some of the original leaders of the party comes into the possession of Winston Smith. Its implied significance is so great that it becomes an important detail in the intellectual struggle between him and O'Brien.[39]

Two other books Orwell reviewed do not have the direct connection to *1984* that *Darkness at Noon* has, but they are nevertheless interesting because they vividly corroborated attitudes and ideas Orwell had already formed, or furnished him with interesting details about life in a totalitarian state, or amplified his knowledge of the atmosphere in the Soviet Union and Hitler's Germany.

The first of these is *An Epic of the Gestapo* by Sir Paul Dukes. The book recounts an investigation the Gestapo allowed Dukes to make in Czechoslovakia into the mysterious disappearance and death of a Czech industrialist named Obry, whose English friends had asked Dukes to undertake the investigation. Owing to his good connections in the diplomatic world, Dukes was given a fairly free hand by the Germans to carry on his work, which ended in his exhuming Obry's body in order to be certain that the man had indeed been run over accidentally by a train while trying to flee Czechoslovakia.

Perhaps the most interesting feature of the book is Dukes's emphasis on the many detailed resemblances between the Nazi and Soviet regimes and especially the way the secret police and propaganda organizations sought to control the bodies and minds of the citizens:

> Just as in Bolshevist Russia, so in Nazi Germany, no department of life escapes the all-seeing eye of ubiquitous secret agents. They tap telephone conversations and postal communications; eavesdrop on trains and trams, in cafés and restaurants; through Youth and other popular organizations they provoke young people to betray parents and elders who criticize the regime; ferret out audacious citizens who, with their ear to toned-down radio sets, listen eagerly for foreign wireless news; and in general act the part of *agents provocateurs*—itself a Russian invention.[40]

Dukes notes the admiration that good Nazis and Communists feel for the Gestapo and the GPU, for they regard the secret police as a sign of the regime's strength.[41] He notes also that *Mein Kampf* had become a sacred book; "like the Bible which it was intended to displace, it must be there, on the bookshelf, on show, but opened only by the devout."[42] We may notice too how often he remarks on the wall posters and other signs bearing slogans like this: "Remember Adolf Hitler is always right,"[43] or even more elaborately:

> He who serves Hitler serves Germany;
> He who serves Germany serves God.[44]

Orwell found Dukes's book "fascinating" and said of it, "Reading this book, one gets some idea of how corrupt a totalitarian society can be. In such a society the practice of lying becomes so habitual that it is almost impossible to believe that anyone else can ever be speaking the truth."[45]

A second book is Erika Mann's *The Lights Go Down*, which contains several true stories typical of the life of ordinary people in Hitler's Reich. The book is packed with details illustrating the manifold ways in which the dictatorship penetrates into every aspect of the citizen's life and usurps the individual's consciousness; the loudspeakers, for example, are everywhere, retailing their statistics, which no one believes except the school children who are required to take notes on what they hear. One especially noteworthy tale concerns a couple, Marie and Peter, who are falsely accused by a neighbor of seeking an illegal abortion. They end by killing themselves in desperation. The irony is that they had been fairly good

Nazi citizens, though dissatisfied with the amount of time they had to spend in activities promoted by the state:

> They always had to be exercising, or learning a "world outlook," or performing some duty, when they wanted to be together, or read, or study. And on the Sundays when they looked forward to a hike into the hills, there would be a "cross-country route march" or some other compulsory assignment of a "military-sports" character.[46]

Orwell called this book a "chronicle of lies, horrors, and absurdities" describing a life so horrible that he could not understand how it could be endured, and this perplexity caused him to think that a book explaining why the regime was accepted would have more practical use.[47]

Finally, we must take notice of a book that was apparently in Orwell's library but which he seems not to have reviewed, Julia de Beausobre's *The Woman Who Could Not Die*. Mme de Beausobre and her husband were arrested in 1932 by the GPU after having been banished to Samarkand for a year. M. de Beausobre was shot in 1933, and his wife, Julia, was jailed in various Soviet prisons and prison camps for a long time before she was at last ransomed by English friends. When her book first appeared in 1938 it did not receive much notice, but after it was reissued in 1948 with an introduction by Rebecca West it secured a rather better reception.

The book is marked by the unquestionable authority with which the writer conveys the reality of what it means to be buried in a Soviet prison. She recounts all the details of life in solitary confinement—the silence, the vigilance of the guards, the painful naked light, the alternating cruelty and kindness. "Strange life!" she comments, "To be forced to the brink of madness, to be set in conditions that make you supremely vulnerable to any sort of illness and yet to be solicitously doctored—twice a day."[48] Except for the "conveyor-belt" system of interrogations, the solitary cell life she endured for a long time was dominated by dreams and fantasies. She testifies to the great bond formed "between the man who is tortured day in, day out, and the man who day in, day out, tortures him."[49] She tried to protect herself, she says, by deliberately forgetting as much as she could of the past, because any mention of it could have been dangerous to her or her husband; but, as she once cries out: "Can you accept a long life with a mind entirely void of memory? The divine gift of Memory!"[50] Despite her physical and mental suffering Julia de Beausobre withstood the interrogations and was temporarily reprieved, but at last she was called again and told, "We only kill those of whom we think very highly and those whom we despise profoundly. You cannot doubt that we think highly of you!" To which she replied, "I shall console myself with that when I am dying."[51]

When such threats as this were ineffectual in making her confess to things she had not done, the GPU transferred her to another prison and thence to Siberia, to which she was sentenced for five years. In the new camp she found that the inmates had careers and families. The prison life engulfed her and them; it was not a hiatus; it was a new, "normal" life. But the rigors of this existence nearly killed Julia; the rats were a particular evil. In large numbers they hurried boldly about the camp searching for food, and Julia could not learn to lie quietly in bed while a rat crawled over her:

> Rat! I realize, jumping to my feet and hurting them so that I sit down quickly on the bed next mine. The woman in it . . . cannot understand my strange behaviour. The others who happen to be awake think me foolish. I suppose I am, why should I mind a rat after all? I must learn not to.[52]

One cannot argue without more evidence that Orwell remembered this book when he wrote 1984, but it touches 1984 at so many points, most notably on the side of the emotions, that the name "Julia"—if nothing more—would appear to survive from Orwell's recollections of Mme de Beausobre's moving narrative.

III

THE INFLUENCE OF JAMES BURNHAM

WHOEVER investigates the background of *1984* must pay particular attention to the work of James Burnham. *The Managerial Revolution* was a seminal work in English;[1] *The Machiavellians*, and *The Struggle for the World* extended and brought up to date some of the generalizations of the earlier book. All three evoked important responses from Orwell in the form of reviews, essays, and numerous allusions; and, as we shall see, *1984* itself can be directly and solidly linked to Burnham's work. I am not the first to have thought so, of course; Hollis, Maddison, Wadsworth, Mander, and Cunningham have written about Orwell's indebtedness. Hollis observed correctly, though without supplying much evidence for his opinion, that the Book by Emmanuel Goldstein is "pure Burnhamism," and Maddison appropriately subtitled his essay on *1984* "A Burnhamite Fantasy."[2]

Burnham is but one of several influential writers classified by Orwell as "political pessimists"; the work of such otherwise widely different thinkers as F. A. Voigt, Peter Drucker, Michael Roberts, Malcolm Muggeridge, Hugh Kingsmill, Bertrand Russell, F. A. Hayek, and Michael Polanyi has tended in the same direction as Burnham's, as did that of Chesterton, Belloc, London, Huxley, and the later Wells. Ways in which some of these writers' ideas are related to Orwell's thinking and to *1984* have already been indicated. What Burnham has to say is worth explaining in even more detail if we are to assess accurately the contribution he made to *1984*.

Between January 1944 and March 1947, Orwell wrote about Burnham on at least five different occasions. His reaction to Burnham's arguments was intense; it is marked by the paradox of love and hate, acceptance and rejection that Richard Voorhees found to be so important a characteristic of Orwell's work. To examine this ambivalence about Burnham closely is to throw fresh light on what Orwell was doing in *1984*.

Behind Burnham's search in *The Managerial Revolution* "to discover," as he put it, "what type . . . of social organization is on the immediate historical horizon" lay his belief that capitalism was dying and that socialism would not, as the Marxists had predicted, take its place.[3] He thought capitalism had proved a failure in several ways: it could not solve the problem of mass unemployment; it could not cushion the violent movements of the business cycle; it could not use its own productive resources or satisfactorily invest its surplus capital; it could not exploit or develop efficiently the backward nations; it was failing to use new technology; and, most important, the ideology of capitalism and of the bourgeoisie was no longer able to command men's enthusiastic assent. Orwell interpreted Burnham's conclusion as a belief that capitalism was obviously doomed.[4]

That socialism, conceived as a classless, democratic, international system of society, was not going to replace capitalism was equally certain. Citing the Russian experience, Burnham showed that the abolition of private property and the vesting of ownership in the state had not produced socialism, and as evidence he noted the survival of the class system in the Soviet Union and the failure of "democracy" to emerge there. Moreover, even though the conditions necessary for socialism had existed in several European countries in the postwar era, the Marxist parties in one country after another, as he said, "have administered the government and have uniformly failed to introduce socialism or make any genuine step toward socialism."[5]

It was a myth that the "workers" were going to seize power. Again basing his theory on historical fact, Burnham cited what must have been for Orwell the heartbreaking example of Catalonia:

> There, just as in Russia, the workers and peasants began taking over direct control of the factories and railroads and farms. There too, not at once, but during the course of the first two years of the Civil War, the *de facto* power slipped from the workers' hands, sometimes voluntarily given up at the persuasion of a political party, sometimes smashed by arms and prison. It was not the troops of Franco who took control away from the people of Catalonia; they had lost control well before Franco's army conquered.[6]

What Burnham thought to be emerging instead was the "managerial society." We are now in a transitional stage of struggle and warfare, he believed, a period comparable to that between feudalism and capitalism, which he thought would come to an end around 1968. By then the "managers," i.e., the technicians, bureaucrats, financial experts, and middle-management executives, would have gained control (which for Burnham means effective ownership) of the means of production, and hence they would have control over the institutions of the state. In language echoed by the Book in *1984*, Burnham says:

> The ideologies expressing the social role and interests and aspirations of the managers . . . have not yet been fully worked out, . . . They are already approximated, however, from several different but similar directions, by, for example: Leninism-Stalinism; fascism-nazism; and, at a more primitive level, by New Dealism and such less influential American ideologies as "technocracy."[7]

The managerial society will not be classless, but it may be called Socialist "for ideological purposes in order to manipulate the favorable mass emotions attached to the historic socialist ideal of a free, classless, and international society and to hide the fact that the managerial economy is in actuality the basis for a new kind of exploiting, class society."[8] Judging from the prevailing tendencies in those countries farthest along the road to the future, Burnham predicted that the managerial society would be totalitarian. To the question of whether or not it would remain so, his answer was that in such a complicated and highly centralized society a one-party monopoly was probably needed for a proper degree of control. Hence the prospect for democracy was not favorable.

What are some of the features of this totalitarian society Burnham thought to be coming into existence on the model of Nazi Germany and Soviet Russia? There are first the managers who, basing their power on state control of the economy, are potentially a "ruling class of an extremity and absoluteness never before known."[9] The managers are identified with the ruling elites of the Communist and Nazi ideologies, i.e., with "the Party," which asserts in the transitional stage its claim to be the vanguard of the masses, thus justifying itself as a ruling class and making the idea of such a class acceptable to its mass following.[10] The managers will exercise their powers through "administrative boards, commissions, bureaus"—a form of corporate as opposed to private exploitation.[11] They will be analogous to a priestly caste, and like the College of Cardinals they will have the corporate power to choose their own leaders and adopt their successors. Their reward will be their right to exercise power and to receive "preferential treatment . . . allotted to them in terms of status in the political-economic structure."[12]

In contrast to that of the managers, the power of the people will be diminished in this new society. The need for a cadre of highly skilled workers would increase, and their welfare would be more closely associated with that of management than heretofore, but the necessity for large numbers of unskilled workers or even for a large proportion of skilled workers in production will be lessened owing to the increased use of machines. Even the usefulness of the "working class" in warfare will diminish, because mass infantry will no longer be widely employed. The masses will, of course, still be useful to the new elite as it struggles for power, for, "as Machiavelli pointed out in his *History of Florence,* the poor, enduring oppressive conditions, were always ready to answer the call for a fight for freedom; but the net result of each revolt was merely to establish a new tyranny."[13]

In the managerial society the "freedom" of the proletarians will be altered; they will be, as they are under capitalism, free from the responsibility of ownership, but their freedom to sell their services to the highest bidder will vanish. "There being only one major employer (the state), there will be no bargaining among competing employers; and the assignment and transfer of jobs, as well as the fixing of rates of pay, will not be left to the accidents of market bargaining."[14]

As for the masses in those parts of the world outside the direct control of the managers, their destiny is implied in Burnham's phrase "the exploitation of backward areas."[15] So far as these people are concerned, the managers will be able to solve a problem that baffled the capitalists, for they will not have to earn a profit. Their aim will simply be that of "organizing production in the most rational way possible, because the state will supply the capital and the motive will be the desire for more control and hence more power."[16]

In theory, Burnham says, managerial society ought to develop into the World State so dear to H. G. Wells, but for practical reasons it probably will not. Instead the "comparatively large number of sovereign states under capitalism is being replaced by a comparatively small number of great nations, or 'super-states,' which will divide the world among them." There will be three "primary super-states," comprising the three regions where the managerial society is most advanced: the United States, Northern Europe, and Japan with part of China. Small, independent states will disappear because they will not be able to defend their sovereignty.[17]

This new political system will be created by warfare, for that is the sole means employed in the past for that purpose, and there is no sign that any other instrumentality is going to replace it. World War II was the first war of the managerial society, but it will not be the last: "There will be much still to be decided after the present struggle is over—though, since war and peace are no longer declared, it may be hard to know when this struggle is over and the next one begins."[18]

The three superstates will therefore continue to fight. "Ostensibly," Burnham says, "these wars will be directed from each base for conquest of the other bases. But it does not seem possible for any one of these to conquer the others; and even two of them in coalition could not win a decisive and lasting victory over the third." The superstates therefore will not be fighting to determine who will rule the strategic bases but to decide "what parts and how much of the *rest* of the world are going to be ruled by each of the three strategic centers." These wars between the superstates have another aspect; that is, they can also be viewed as "wars of the metropolitan centers against the backward areas and peoples."[19]

The new order that Burnham thus describes will be a hierarchical society in which the ruling class will seek to increase its power, first by defeating the capitalists and then by warring on the masses. There will, of course, be resistance; among the managers there will also be fighting over the spoils until some group becomes dominant and consolidates its control. Burnham does not try to foresee what will happen then, but the direction of his thinking is clear. As he says, "Unfortunately, we already know what two of the aims of managerial planning are: the more effective prosecution of war, and the support of the power and privilege of a new ruling class."[20]

Burnham concedes that the superior powers of direction afforded by managerial society may be used for the benefit of mankind at large. "Just as many new inventions can be used equally well to kill men or to grow better food, so may there be plans for freeing humanity or for enslaving it further."[21] But the latter alternative is more probable, given the fact that the "new, rising social order is, as against the old, more likely to resort on a large scale to lies, terror, persecution."[22]

Managerial society will have its own kind of crisis. Breakdowns in bureaucratic administration will be inevitable because the system cannot readily accommodate itself to a sudden change from war to peace or abrupt changes in technology, just as it cannot easily deal with "mass movements of dissatisfaction and revolt which, with the state and economy fused, would be automatically at once political and economic in character and effect."[23] That any rebellion would actually occur is doubtful, however, since the devotion of the masses to democracy is questionable, and they can be duped into exchanging their freedom for such things as jobs, food, or security. Since the new ruling class will be more powerful than any known heretofore, and since in the transitional dictatorships that Burnham observed in Russia, Germany, and Italy "nearly every side of life, business and art and science and education and religion and recreation and morality are not merely influenced by but directly subjected to the totalitarian regime,"[24] one may conclude that managerial society will not mean an increase in personal liberty and that, if not permanent, it will be very long lasting.

Even this brief summary of *The Managerial Revolution* should be enough to show why the author of *1984* found Burnham's ideas arresting, both in themselves and for the ready acceptance they gained from intellectuals.[25] At first Orwell's reaction was antagonistic, partly because he suspected Burnham of being anti-British. Later on, fortunately, this suspicion was allayed by Burnham's denial of the charge and Orwell's growing awareness of what Burnham's position really was.

Burnham was wrong, said Orwell in 1944, in his prediction that Germany would first defeat Britain and then attack Russia; he was equally mistaken in his view that totalitarianism was the inevitable form of future society. Writing in *Tribune*, Orwell said:

> The basic error of this school of thought is its contempt for the common man. A totalitarian society, it is felt, *must* be stronger than a democratic one: the expert's opinion *must* be worth more than the ordinary man's. The German army had won the first battles: therefore it must win the last one. The great strength of democracy, its power of criticism, was ignored.[26]

Nor did he share the view of the future that he attributed to Burnham. "Where Burnham and his fellow-thinkers are wrong," he went on, "is in trying to spread the idea that totalitarianism is *unavoidable*, and that therefore we must do nothing to oppose it."

Two months later, in a letter to *Tribune*, Burnham replied to Orwell's criticism. He denied having said that totalitarianism in the major nations was unavoidable, only that it was probable. He denied also having said that the German army was invincible or that Germany, Japan, and the United States would be the three superstates of the future. He rejected Orwell's implication that he was anti-British, but he did acknowledge believing that the Stalinist regime was "the worst so far known in history."[27]

In a rebuttal, printed with Burnham's letter, Orwell restated his understanding of Burnham's double thesis: that power cannot be restrained and that both democracy and socialism are at present impossible, and he added, "If democracy is impossible and all rulers are as described, what prospect can there be except totalitarianism?" Orwell also repeated his analysis of Burnham's predictions that

Germany would first defeat Britain and then Russia and concluded: "We could all be true prophets if we were allowed to alter our prophecies after the event."

The Machiavellians may be read as a commentary on *The Managerial Revolution,* and for the purposes of this study it is significant for two reasons. The first is its analysis of the human desire for power over men and things. Following Machiavelli, Burnham defines politics as "the study of the struggles for power among men."[28] Man's insatiable appetite for power is the dynamo of political conduct, causing perpetual change and political instability. Every society is composed of three groups: a governing elite, a nongoverning elite, and the mass of people. "The primary object of every elite, or ruling class, is to maintain its own power and privilege," and to do so it will always use force and fraud.[29]

On this question of the struggle for power, Orwell offered this summary of Burnham's analysis of Machiavelli, Mosca, Pareto, Michels, and Sorel:

> Progress is largely an illusion. Democracy is impossible, though useful as a myth to deceive the masses.
>
> Society is inevitably ruled by oligarchies who hold their position by means of force and fraud, and whose sole objective is power and still more power for themselves. No revolution means more than a change of rulers.
>
> Man, as a political animal, is moved solely by selfish motives, except so far as he is under the influence of myths.
>
> Conscious, planned action for the good of the community is impossible, since each group is simply trying to secure its own advantage.
>
> Politics is, and can be, nothing except a struggle for power. Human equality, human fraternity are empty phrases.
>
> All moral codes, all "idealistic" conceptions of politics, all visions of a better society in the future are simply lies, conscious or unconscious, covering the naked struggle for power.[30]

The second feature in *The Machiavellians* that is especially noteworthy is Burnham's discussion of whether or not an elite might rule "scientifically." That is, using the large amount of new knowledge about administration and organization, could it maintain itself in power while pursuing with objectivity "consciously understood and deliberately chosen goals"?[31] Burnham's answer to this question is a tentative yes, and the reason for his answer is of considerable interest to students of *1984.* He notes the dilemma faced by any elite trying to rule scientifically: the political life of most men in society necessitates a belief in myths, although a scientific outlook will not permit one to believe them. Nevertheless, he said:

> The leaders must profess, indeed foster, belief in the myths, or the fabric of society will crack and they be overthrown. In short, the leaders, if they themselves are scientific, must lie. It is hard to lie all the time in public but to keep privately an objective regard for the truth. Not only is it hard; it is often ineffective, for lies are often not convincing when told with a divided heart. The tendency is for the deceivers to become self-deceived, to believe their own myths. When this happens, they are no longer scientific. Sincerity is bought at the price of truth.[32]

The obvious interest of this passage lies in its relation to double-think, and we will return to that connection later.

Orwell criticized *The Machiavellians* even more severely than *The Managerial Revolution,* probably because it overemphasized selfishness as the primary human motive and force and fraud as the chief means used by the leaders to achieve their aims. Alluding to the satisfaction one gets from doing what is forbidden, he observed that the same pleasure results from adopting certain political theories:

> Any theory which is obviously dishonest and immoral ("realistic" is the favourite word at this moment) will find adherents who accept it just for that reason. Whether the theory works, whether it attains the result aimed at will hardly be questioned. The mere fact that it throws ordinary decency overboard will be accepted as proof of its grown-upness and consequently of its efficacy.[33]

Commenting adversely on Burnham's outlook, Orwell goes on to point out that it is no more scientific than "the idealistic creeds it professes to debunk." He interprets Burnham's premise to be that "a relatively decent society . . . in which everyone has enough to eat and wars are a thing of the past, is impossible," but in his opinion Burnham made no effort to prove that conclusion. In fact, Burnham based it on the tacit assumption that what has not existed in the past will not exist in the future.

In this context one may note, however, that in 1938 Orwell had been speculating in a similarly pessimistic vein:

> It would seem that what you get over and over again is a movement of the proletariat which is promptly canalised and betrayed by

astute people at the top, and then the growth of a new governing class. The one thing that never arrives is equality. The mass of the people never get the chance to bring their innate decency into the control of affairs, so that one is almost driven to the cynical thought that men are only decent when they are powerless.[34]

But in 1944 Orwell was arguing that Machiavelli's pessimism about the possibility of a decent future for all human beings had been invalidated by modern technology. And by the pragmatic test of history, the results of World War II for example, Machiavelli is also discredited: "It would seem," he says, "that the theory that there is no such thing as a 'good' motive in politics, that nothing counts except force and fraud, has a hole in it somewhere, and that the Machiavellian system fails, even by its own test of material success."[35] The best guide to action that neo-Machiavellians like Burnham can offer is that dishonesty, not honesty, is the best policy: "The fact that this shallow piece of naughtiness can—just because it sounds 'realistic' and grown-up—be accepted without any examination does not speak well for the Anglo-American intelligentsia."[36]

Somewhat later, in October 1945, an article by Orwell appeared under the title "You and the Atomic Bomb." Acknowledging that the new weapon had further tipped the balance of power toward the state as against the individual and that this implied an additional loss of personal freedom, Orwell alluded to Burnham rather more generously than he had done earlier. He repeated that Burnham's prophecy of a German victory had been falsified by events. Now, however, he added:

> This was a miscalculation, but it does not affect the main argument. For Burnham's geographical picture of the new world has turned out to be correct. More and more obviously the surface of the earth is being parcelled off into three great empires, each self-contained and cut off from contact with the outer world, and each ruled, under one disguise or another, by a self-elected oligarchy. The haggling as to where the frontiers are to be drawn is still going on, and will continue for some years, and the third of the three super-states— East Asia, dominated by China—is still potential rather than actual. But the general drift is unmistakable, and every scientific discovery of recent years has accelerated it.[37]

In the same context he observes that the trend toward what he calls superstates "has been obvious for years, and was pointed out by a few observers even before 1914." This last qualification, however, in no way detracts from his tribute to Burnham.

Orwell's essay "Second Thoughts on James Burnham" (1946) elaborates ideas which Orwell had already expressed in print. By this time his approval of some of what Burnham says is clear enough, though it is sometimes grudging: "As an interpretation of what is *happening*, Burnham's theory is extremely plausible, to put it at the lowest. The events of, at any rate, the last fifteen years in the USSR can be far more easily explained by this theory than by any other."[38] He admits also that "if one considers the world movement as a whole, his conclusions are difficult to resist," and that "Burnham has probably been more right than wrong about the present and the immediate past."[39]

But if Burnham's conclusions are difficult to resist, Orwell nevertheless resists them. He insists that what Burnham is saying is not new, and he again criticizes Burnham for asserting that the drift toward a totalitarian state ruled by an oligarchy is inevitable. Burnham's tendency to predict a continuation of what is happening, he says, is "a major mental disease, and its roots lie partly in cowardice and partly in the worship of power."[40]

This is the same disease that Chesterton had commented on in *The Napoleon of Notting Hill,* and Orwell also found it in the Russophile intelligentsia in England who hoped to augment their own power as the result of some drastic social change. One of the worst evils of this power worship was its blurring of political judgment—for example, the wish for something different interfering with the ability to see that social change is not apocalyptic but rather gradual and slow.[41]

In 1947, Orwell published his final commentary on Burnham's ideas (excluding *1984*) in a long review of *The Struggle for the World*.[42] According to Burnham this was the prospect: The atom bomb had altered the relation between the great powers; the Soviet Union might soon possess the bomb, and unless the United States acted quickly it would enter the inevitable war against the Soviet Union without much hope of winning. What the United States had to do was to propose an immediate union with Great Britain and the Dominions and then draw Western Europe into its orbit. It must establish itself as the enemy of communism throughout the world and wipe out domestic communism. It must have a clear plan for organizing the world and be prepared to carry out the plan even if it required the use of atomic bombs. Unless the United States did all this, the experts and fanatics ruling the Soviet Union, helped by the threat of the bomb, would conquer the world.

Orwell's first comment on the book is that Burnham was in effect advocating a preventive war; his second, that Burnham had abandoned his belief in the inevitable victory of totalitarianism and become "the champion of old-style democracy." In the third place he praises Burnham for his intellectual courage, his regard for real issues, and his honesty in dealing with the facts of international life as he understands them. It is not, one suspects, because of any mellowing in Orwell that his comments on Burnham are more generous here, but rather that Burnham had changed in ways that Orwell approved, that is, no longer interpreting history in purely Machiavellian terms.

Orwell still found fault with Burnham, however, though for different reasons. He thought that Burnham's picture of the dedicated, fanatical Communist was exaggerated, largely because Burnham did not assign sufficient significance to the rapid turnover in Communist party membership. He agreed that there were a "few hundred thousand or a few million fanatical, dehumanized people, mostly inside the U.S.S.R., who are the nucleus of the movement." He thought it was also true that some secret Communists are dangerous and that Communist fractions in the labor movement exert power far out of proportion to their numbers. Still, when this was said, the fact of rapid turnover in membership remained, the disillusioned fellow traveler was a familiar figure, and the patriotism of most people in time of crisis was such as to reduce to a minimum the possibility of the Russians' having a powerful fifth column in the countries they might threaten.

Orwell's analysis of this point led him to a more familiar criticism of Burnham—that he overstates his case: "He is too fond of apocalyptic visions, too ready to believe that the muddled processes of history will happen suddenly and logically." Furthermore, Burnham, like many intellectuals, tended to compress the time scale; in this instance, he talked of a margin of five or ten years. "But," Orwell asked:

> . . . suppose he is wrong. Suppose the ship is not sinking, only leaking. Suppose that Communism is not yet strong enough to swallow the world and that the danger of war can be staved off for twenty years or more: then we don't have to accept Burnham's remedy—or, at least, we don't have to accept it immediately and without question.[43]

Burnham saw everything in the darkest colors, but Orwell thought we had another alternative, given more time, and this was making democratic socialism work, not just in Norway or New Zealand but over as large an area as Western Europe and Africa. He acknowledged the enormous impediments in the way of his proposal, but he believed it possible if enough people wanted it, and if peace could be assured for the ten or twenty years it would take to bring it about. Such a project, moreover, would rob the Russian dictatorship of any pretext for existing and significantly lessen the appeal of communism.

Finally Orwell objected that "the tendency of writers like Burnham, whose key concept is 'realism,' is to overrate that part played in human affairs by sheer force." He admitted that Burnham was not always wrong and agreed that the same moral code does not apply in politics that applies in private life, but he felt that Burnham's view of the world was always somewhat distorted. The reason lay in Burnham's tendency to be preoccupied with power and to exaggerate its importance. Thinking, as he characteristically did, "of monsters and cataclysms," Burnham lacked perspective. Otherwise, Orwell thought, he might see more clearly that what was happening did not necessarily have to continue.

He might see, too, that a democracy is not handicapped by the rigidity of a totalitarian state. Its power of self-criticism would save it from the errors in politics and strategy that totalitarian governments commit. Specifically Orwell notes two possibilities that Burnham, inhibited by his preoccupation with power, fails to grasp. One is that "the Russian regime may become more liberal and less dangerous a generation hence"; the other is that the "great powers will be simply too frightened of the effects of atomic weapons ever to make use of them." In Orwell's opinion, possibilities like these are too dull for Burnham, for whom the choice must be all or nothing, but "history never happens quite so melodramatically as that."

Perhaps history's melodramas are muted by actuality, but art is not so inhibited. It is free to distort the time scale or to assume that the impossible can be treated as if it were probable—all in the interest of a more profound truth than that of the actual. This is what Orwell did in 1984 when by projecting the logical implications of Burnham's arguments into the future he sought to refute them.

PART TWO

The Intellectuals

IV

THE POLITICS OF POWER

WHEN the history of intellectuals in the twentieth century is written, some part of it will be devoted to Orwell's analysis and criticism of his fellow intellectuals. *1984* is very much a book about intellectuals, their beliefs, and their ways of thinking and feeling. Any utopia book must be so, since such books stress the importance of rationality and a rational control of human affairs, but in writing *1984* Orwell was principally interested in working out the consequences of the tendencies he saw about him rather than explaining how they developed. The reasons why O'Brien and his kind can exercise their tyranny are implicit in the novel, but only in his earlier essays and articles does Orwell explicitly show his beliefs about the attraction of power, the kinds of people who succumbed to it, and the organizations and systems of thought through which the leaders exerted power.

Thus, long before *1984*, Orwell had begun to single out and attack certain movements and institutions in which intellectuals were prominent, because they endangered freedom of thought and represented efforts by elitists to gain power. His journalism attests his skeptical view of the intelligentsia and his mistrust of the press, as well as his specific opposition to certain groups—Socialists, Communists, pacifists, Roman Catholics—that appealed to the intellectual's fascination with power, his love of order, and his need for some faith and some activity worthy of his talents.

The terms "intellectuals," "intelligentsia," "literary intelligentsia," and "politico-literary intellectuals" appear often in Orwell's writings, seldom in favorable contexts. During the war especially, Orwell was accused of being prejudiced against intellectuals. Alex Comfort, whose pacifism he attacked, wrote of him in 1942, "Mr. Orwell is intellectual-hunting again,"[1] as one might say, "Hieronimo is mad again." Orwell's reply to this charge, expressed in language rather below his usual standard, helps to clarify his definition of what an intellectual ought to be:

> I have used a lot of ink and done myself a lot of harm by attacking the successive literary cliques which have infested this country, not

because they were intellectuals but precisely because they were *not* what I mean by true intellectuals. The life of a clique is about five years and I have been writing long enough to see three of them come and two go—the Catholic gang, the Stalinist gang, and the present pacifist or, as they are sometimes nicknamed, Fascifist gang. My case against all of them is that they write mentally dishonest propaganda and degrade literary criticism to mutual arse-licking.[2]

He went on to condemn the peace propaganda that avoided mentioning Hitler's invasion of Russia, and said it was not what he meant by intellectual honesty. "It is just because I do take the function of the intelligentsia seriously that I don't like the sneers, libels, parrot phrases and financially profitable back-scratching which flourish in our English literary world."

Such statements as these, uttered in the heat of controversy and in the midst of a world war in which Great Britain was fighting to survive, are perhaps too sharply expressed; but it is noteworthy that even in this context Orwell sought to distinguish between the Alex Comfort who had written an admirable poem and the Alex Comfort who wrote "lifeless propaganda tracts dressed up as novels." It is noteworthy also that at least one critic felt that his attacks were effective. In Conor Cruise O'Brien's judgment Orwell's writings "shook the confidence of the English left, perhaps permanently." Writing in 1964, he said:

> The cant of the left, that cant which has so far proved indispensable to the victory of any mass movement, was almost destroyed by Orwell's attacks, which put out of action so much cant-producing machinery in its factories: the minds of left-wing intellectuals. His effect on the English left might be compared to that of Voltaire on the French nobility: he weakened their belief in their own ideology, made them ashamed of their cliches, left them intellectually more scrupulous and more defenceless.[3]

The intellectuals whom Orwell observed tacitly or overtly assenting to totalitarian ideas and actions differed, of course, in their allegiances.[4] Some were Russophiles and within this grouping were further divided according to their loyalties to particular leaders. Others were admirers of fascism and the Nazi brand of tyranny. Still others embraced the orthodoxy of the Roman Catholic church. Orwell saw little to choose between these various systems. To him, they all had the same disastrous consequences for ordinary people. Only the leaders had any freedom; the rest were permitted at best to be followers. At worst—that is, if they were not sufficiently docile—they were forced into slavery or killed.

The prospect of exercising power themselves—or at least admiration for those who could grasp that power—was one of the great forces which inclined intellectuals on both the Left and the Right toward supporting the tyrants:

> A tyrant is all the more admired if he happens to be a bloodstained crook as well, and "the end justifies the means" often becomes, in effect, "the means justify themselves provided they are dirty enough." This idea colours the outlook of all sympathisers with totalitarianism, and accounts, for instance, for the positive delight with which many English intellectuals greeted the Nazi-Soviet pact.[5]

Power and cruelty go together, and although Orwell acknowledged that some English intellectuals were led by "genuinely progressive impulses" to admire the Soviet Union, still power-worship was probably the strongest motive of the Russophiles, most of whom were members of Burnham's managerial class.[6]

Perhaps it is indicative of Orwell's "Englishness" that he found fault with contemporary intellectuals for taking so many of their ideas from continental Europe, having been "infected by habits of thought that derive ultimately from Machiavelli."[7] He thought, too, that the process by which some English intellectuals had come to sympathize with the totalitarians had begun with writers at least as far back as Carlyle and Creasy. The infection, he found, was being transmitted to the common people by writers like James Hadley Chase—"Carlyle for the masses"—whose violent and amoral novels were at one time extremely popular.

But the development of totalitarian ideas was less significant to Orwell than their current acceptance by intellectuals of both the Right and the Left. "The truth is, of course, that the countless English intellectuals who kiss the arse of Stalin are not different from the minority who give their allegiance to Hitler or Mussolini," he said in an article he wrote for *Horizon*, although the remark was censored by someone on the editorial staff.[8]

Insofar as the intellectuals of the Left opposed Hitler, Orwell considered their actions to be more honorable than their theories. Nevertheless, he felt that they were no better than their opponents on the Right in their willingness to enter into what he called "the evil world of 'realism' and power politics."[9] Left-wing intellectuals supported Chiang Kai-Shek; and Churchill, he said, was the darling of the *Daily Worker*. They were pleased by the pictures of Stalin shaking hands with Hitler, and they defended the Nazi-Soviet pact.

The truth was, he thought, that "in a totalitarian age each man worships power in a form he can understand; the daydream of each is appropriate to his intellectual maturity, but its content is the same: "A twelve-year-old boy worships Jack Dempsey. An adolescent in a Glasgow slum worships Al Capone. An aspiring pupil at a business college worships Lord Nuffield. A *New Statesman* reader worships Stalin."[10] This is perhaps a fanciful explanation for power worship, existing principally to lend force to the last sentence, but intellectuals can find a more practical reason in the example set by the leaders of the Soviet Union. For the Communist party to maintain its dominant position in the state, its leaders had to abandon much of Marx's teaching: "The 'dictatorship of the proletariat' had to mean the dictatorship of a handful of intellectuals, ruling through terrorism."[11] English intellectuals thus had before them a demonstration of what could be done by those who had seized power and were, at any price, determined to hold it.

Furthermore, as Orwell thought, many of the Russophiles in England, members of Burnham's managerial class, were beginning to glimpse the opportunity to become rulers in their own country, to secure more power and prestige for themselves. In the Soviet Union they saw:

> . . . a system which eliminates the upper class, keeps the working class in its place, and hands unlimited power to people very similar to themselves. It was only *after* the Soviet régime became unmistakably totalitarian that English intellectuals, in large numbers, began to show an interest in it. Burnham, although the English russophile intelligentsia would repudiate him, is really voicing their secret wish: the wish to destroy the old, equalitarian version of Socialism and usher in a hierarchical society where the intellectual can at last get his hands on the whip.[12]

A specific example of the intellectuals' deference to power was their attitude toward the premature rising in Warsaw in 1944, which turned out to be a disaster for the Polish resistance. Amid the controversy over who was to blame, Orwell observed that the first concern of left-wing intellectuals was to find out what Soviet policy was—not whether it was right or wrong. They wished to make the Soviet Union appear to be right in any circumstances.

Orwell had little respect for the reasons they gave for yielding so readily to the Russian claims. He said their attitude "is defended, if at all, solely on grounds of power. The Russians are powerful in eastern Europe, we are not: therefore we must not oppose them. This involves the principle, of its nature alien to Socialism, that you must not protest against an evil which you cannot prevent."[13]

Orwell found other arguments to advance against intellectuals who, thinking they were thus being "realistic," stood mute when faced with questions about the nature and use of power. In the first place, he said, power politics did not invariably pay. Mussolini was a professed student and follower of Machiavelli, and he failed. Nazi Germany was being beaten by other forces, at least some of whom did not imitate its supposedly realistic unscrupulousness. Second, even if a dictator has a great force at his command, it is often not enough to secure the ends he desires. As he pointed out in rebutting Burnham, Orwell believed that a system based on force alone lacks the strength that a democracy derives from self-criticism, whose operation can sometimes prevent fatal mistakes.[14]

In the third place, Machiavelli's theory was out of date. Even if it could be proved that at one time the use of force and fraud was needed to exploit the labor of ignorant masses in order to subsidize an elite who would carry on the arts of civilization, this was no longer true. As Orwell realized, the conditions of modern industrial life make a society of equal human beings at least technically possible. The human labor once needed to liberate even a minority can be replaced by machines; and the majority of people, like the elite in fifteenth-century Florence, could be freed to cultivate their talents.

Finally, to show that the Devil can be quoted at need, Orwell pointed out that Marx himself rejected the purely materialistic and quantitative measure of power. Quoting Marx's, "Religion is the sigh of the soul in a soulless world. Religion is the opium of the people," Orwell went on to ask: "What is he saying except that man does *not* live by bread alone, that hatred is *not* enough, that a world worth living in cannot be founded on 'realism' and machine-guns."[15]

To ridicule those intellectuals who resorted to doublethink in order to preserve their belief that human history is determined by force alone, Orwell formulated what he called the Theory of Catastrophic Gradualism. He attributed this theory to those who wished to "justify some action which conflicts with the sense of decency of the average human being." This is how he states its essence:

Nothing is ever achieved without bloodshed, lies, tyranny and injustice, but on the other hand no considerable change for the better
is to be expected as the result of even the greatest upheaval. . . .
One must not protest against purges, deportations, secret police
forces and so forth, because this is the price that has to be paid for
progress; but on the other hand "human nature" will always see to
it that progress is slow or even imperceptible.[16]

The theory developed, he thought, because intellectuals needed to
explain the failure of the Russian revolution. To admit that failure
would be to "repudiate the whole theory of totalitarianism, which
few English intellectuals have the courage to do." It was this need,
he said, that induced Kingsley Martin to liken Stalin to Henry VIII
and to be unmoved by a few million "liquidations."[17]

Orwell identified the connection between this routine belief in
progress and the acceptance of tyranny: "If each epoch is as a matter
of course better than the last, then any crime or force that pushes the
historical process forward can be justified." We need to redefine the
idea of progress, he said, and to look afresh at the notion that history
is predetermined. In any event, the absurdity of this theory, and the
state of the world in 1946, indicated to him that Arthur Koestler was
right in thinking that the Yogi had to be called to the aid of the
Commisar in order to curb men's desire for power. It would not do
to follow either the "practical men [who] have led us to the edge of
the abyss," or "the intellectuals in whom acceptance of power politics
has killed first the moral sense, and then the sense of reality."[18]

Thus Orwell in his time, like Benda a generation or so earlier,
came to believe that the intellectuals had betrayed their trust and
repudiated their obligation to think.[19] They had been so corrupted
by the desire to get their hands on the whip that they had accepted
without analysis or protest the totalitarian outlook: "The sin of nearly
all left-wingers from 1933 onwards is that they have wanted to be
anti-Fascist without being anti-totalitarian."[20] This failure to follow
the truth where it led them and to declare it when they found it
fostered the evasions and compromises they adopted to defend totalitarianism. And it is Orwell's perception of this unsoundness in the
intellectual movements of his day that informs *1984*.[21]

V

BELIEVERS AND UNBELIEVERS

ENGLAND'S protection against tyranni-
cal collectivism, Orwell thought, lay in certain traditional features of
English life. One of these was a general sympathy for the underdog,
"a tendency," as he said, "to support the weaker side merely because
it is weaker."[1] Another was a strong and widespread belief in an
almost absolute standard of right and wrong. Orwell considered such
a standard to be as necessary in politics as it was in ordinary life,
and he devoted an essay to outlining his disagreement with a Communist scientist, J. D. Bernal, who argued that political expediency
was more important than moral principle. Such a position, Orwell
said, implied that "public spirit and common decency pull in opposite directions"; and if such were true, we would have to keep
changing our ideas of right and wrong "from year to year, and if
necessary from minute to minute." He observed that Communists
defined morality by political objectives, so that "any virtue can become a vice, and any vice a virtue, according to the political needs of
the moment." For Bernal, he noted, power and virtue were related—
whatever works is good—and therefore questions provoked by individual conscience or a traditional moral code were irrelevant. He
summed up Bernal's doctrine as "anything is right that furthers the
aims of Russian foreign policy."[2]

The common man, unlike a scientist trained in Marxism, was
reluctant to change his moral attitudes, which were about a century
behind the times. Most Englishmen, Orwell said, were still "living in
the mental world of Dickens."[3] Their moral credo found its best expression in Christianity, not as elaborated doctrine but as a code of
conduct. Though he detected even among ordinary people a growing
acceptance of expediency and callousness "in the face of the most
atrocious crimes and sufferings,"[4] nevertheless he thought them on
the whole still living in a "world of absolute good and evil from
which the intellectuals have long since escaped."[5] In another place
he said that common people retained enough of the Christian ethic to
condemn the belief that might is right; it was the intellectuals who
joined the cult of the power worshippers.[6] This is not owing to any
special virtue, or at least not to one consciously cherished by ordinary

men, but rather to their general indifference to intellectual matters: "An ordinary Englishman, Conservative, Socialist, Catholic, Communist, or what not, almost never grasps the full logical implications of the creed he professes: almost always he utters heresies without noticing it. Orthodoxies, whether of the Right or the Left, flourish chiefly among the literary intelligentsia, the people who ought in theory to be the guardians of freedom of thought."[7] Despite this condemnation he acknowledged the plight of the modern intellectuals who became cynical or turned to Catholicism, and he understood better than most the reasons for their despair.

Hope defeated is one of the permanent themes of human history, but even so it is remarkable how often and how rapidly the cycle recurs among intellectuals in recent times. John Lehmann observed that from Auden's *Spain* to Orwell's *Homage to Catalonia* the same parabola is described that marked World War I: idealistic enthusiasm for a worthy cause mobilizes a crusade against supposed tyranny that soon founders in disillusionment and a determination not to be fooled again.[8] The credulity and disillusion are equally exaggerated. The motion of the cycle is violent because ideas and emotions do not rest on a foundation of belief that might restrain their excesses, except perhaps the belief that anything is better than what exists. This instability is readily observable among intellectuals, and it is symptomatic of a more profound malaise.

Orwell more than once tells the story of playing a "rather cruel trick" on a wasp which was sucking jam on his plate. He cut the wasp in half, but the wasp went on with his meal: "Only when he tried to fly away did he grasp the dreadful thing that had happened to him. It is the same with modern man. The thing that has been cut away is his soul."[9] Ironically, the thinking man was very often the one who worked this destruction on others. To him the operation was necessary, says Orwell, to remove the contradiction between the actual workings of capitalist society and the Christian faith that another world existed free of the injustice of this one; that promise was a lie thoughtful men could not tolerate, hence their rebelliousness and disaffection.

Literary men from Gibbon and Voltaire to Shaw and Joyce were therefore "destroyers, wreckers, saboteurs," but the truth they supposed they were offering as compensation had no saving virtue:

> For two hundred years we had sawed and sawed and sawed at the branch we were sitting on. And in the end, much more suddenly than anyone had foreseen, our efforts were rewarded, and down

we came. But unfortunately there had been a little mistake. The thing at the bottom was not a bed of roses after all, it was a cesspool full of barbed wire.[10]

To the metaphor of the wasp he added this remark: ". . . amputation of the soul *isn't* just a simple surgical job. . . . The wound has a tendency to go septic."[11]

Faced with an increasing awareness of the development Orwell perceived, intellectuals of the nineteenth and twentieth centuries tended to assume one of two initially contradictory attitudes. The first is manifested by writers who realized that what they valued was disappearing but who believed they could not arrest or reverse the process. For Orwell, "The Scholar Gypsy" expressed what was perhaps the prevailing literary attitude of the last hundred years "with its railing against the 'strange disease of modern life' and its magnificent defeatist simile in the final stanza."[12] And the early poems of T. S. Eliot, with their "glowing despair," were "an end-product, the last gasp of a cultural tradition, poems which spoke only for the cultivated third-generation *rentier,* for people able to feel and criticize but no longer able to act."[13] Recalling that E. M. Forster praised "Prufrock" because it was about people who were "ineffectual and weak" and because it was "innocent of public spirit," he himself felt that these poems, evoking the spirit of "conscious futility," had left no place for "the qualities by which any society which is to last longer than a generation actually has to be sustained—industry, courage, patriotism, frugality, philoprogenitiveness."[14]

The second principal response to the loss of a confident spiritual life based on faith in the Divine was typified by Shaw and Wells, with their root and branch criticism of the defects of capitalist, Christian society and their advocacy of a new order. Shaw wanted to apply Marxism to every aspect of human affairs. Wells foresaw the earthly paradise as the result of orderly progress through the dissemination and use of scientific knowledge. Shaw's buoyant and witty hopefulness degenerated into praise for Hitler and Stalin, and then, happily, concluded in religious ecstasy—Marx's "sigh of the soul in a soulless world." Wells gave mankind up in disgust, concluding that it had reached the end of its tether and gone insane.[15]

Thus the intellectuals, carrying on what they may have thought was their necessary historical task of amputating society's soul, had also accomplished their own disaffection. What Arnold had anticipated, "the infection of our mental strife," had culminated in Henry Miller's acceptance of defeat: twitching passivity inside the whale.

Conscious of living in what they thought to be a dying society, often deceived by false promises of a new world, intellectuals had also an immediately practical reason for their disaffection. "In the last twenty years," Orwell said, "particularly in Britain and America and almost as much in France, there has been no real job, no place in the structure of society, . . . for the thinking man, as such, to make himself or feel himself *useful*."[16]

Things had been different in the nineteenth century. As Orwell interpreted the history of the immediate past, the need to administer a vast empire had permitted men to unite intelligence and action in their work, free of any very close supervision. Since then, intelligence and action had been divorced. Thinking, such as it was, was centralized in Whitehall, and the men in the field did what they were told. Furthermore, the aims and workings of the Empire had become so outdated and unjust that the intelligentsia would have revolted even if they had been offered otherwise attractive jobs, just as Orwell had given up his police work in Burma. Writing of people like himself, educated and needing work, but with aspirations toward something more than money, he said:

> They lived in a society which automatically deprived them of function and in which the best way to prosper was to be stupid. That is the explanation of their never-failing discontent. In every other way they had opportunities such as the world has never before seen. They had ease, money, security, liberty of thought and even completer moral liberty. Life in Bloomsbury during the last twenty years has been what the moral rebels all through the ages have dreamed about. And yet on the whole the people who were favoured in this way weren't happy, didn't really like the things they ostensibly asked for. They would sooner have had a genuine function in a society which might give them less but took them more seriously.[17]

The divorce between intelligence and action is demonstrated also in the political history of England in the twenties and thirties. "If you had the kind of brain that could understand the poems of T. S. Eliot or the theories of Karl Marx, the higher-ups would see to it that you were kept out of any important job. The intellectuals could find a function for themselves only in the literary reviews and the left-wing political parties."[18]

The intelligentsia, therefore, especially the intelligentsia of the Left so conspicuous in the intellectual world during the thirties, was discontented and mistrustful. Without enough satisfying and praiseworthy jobs, dependent for its income on a capitalism it despised, leading an exceptionally secure life, this group was remarkable for "its extraordinarily negative outlook, its lack of any firm beliefs or positive aims, and its power of harbouring illusions that would not be possible to people in less sheltered places."[19] These show up not only in hatred of things as they are, but also, judging from the work of the *New Statesman* and such men as Cole, Crossman, and Laski, in exaggerated suspicion and criticism of the Labour party—the chief practical means in Britain by which things might be made better. Its leaders, said Orwell, were suspected of wanting "not actually to sell out to the enemy, but to slow down the rate of change and to keep the social structure as nearly intact as possible."[20]

Feeling useless and dependent one naturally also feels inferior. Auden said that the poet should either try to look like a stockbroker or, since he is a parasite, leave the dying middle class and attach himself to the proletariat.[21] Of this "Proletcult" Orwell remarked, "In the nineteen-thirties we saw a whole literary generation, or at least the most prominent members of a generation, either pretending to be proletarians or indulging in public orgies of self-hatred because they were not proletarians."[22] Orwell's friend, Cyril Connolly, was an exception, since he was as disdainful of the beehive state as an aristocrat should be. Yet, as Orwell remarked, he self-consciously accuses himself in *The Unquiet Grave* of being "an end-product, a mere ghost, like the cultivated pagans of 400 A.D. On almost every page [his] book exhibits that queer product of capitalist democracy, an inferiority complex resulting from a private income." Communists and fellow travelers, he went on to say, shared Connolly's assumptions about society but rejected his clinging to the lost cause of individualism. They chose collectivism and yielded up their "intellectual integrity in a frenzy of masochism."[23]

When Orwell attacked such intellectuals who sought escape through orthodoxies of one kind or another, he usually aimed at Communists and others on the political Left, but he also had some harsh things to say about the Roman Catholic church and Roman Catholic intellectuals. He praised Chesterton, Belloc, and Maritain because he thought their influence beneficial in countering the "too easy optimism and ill-thought-out materialism" of left-wing intellectuals. But "the Christian humanist is a rare animal," he said, and his respect for the message of those few did little more than qualify his general disapproval of the Roman Catholic church and writers who adhered to it.[24]

Orwell's Protestant teaching may have prejudiced him against Catholicism; but he thought any orthodoxy—Communist or Catholic —severely limited the individual's capacity to judge matters for himself. Very early in his career, in 1932, he wrote that there could be "very little real contact of mind between believer and unbeliever." He then went on to strike in two directions with an allusion to the "Hebrew-like pride and exclusiveness of the genuine Catholic mind." The genuine Catholic, he said, was one who could see no possibility of salvation outside the church and who considered that "dogmatic intolerance is a duty to the infinite truth."[25]

In 1946 he was still expressing similar opinions, alluding to the heretic as a courageous figure who, like Daniel, "refused to outrage his own conscience." He believed the Catholic church resembled the Communist party in restraining freedom of thought under the pretense of inculcating a necessary and beneficial discipline, when the real issue was truth versus lies and when both were meanwhile accusing their opponents of dishonesty. Both creeds, he asserted, had developed into theocracies, insisting on their infallibility and rewriting history when that appeared necessary to authenticate the myths that kept their ruling castes in power.[26]

Orthodoxy had another harmful effect in that it separated intellectuals from the common people of England who, sustained by tradition, took no interest in a refined theology or religious abstractions. To them, the observance of Christian conventions was part of a normal life, and they had no more fear of judgment than George Eliot's character Dolly Winthrop in her summing up: "And if we'n done our part, it isn't to be believed as Them as are above us 'ull be worse nor we are, and come short of Their'n."[27] Only the educated among the British could be persuaded to go against this inherited tolerance. "The ruthless ideologies of the Continent—not merely communism and fascism, but anarchism, Trotskyism, and even ultramontane Catholicism—are accepted in their pure form only by the intelligentsia, who constitute a sort of island of bigotry amid the general vagueness."[28]

Orthodoxy was particularly inimical to literature. Orwell was ready to concede that one might write poetry under an imposed orthodoxy, but he considered prose to be "the product of rationalism, of the Protestant centuries, of the autonomous individual." Historically, he said, it had reached its highest peaks when democracy and free speculation prevailed. This he explained on the grounds that these periods offered the writer subjects that could engage his whole mind and about which he need not be guarded.

"The fact is," he said, "that certain themes cannot be celebrated in words and tyranny is one of them. No one ever wrote a good book in praise of the Inquisition."[29]

A rather more unusual reason for Orwell's criticism of orthodoxy among Catholic intellectuals was that it caused them to practice doublethink even in matters of religion. Their claim to be orthodox Roman Catholics meant that they had to believe in personal immortality, the divinity of Christ, and other Catholic dogmas. But many Catholic intellectuals tried to evade the consequences of these beliefs by calling them myths—something one does not have to accept literally:

> Thus the Catholic intellectual is able, for controversial purposes, to play a sort of handy-pandy game, repeating the articles of the Creed in exactly the same terms as his forefathers, while defending himself from the charge of superstition by explaining that he is speaking in parables. Substantially his claim is that though he himself doesn't believe in any very definite way in life after death, there has been no change in Christian belief, since our ancestors didn't really believe in it either. Meanwhile a vitally important fact—that one of the props of Western civilization has been knocked away—is obscured.[30]

This loss weighed heavily on Orwell because he thought that the major difficulty of contemporary life was finding a faith to replace the belief in personal immortality. His hopes for socialism and a better world for most human beings hinged on evolving a system of good and evil independent of a belief in heaven and hell. It was necessary first to satisfy hunger. Physical necessity came before the need in all men to know the good, but the priority was only one of time, not importance. He blamed Catholic intellectuals for obscuring the decay of belief in Christianity which they themselves exemplified. Such people, he said, who "cling to the letter of the Creeds while reading into them meanings they were never meant to have, and who snigger at anyone simple enough to suppose that the Fathers of the Church meant what they said, are simply raising smoke-screens to conceal their own disbelief from themselves."[31]

Apart from these faults, Orwell disliked Catholic intellectuals because they supported what he thought were reactionary causes. Certain groups among them, he believed, wished for a Fascist victory.[32] Analyzing their status in England in 1941, he distinguished between the large mass of Roman Catholics, some two million poor Irish laborers who were not Fascist in sympathy, and the upper and middle class Roman Catholics. Large numbers of the latter, he said further, held posts in the Foreign Office and in the Consular Service, and many were influential in the press. All these he believed to be anti-Soviet and pro-Fascist. "No one who has studied Catholic literature during the last ten years can doubt that the bulk of the hierarchy and the intelligentsia would side with Germany as against Russia if they had a quarter of a chance."[33]

Roman Catholics by birth he thought less ultramontane and more patriotic than the converted intellectuals, who had much the same mentality in his opinion as the British Communists. He foresaw the probability that they would favor a compromise peace, and if England were defeated, would support the new government as readily as some Catholics had supported the Pétain government in France. "They are the only really conscious, logical, intelligent enemies that democracy has got in England," he wrote in *Partisan Review*, "and it is a mistake to despise them."[34]

For such professional Roman Catholic intellectuals as "Timothy Shy" (D. B. Wyndham Lewis) and "Beachcomber" (J. B. Morton) he had only contempt, pointing out in 1944 that they had always championed reactionary leaders and causes—Mussolini, Pilsudski, Franco, appeasement, flogging, literary censorship—and charging that "between them they have found good words for everything that any decent person instinctively objects to."[35] They also were against England and the Protestant countries, he said; like Chesterton, they constantly exalted the peasants and the Roman Catholic countries, to the point of regretting the failure of the Spanish Armada. In Orwell's opinion Chesterton, at least, had courage; but the two popular journalists were cowards. They were afraid to attack the rich and powerful and afraid to be anti-Russian when the Russians were popular in England.

Although he severely criticized Roman Catholics, it must not be supposed that Orwell's opposition was altogether indiscriminate. He used to recite Hopkins' poem "Felix Randal" while on guard duty in Spain, and in one of his talks for the B.B.C. he chose it for analysis as probably the best short poem in English. He admired it because of the poem's remarkable fusion of Christian feeling about death and a loving regard for rural England. Furthermore, he realized that Hopkins benefited by being a Jesuit priest, which a bigot could not have done.[36] Similarly, he admired Chesterton as a writer and thinker and praised him for opposing the Boer War, though he condemned the anti-Semitic strain he found in him and Belloc.[37] As a reviewer, too, he was always fair to such Catholic writers as Christopher Dawson and F. J. Sheed, responding generously to their moderation and intelligence.

And despite his criticisms of orthodoxy he was able to recognize its usefulness, particularly to those who were no longer young. Reviewing some of T. S. Eliot's later poems he observed that they have little of the vitality apparent in those Eliot wrote as a young man, even though that vitality was the expression of "conscious futility," which Orwell thought an appropriate attitude for a young man though impossible for an older one to maintain:

> Sooner or later one is obliged to adopt a positive attitude towards life and society. It would be putting it too crudely to say that every poet in our time must either die young, enter the Catholic Church, or join the Communist Party, but in fact the escape from consciousness of futility is along those general lines.[38]

Toward the end of his life he showed a more than superficial interest in those Roman Catholic writers who advocated social reforms within the boundaries of the papal encyclicals, though he did not accept their belief that it was possible to reconcile Christian doctrine with the social changes he thought necessary. It seemed to him that the gap between "humanism" and Christian doctrine and institutions was too great ever to be bridged. The first was this-worldly, necessarily materialistic, and democratic; the second other-worldly, looking to a life beyond the grave which it is our duty to prepare for, probably ascetic, and at least potentially totalitarian.

VI

COMMUNISTS AND SOCIALISTS

BECAUSE Orwell attacked the Communists and the Soviet Union so often and so savagely and because of his insight into the attraction exerted by the party, some have thought that he was once a Communist or at least a fellow traveler. There is no evidence to support this belief. Not all those whose political ideals are tempered by skepticism are disappointed Communists. C. S. Lewis was mistaken, I think, when he wrote of *Animal Farm* and *1984* that "both are very bitter, honest, and honourable recantations."[1] Harry Pollitt, the Communist leader, was also wrong when he called *The Road to Wigan Pier* the work of a "disillusioned little middle-class boy,"[2] if by "recantations" and "disillusioned" these critics interpret Orwell's books as evidence of disappointed expectations that communism was a form of socialism which would set the world to rights.

Randall Swingler, a Communist writer, claimed that Orwell had been among those to whom at one time the Soviet myth had made a strong appeal; in reply Orwell wrote in 1946: "I could never be disappointed by the Stalin regime, because I never expected any good to come of it," and he denied that there was in his published work any word suggesting a "messianic hope and consequent disappointment." Further, he said, "I have never fundamentally altered my attitude towards the Soviet regime since I first began to pay attention to it some time in the nineteen-twenties. But so far from disappointing me, it has actually turned out somewhat better than I would have predicted fifteen years ago."[3]

Orwell's publisher, Frederic Warburg, wrote that in 1936 Orwell "loathed" the Communists and fellow travelers whom he knew through the Left Book Club, and that he "disliked with almost equal intensity" the members of the Independent Labour party and the followers of Cripps. He joined the I.L.P. after his return from Spain, largely as a gesture of solidarity toward his former comrades in the P.O.U.M., with which the I.L.P. was affiliated, and out of affection for John McNair, who had helped him so much in Spain, but he was not a member very long.[4] His reason for resigning is clear:

What I saw in Spain, and what I have seen since of the inner workings of left-wing political parties, have given me a horror of politics. I was for a while a member of the Independent Labour Party, but left them at the beginning of the present war because I considered that they were talking nonsense and proposing a line of policy that could only make things easier for Hitler. In sentiment I am definitely "left," but I believe that a writer can only remain honest if he keeps free of party labels.[5]

Orwell was no more a Marxist than he was a disillusioned ex-Communist or fellow traveler. He knew a great deal about Marxism, and he regarded Marx's theory as a "useful instrument for testing other theories of thought" because it forced one to consider the economic basis of society and to ask, "Who owns what and how much?" At its best, however, such testing amounted, he said, to an up-to-date version of "Where your treasure lies, there will your heart lie also." A Marxist analysis of "any historical event tends to be a hurried snap-judgment based on the principle of *cui bono?* Something rather like the 'realism' of the saloon-bar cynic who *always* assumes that the bishop is keeping a mistress and the trade-union leader is in the pay of the boss."[6]

The radical defect of Marxism, he thought, was that with its exclusive stress on class consciousness and the class struggle as the mainsprings of action and its denial of the importance of religion, morality, and patriotism, which it wrote off as "superstructure," it made people incapable of understanding human beings; orthodox Marxists, possessing the truth, "never bother to discover what is going on inside other people's heads."[7] Furthermore, he said, "Men will not die for things called capitalism and feudalism, and will die for things called liberty or loyalty, and to ignore one set of motives is as misleading as to ignore the others."[8]

This denigration of some human motives made Marxist predictions not only wrong but "more sensationally wrong than those of much simpler people. . . . Long *after* Hitler came to power, official Marxism was declaring that Hitler was of no importance and could achieve nothing. On the other hand, people who had hardly heard of Marx but who knew the power of faith had seen Hitler coming years earlier."[9] Orwell did not exaggerate this point. In January 1933, for example, Stalin made a speech in which among other things he predicted the coming victory of the German working class over Hitler. Twenty-three days later Hitler began his rule, and soon afterwards the enfeebled German Communist party announced a new slogan, "The worse, the better!" a prelude to its own rapid destruction.[10] The German Communists had a rhyming verse expressive of their illusion: "First the S.P.D., then the N.S.D.A.P., and in the end the K.P.D."[11] As another example, Kingsley Martin remembers John Strachey speaking at a great meeting organized by the Left Book Club only a few days before the Nazi-Soviet pact. "I can still recall the confident, resonant voice of John Strachey as he said: 'Nothing is so certain amid the shifting sands of politics today as the absolute knowledge that the Soviet Union will never yield an inch to Nazi Germany.' "[12]

It is easier to say what Orwell thought would destroy the world than what would save it. For many years he pinned his hopes on socialism, or at least a moralized form of socialism that would embody what he once called the "liberal values." A succinct statement of these is to be found in his praise of Thomas Mann for his belief in freedom of the intellect, in human brotherhood, in the existence of objective truth: "One has only to compare his [Mann's] remarks on Hitler and Mussolini with, say, those of Bernard Shaw to see that respect for human decency is not a bad guide, even in international politics."[13]

Orwell's skepticism was temperamental. As an adolescent at Eton he was called Cynicus and was, he says, a snob and a revolutionary. Cyril Connolly thought him a true rebel, not a stage one, and believed he had a power of intelligent prophecy. "Whoever wins this war, we shall emerge a second-rate nation," he said to Connolly during the First World War.[14] He read advanced writers like Shaw, Galsworthy, Wells, and London and shared with some of his contemporaries a more than ordinarily violent reaction against his elders, whom he held responsible for the horrors and failures of World War I. This feeling of rebelliousness was colored also by the sense of having missed a chance to prove themselves—what Isherwood later called "the Test," that is, the public demonstration of one's manhood. The snobbishness came from an upbringing which, like Ernest Pontifex, he had not yet learned to modify with much assurance, so that at this period he felt that he "spent half the time in denouncing the capitalist system and the other half in raging over the insolence of bus-conductors."[15]

When he returned from Burma with a fund of firsthand experience earned in the service of a dying imperialism he was wholly on the side of the oppressed against their oppressors, against "every form of man's dominion over man."[16] It was this attitude derived from this background which determined his feelings about socialism. He thought that socialism was elementary common sense—in the midst of abundance there was no good reason why everyone should not have a fair share; but the root of his adherence to socialism was moral conviction, the same feeling that led him to fight in Spain and to have the Ukrainian edition of *Animal Farm* smuggled into the Soviet Union. He rejected doctrinaire socialism and Marxism, but that did not prevent him from advocating the common ownership of the means of production, a classless society, approximate equality of incomes, and a revolution in the system of education. In fact he published a six-point program along those lines in 1941, at a time when he supposed a revolution was possible in England, but he was not rigid about its provisions.[17]

If in 1936 Orwell believed that the Socialist aim of "justice and liberty" was being frustrated by the stupidities of capitalism,[18] nevertheless in 1941 he was still asserting his faith in its eventual fulfillment, so long as the more acute danger of fascism could be surmounted:

> The whole English-speaking world is haunted by the idea of human equality, and though it would be simply a lie to say that either we or the Americans have ever acted up to our professions, still, the *idea* is there, and it is capable of one day becoming a reality. From the English-speaking culture, if it does not perish, a society of free and equal human beings will ultimately arise.[19]

The early years of World War II confirmed Orwell's belief that despite its imperfections socialism was the best solution to society's problems because it offered the best hope of natural justice and efficiency. The first part of *The Road to Wigan Pier* is a detailed demonstration of the inhumanity of capitalism, and this he continued to take for granted. The political and military disasters of 1940 and 1941 were, to him, conclusive proof that even in a time of crisis capitalism was incapable of organizing the men and materials needed to defeat the more single-minded and efficient Fascists. "Hitler's conquest of Europe . . . was a *physical* debunking of capitalism," he said. "War, for all its evil, is at any rate an unanswerable test of strength, like a try-your-grip machine. Great strength returns the penny, and there is no way of faking the result."[20]

Despite capitalism's seemingly obvious failures, the possibility that socialism would replace it was not strong, he thought, and one reason was that so many of the wrong people advocated it. In a memorable sentence that offended many, Orwell wrote: "One sometimes gets the impression that the mere words 'Socialism' and 'Communism' draw towards them . . . every fruit-juice drinker, nudist, sandal-wearer, sex-maniac, Quaker, 'Nature Cure' quack, pacifist, and feminist in England."[21] In a word, Socialists were likely to be cranks, and the ordinary man who might otherwise be attracted to socialism was naturally put off by them.

Orwell found one clue to the literary intelligentsia's attraction to communism in the literature of the preceding twenty years. Its keynote was expressed in such phrases as "the tragic sense of life" or "cosmic despair." The principal writers seemed to him reactionary and pessimist, deploring the civilization they lived in, hostile to the Victorian values in which they had been reared, despairing about the future. These sentiments, he thought, were not necessarily the result of the war, since few of these writers were directly affected by it. Instead, paradoxically, their sentiments were luxuries; they could feel as they did because they were living in exceptionally comfortable times, "the golden age of the *rentier-intellectual*, a period of irresponsibility such as the world had never seen before."[22] So they could express what they believed to be the hopelessness of the age without paying a penalty, and certainly without any sense of being obliged to remedy its ills.

At their first meeting, Stephen Spender, aged twenty, asked T. S. Eliot, aged forty, what he thought of the future of western civilization. In answer Eliot said it had none except "internecine conflict." Spender did not quite understand what this meant until Eliot made it plainer: "People killing one another in the streets."[23] Yeats foresaw equal horrors—first the political age, then the age of the psychologists, then, worst of all, the age of Yeats's people, the spiritualists. Spender and his fellows accepted this verdict and reacted accordingly: "It seemed that with us the thin wall which surrounded their little situation of independence and which enabled them to retain their air of being the last of the Romans had broken down. A new generation had arisen which proclaimed that bourgeois civilization was at an end, and which assumed the certainty of revolution."[24]

It was not yet certain, however, what affirmation, if any, these young intellectuals were going to make or what the revolutionary future would be like. John Lehmann recalls talking to Spender in the Christmas holidays of 1930 and being urged to come to Germany, which, Spender told him, "had escaped from the mortal sickness of Western civilization; . . . there youth had started to live again, free of the shackles of the past, a life without inhibition, inspired by hope, natural humanity and brotherhood in the springs of being." Isherwood was already there, living "in stark poverty," and Auden was sympathetic to his experiments.[25]

John Strachey and Oswald Mosley resigned from the Labour party in 1931 to form the New Party, which developed into the British Union of Fascists, but this line of development did not go much further, except with people like William Joyce. Instead, as Orwell says, "Suddenly we have got out of the twilight of the gods into a sort of Boy Scout atmosphere of bare knees and community singing. The typical literary man ceases to be a cultured ex-patriate with a leaning towards the Church, and becomes an eager-minded schoolboy with a leaning towards communism."[26]

This movement toward communism, largely confined to intellectuals, becomes more understandable when we recall the thesis of John Strachey's *The Coming Struggle for Power*, one of the most influential books of the thirties: "Communism offers no one of this generation a ticket to Utopia. But it does offer to intellectual workers of every kind the one road of escape out of a paralyzing atmosphere of capitalist decay, into a social environment which will give limitless stimulus to the achievements of the mind of man."[27] Page after page of this book contrasts the dreary hopelessness of the capitalist world with the "exhilaration of living" in the Soviet Union. Translated into the life of a young man like Philip Toynbee, who was a Communist party organizer and a president of the Oxford Union, this became "the whole marvelous atmosphere of conspiracy and purpose," and he described himself in the winter of 1936 as going about organizing Spanish Defence Committees like "a moth laying its eggs in a clothes cupboard."[28]

Large numbers of the laboring class could not find work and therefore felt useless and guilty—as a minor classic like *Love on the Dole* shows vividly. Orwell believed that these feelings could be relieved by work, almost any work, but the loss of purpose among the middle-class intellectuals whom we have called unbelievers was something different. To Orwell "middle-class unemployment" meant not having a job whose value was self-evident to its possessor. To these "unemployed," the Communist party supplied a channel through which "all the loyalties and superstitions that the intellect had seemingly banished could come rushing back under the thinnest of disguises. Patriotism, religion, empire, military glory—all in one word, Russia."[29]

As the comfort and security of English life had sheltered the pessimists in the twenties, so in the thirties the same shield protected the inexperienced—those it is now customary to call "idealists." Like Auden at that stage in his life, they could accept what he called "the necessary murder" without knowing what this meant. As Koestler says, "The necessary lie; the necessary slander;

the necessary intimidation of the masses to preserve them from short-sighted errors; the necessary liquidation of oppositional groups and hostile classes; the necessary sacrifice of a whole generation in the interest of the next—it may all sound monstrous and yet it was so easy to accept while rolling along the single track of faith."[30] Faith and money protected ignorance. And this also helps to explain the enormous turnover in the Communist party's ranks, for as soon as many of these intellectuals found out that—as in Spain—hardship, stultifying discipline, sacrifice, and death were implied in their allegiance, they left the party, though without in some cases ever wholly forgetting its glamour. When Orwell in 1946 reformulated this explanation of the appeal of communism he treated it under the rubric of nationalism, the English Communist being one who has transferred his loyalty from England to the Soviet Union; it was "a way of attaining salvation without altering one's conduct."[31]

If the discovery of a faith that would replace the lost faith in Britain was one profound appeal that communism made to British intellectuals, the "fight against fascism," though essentially negative, was more immediate and spectacular. After the Communists' success in helping Hitler destroy social democracy in Germany, a success which must soon have seemed like suicide, they turned rather more profitably to the tactic of the Popular Front. No formal alliance was ever achieved in Great Britain, as it was in France, among the parties of the Left, because the leadership of the Labour party was too canny to be seduced. Nevertheless, what we now call simply "Spain" stirred intellectuals even more than the struggle against Germany.

The mass of people were indifferent; and even on the Left, where all sorts of activities supporting the Republicans were carried on with dash and intensity, men were cautious about going to Spain to fight. The "Cook's tours" to Spain taken by writers, painters, politicians, and intellectuals are notorious. But in contrast some men were more in earnest. There were 2,762 volunteers in the Republican forces, and the casualties among them—543 killed, 1,763 wounded—justify the prudence of those who stayed home.[32]

This contrast between profession and act was never directly mentioned by Orwell, but he was struck by the emotions that the events in Spain aroused: "By 1937 the whole of the intelligentsia was mentally at war," he said. What he found "truly frightening about the war in Spain was . . . the immediate reappearance in left-wing circles of the mental atmosphere of the Great War. The very people who for twenty years had sniggered over their own superiority to war hysteria were the ones who rushed straight back into the mental slum of 1915."[33] Julian Symons tells us that for the "Artists" and "Pragmatists" in his pyramid of intellectuals peace was as dirty a word as fascism, and he points to the symbolic contrast between Aldous Huxley's pamphlet in support of pacifism, *What Are You Going to Do About It?* and Day Lewis's implicitly violent reply, *We Are Not Going to Do Nothing.*[34]

Power-hunger, reaction against an older generation, discovery of a new faith, the genuine and fashionable pull of "Spain" were all motives working to draw intellectuals toward communism or socialism, but they were not having the same effect on the general public. Industrial stagnation and unemployment in the 1930s did not drive the mass of people toward socialism, perhaps because the moral bankruptcy of the Labour party was so apparent. Orwell remarked that "only the intellectuals, the least useful section of the middle class," gravitated toward the movement. Leftists were mistaken and insensitive, he thought, in continuing to advocate a popular revolution that in fact none of them wanted or expected; the labor leaders wanted to go on drawing their salaries, the Communists wanted to continue being martyrs, and "the left-wing intelligentsia wanted to go on and on, sniggering at the Blimps, sapping away at middle-class morale, but still keeping their favoured position as hangers-on of the dividend drawers."[35]

Orwell was one of the few contemporary writers who have tried to explain what other reasons should have attracted these people to socialism. What inspired "the intellectual, tract-writing type of Socialist with his pullover, his fuzzy hair, and his Marxian quotation"?[36] It was certainly not love of the working class or a desire for justice, since these motives—if they were sincere—should have long since produced a change in the way such intellectuals lived, quite apart from any expectation that the coming of socialism was imminent:

> Look at any bourgeois Socialist. Look at Comrade X, member of the C.P.G.B. and author of *Marxism for Infants*. Comrade X, it so happens, is an old Etonian. He would be ready to die on the barricades, in theory anyway, but you notice that he still leaves his bottom waistcoat button undone. He idealises the proletariat, but it is remarkable how little his habits resemble theirs.[37]

Generally speaking, Orwell found many intellectual advocates of socialism to be animated by two other motives: a sense of order and a generalized hatred. "The underlying motive of many Socialists, I believe, is simply a hypertrophied sense of order. The present state of affairs offends them not because it causes misery, still less because it makes freedom impossible, but because it is untidy; what they desire, basically, is to reduce the world to something re-sembling a chessboard."[38] Shaw was for Orwell an example of those wanting to exert power; he had little understanding of working-class life and he thought of the poor chiefly as material to be worked on. According to that view, Orwell said, "Poverty and, what is more, the habits of mind created by poverty, are something to be abolished *from above,* by violence if necessary; perhaps even preferably by violence."[39] Another intellectual, Beatrice Webb, becomes in Orwell's reading of her autobiography the picture of a "high-minded Socialist slum-visitor. The truth is that to many people, calling themselves Socialists, revolution does not mean a movement of the masses with which they hope to associate them-selves; it means a set of reforms which 'we,' the clever ones, are going to impose upon 'them,' the Lower Orders."[40] The vision of a self-conscious elite imposing its will on human material, violently if necessary, is one that stayed in Orwell's mind, partly, no doubt, because it was being acted out in Italy, Germany, and the Soviet Union. It is, of course, an important feature of the intellectual struc-ture of *1984* and the parable of *Animal Farm.*

A second motive which Orwell finds at work among intellec-tuals, and a powerful one, is hatred, "a sort of queer, theoretical, *in vacuo* hatred—against the exploiters. Hence the grand old Socialist sport of denouncing the bourgeoisie."[41] And he finds this feeling especially noticeable in a book like Mirsky's *The Intelligentsia of Great Britain,* which gives the impression that communism is nothing but hatred, there being no other discoverable motive for Mirsky's malice.

Orwell's opposition to the Communists he knew, and to many of the Socialists as well, came partly of course from his natural skepticism, but he also had reasoned arguments to support his stand. First, anyone with totalitarian aims had in the nature of things to be dishonest. Franz Borkenau, whose work Orwell re-viewed so favorably, has an interesting comment in this connection:

> Already in his pamphlet about "Left-wing Communism" Lenin had suggested that the communists should offer support to the socialists in their attempts to get increased power—on condition that such an offer must never be honest; the communist support for their allies would be "like the support the rope gives to the hanged man."

This dishonesty was not a tactical device, but the essence of the whole manoeuvre. For a communist to co-operate honestly with social-democrats would be tantamount to becoming a social-democratic traitor himself. *Dishonesty, in every tactical alliance, was the basic guarantee of orthodoxy.*[42]

This is, of course, one of the themes of *1984*. Unlike Bishop Warburton, who claimed that "orthodoxy is my doxy; heterodoxy is other people's doxy," Orwell thought that anyone's orthodoxy killed the free working of the mind and heart.[43] The prevalence of orthodoxies of whatever sort had reduced the possibility that truthful history might be written, and their corrupting effect on intellectuals was such that "the bulk of the English literary intelligentsia has looked on at torture, massacre and aggression without expressing disapproval, and perhaps in the long run without feeling it."[44]

Second, Orwell opposed the Communists because by their tactics and their lies they had injured the Socialist cause. The case for socialism has been too often argued by "unsatisfactory or even inhuman types" acting upon questionable motives. The bad impression they make on the ordinary man may, in time of crisis, drive him still farther to the Right, even though he might on rational grounds have accepted a Socialist solution.[45] The Communists in the Labour party, he said, and all the left-wing members of the Labour movement were chiefly important for "the part they played in alienating the middle classes from Socialism."[46] It is worth remarking that at a critical moment early in the war, when Orwell made a direct and rather naive appeal in *The English Revolution* for a Socialist take-over of the government, he was careful to reject explicitly the Communist creed and that of the "more soft-boiled intellectuals of the Left" because he believed they were inimical to the success of a specifically English Socialist movement.[47]

Third, in the Soviet Union they had created a hierarchical society whose ruling class was as ruthless as any other in maintaining itself in power. *Animal Farm* derived partly from his conviction that the Soviet Union had to be stripped of the myth that it was a Socialist country if the real Socialist movement were to be revived.[48]

Among all his other reasons for resisting communism, not the least important was his belief that a decent human life and a literature of any permanent value live on honesty the way a man lives on air. Totalitarianism, by compelling a writer to suppress what he spontaneously thinks and feels, and by deciding for him from week to week and even day to day the approved ways of thinking and feeling, necessarily ends by destroying literature, as it destroys mutual trust, and therefore it must be opposed.[49]

The crypto-Communists deserve especial notice here for reasons directly related to those just described. Orwell quarreled bitterly with two of them in print and occasionally attacked others. "Cryptos" were persons whose membership or close association with the party was kept secret, not so much for purposes of espionage, but because they could be more useful in other ways if their affiliation was not generally known. J. B. S. Haldane and his wife, for example, concealed their membership in the party for several years.[50] Mrs. Haldane worked for the Comintern and served as a Labour party member of the St. Pancras Borough Council; Professor Haldane wrote scientific articles for the *Daily Worker* and was active in front organizations.

Orwell sharply criticized the cryptos and fellow travelers for their part in the People's Convention, a Communist front led by D. N. Pritt, whom he described as "a Labour MP . . . always claimed by Communists as an 'underground' member of their party, evidently with truth."[51] During the period between the British declaration of war on Germany and the German invasion of the Soviet Union, this Communist front advocated what amounted to Lenin's policy of "revolutionary defeatism." That is, they sought to weaken British morale by maintaining that the war against Germany was an imperialist war which the masses should oppose. They would thus help to prepare the ground for the revolt which would follow when Britain was sufficiently weakened by military defeat and domestic turmoil. But of course this policy and the People's Convention itself ended on June 22, 1941. On December 17, 1943, *Tribune* had pointed out that the Communists and fellow travelers then demonstrating most against Oswald Mosley's release from internment were, at the time Mosley was interned, also pursuing a "'stop the war' campaign barely distinguishable from Mosley's own."[52]

D. N. Pritt objected to this statement, saying that it had been made on previous occasions "by some of the worst elements of our various political groupings," but leaving unspecified who these "worst elements" might be. In response to Pritt's effort to rewrite history, Orwell pointed out that the backers of the People's Convention had been promoting a "stop the war" campaign since the autumn of 1939. He cited R. Palme Dutt's pamphlet "Why This War?" and D. N. Pritt's own book *Choose Your Future* as examples of what he meant, and he also noted that *The Betrayal of the Left,* edited by Victor Gollancz, had exposed in detail the antiwar activities of Pritt's organization.[53]

In the general election of 1945, a group of crypto-Communists— some twenty or thirty was Orwell's estimate—were elected to Parliament ostensibly as members of the Labour party. The Communists were numerically weak, and open members of the Communist party had been excluded from the Labour party for years; but they had already secured important positions of leadership in several unions, and Orwell thought that if, through the cryptos, "they could get inside the Labour Party as an organized body, they might be able to do enormous mischief."[54] As one of these underground Communist M.P.'s he named Konni Zilliacus and said that if in fact Zilliacus was not a Communist he was "reliably sympathetic." In a letter published in the correspondence columns of *Tribune*, Zilliacus denied Orwell's charges. He also said that Orwell had lied in making these allegations and had been guilty of "a quite despicable thing" in slandering a Member of Parliament in the American press.[55]

In reply Orwell said that naturally Zilliacus would not admit he was a Communist, since the whole effectiveness of the cryptos depended on their not being identified as Communists. He also amplified his charge that the group's policy was "barely distinguishable from that of the C.P." In effect, he said, they were "publicity agents of the U.S.S.R. in this country, and . . . when Soviet and British interests appear to them to clash, they will support the Soviet interest." He admitted that he could not prove in a court of law that they were Communists any more than he could have proved before the war "that the Catholic Church was sympathetic to Fascism." But he insisted on his right to criticize public figures like Zilliacus and concluded by saying that he could not be intimidated from continuing his efforts to "counter totalitarian propaganda."[56]

Others entered the controversy. Some denounced Orwell for red-baiting, and some supported his statements, noting that Zilliacus had indeed said such things as Orwell cited—for example, that in the part of Germany under Soviet control he found "democracy in the full sense of the word, in the sense that Lincoln defined it."[57] Zilliacus maintained in another letter that he did not understand whether Orwell had withdrawn or repeated his "lie" and indirectly threatened to sue Orwell for libel and charge him with breaching parliamentary privilege.[58] A week later Orwell repeated his accusations and added, "At this stage I cannot prove that he is lying, but I see no reason for supposing that he is telling the truth."[59] In a final letter Zilliacus said that what he objected to was being libeled, but either he did not mean this seriously or other considerations influenced him, for he never sued Orwell.

Finally, it should be said that although Orwell did not think socialism would restrict liberty as communism did, he believed its hedonism was a threat. He had found this line of thought developing from Shaw and Wells and their followers—progress toward comfort through machines—and he felt it to be personally repugnant and intellectually shallow. That machines would "liberate" human beings was objectionable to him as idea and ideal. "Man," he said, "is not as the vulgarer hedonists seem to suppose, a kind of walking stomach; he has also got a hand, an eye and a brain. Cease to use your hands, and you have lopped off a huge chunk of your consciousness." A fully mechanized world in which a man's chance of working—in effect his chance of living—was minimized would be a world populated by beings who were less than fully human.[60]

Intellectuals, of all people, ought to see the error in identifying socialism with the consumer mentality which accompanies machine civilization; and they ought also, he thought, to make it clear that socialism might result in a lowering of the standard of living, including their own. The argument for "comfort" falsified human nature; Hitler's insanity was more appealing than Wells's common-sense hedonism.[61] Progressive thinkers, mistakenly assuming that people most desire ease, security, and avoidance of pain, knew less about human nature than the Fascists. "All three of the great dictators have enhanced their power by imposing intolerable burdens on their peoples. Whereas Socialism, and even capitalism in a more grudging way, have said to people 'I offer you a good time,' Hitler has said to them, 'I offer you struggle, danger and death,' and as a result a whole nation flings itself at his feet."[62]

The ardent response to this appeal may not endure, but in a crisis it is effective, because it calls to a side of human nature that is not touched by the philosophy of the machine worshippers. "The Socialist who finds his children playing with tin soldiers is usually upset, but he is never able to think of a substitute for the tin soldiers; tin pacifists won't do."[63] In fact, Orwell believed in these possibilities: "Building a Socialist on the bones of a Blimp, the power of one kind of loyalty to transmute itself into another, the spiritual need for patriotism and the military virtues, for which, however little the boiled rabbits of the Left may like them, no substitute has yet been found."[64]

In *The Road to Wigan Pier,* Orwell analyzed some of the present dangers to human beings in a machine civilization, but as time went on he became even more concerned that state control of the machines which were to improve life would eventually destroy individual freedom. In a talk broadcast by the B. B. C. he noted that the disappearance of economic liberty was necessarily affecting intellectual liberty. In the nineteenth century, he said, "Socialism was usually thought of as a sort of moralized liberalism," but with the rise of totalitarianism this idea was shown to be incomplete.[65] His reviews of books by Harold Laski and Friedrich Hayek assert that state control of property and planned production could lead to a collectivism that was the reverse of democratic and equalitarian, since it placed so much power in the hands of a minority. Hilaire Belloc's recognition of this possibility as early as 1914, when he published *The Servile State,* was, as we saw, one reason Orwell had been impressed by that work.

Orwell's analysis of socialism and communism is practical in its bearing, but it is at bottom moral, being based on a view of what ought to be; and this is what socialism always was for Orwell. As a man of action who was also a man of the Left, he retained until the end of his life the desire to see socialism flourishing somewhere, and his elaboration of this desire as well as his attacks on those who discredited the ideal prove his continuing hope in socialism's future.

VII

PACIFISTS

ORWELL'S long-standing quarrel with pacifist intellectuals was intensified by World War II, and it became especially bitter when Britain was fighting alone and Goebbels was boasting that the country would be "reduced to degradation and poverty." The antagonism was profoundly based in his temperament and education. Temperamentally he was a man of action not averse to violence, and his education, he says, made a patriot of him almost against his will. But good reasons for this quarrel also existed in the intellectuals' reactions to political developments of the thirties and forties, though unfortunately the extraordinary complications of the period are barriers to an easy understanding of them. Reversals of opinion and contradictions in action manifested by nearly all the antagonists are virtually impossible to chronicle with both copiousness of detail and clarity of outline. As a book like Kingsley Martin's *Editor* shows, even in retrospect the thread of consistency (assuming one existed) is hard to discern in the tangled mass of self-contradictions so characteristic of political thinking during this period.

For example, Hugh Dalton, a moderate Labour party politician, urged his colleagues in the party to support rearmament against the Germans, whom he called "a race of carnivorous sheep." But as A. L. Rowse wryly says, "It did not do him much good inside the Labour Party, which was dedicated to the lunacy of collective security without rearming." The distinction usually denoted by the terms Left and Right, implying different principles and hence different policies, tended to disappear, smothered by the momentous decisions being taken at this time. Mr. Chamberlain's inner circle— men like Dawson, Halifax, Simon, Hoare, Runciman—were right-wingers who were beaten before the fighting started: "The plain truth is that their deepest instinct was defeatist, their highest wisdom surrender."[1] And on the Left the same end was in sight, if not the same motive. A professional pacifist, George Lansbury, M.P., President of the Peace Pledge Union, addressing Parliament on September 3, 1939, the day it reluctantly declared war, said:

The cause that I and a handful of friends represent is this morning going down to ruin. But I think that we ought to take heart and courage from the fact that after two thousand years of war and strife, at least those who enter upon this colossal struggle have to admit that force has not settled and cannot settle anything.[2]

Lansbury was alluding, of course, to Chamberlain and his followers and not to Hitler.

As the outcome of the war became more predictable and the controversy with the pacifists began to die away, Orwell himself pointed to some of his own errors and apologized for them. It is therefore not so much a matter here of defending the positions he took as of trying to understand what happened to his views about war and pacifists and how these bear on his conception of the role of the intellectual.

Orwell's first poem, "Awake! Young Men of England," was published in 1914, when he was eleven years old; it expresses well the attitudes of those who distributed white feathers and read W. J. Locke's *The Red Planet* approvingly. In these verses, the youthful poet asks for the strength of the lion and the wisdom of the fox so that he can successfully oppose the Germans. Thinking of the blows being struck at England and of the soldiers who sacrificed themselves, he called upon the young to come to England's help:

> Awake! Oh you young men of England,
> For if, when your Country's in need
> You do not enlist by the thousand,
> You truly are cowards indeed.[3]

His second published poem, written to mark the death of Lord Kitchener in 1916, makes a hero of Kitchener for his devotion to duty and says that those who imitate him will be free from fear and malice. The attitudes the poem implies were encouraged by the atmosphere of militarism in which Orwell grew up, by the military training groups in which he participated while at school, and by the five years he spent as a member of the paramilitary police force in Burma.

Paradoxically, his service in Burma produced in Orwell a feeling of revulsion against the Empire, without diminishing his patriotism. Similarly, the military training in school led naturally to the pacifist reaction through which many young men passed in the twenties. But in Orwell this was qualified by the resentful fear that those who had not been in the war had missed something important—Isherwood's Test—and he was persuaded that the war in Spain attracted some men of his age precisely because they needed to make up for escaping World War I.

Like many men, Orwell hated war but saw something in it that moved him against his will. War was barbarous and turned men into savages; it stimulated hatred and dishonesty and thus attacked the roots of civilization, although war hysteria was less common among soldiers than among civilians.[4] Nevertheless, when he left the front in Spain, after having been wounded, and saw the troops moving up to replace the casualties, he reflected:

> It was like an allegorical picture of war; the trainload of fresh men gliding proudly up the line, the maimed men sliding slowly down, and all the while the guns on the open trucks making one's heart leap up as guns always do, and reviving that pernicious feeling, so difficult to get rid of, that war *is* glorious after all.[5]

The appeal of Spain had been so pure at first that the revulsion, when it came to Orwell, was intense. An intimation of his changed feelings appears in a review of *The Men I Killed* by Brigadier General F. P. Crozier, one of the founders of the Peace Pledge Union. Orwell observed that as a pacifist General Crozier made an impressive figure, "like the reformed burglar at a Salvation Army meeting." But the book seemed ineffective because it would not increase the public's active opposition to war. First, it did not make plain that what he called the "moneyed class" tolerate foreign wars only when war is profitable. Secondly, it did not help people see that war propaganda is usually disguised as peace propaganda. Without finding fault with the pacifists, Orwell did criticize those who did not distinguish between foreign and civil wars; in effect they were saying that "violence may be used by the rich against the poor but not by the poor against the rich."[6]

In a letter to Jack Common, he wrote, "To me the idea of war is pure nightmare." In the same letter, after asserting that many left-wing intellectuals had become jingoes because they could not find under the prevailing conditions any satisfying peacetime activity, he spoke of the many things he wanted to go on doing as long as he could. "The idea," he said, "that I've got to abandon them and either be bumped off or depart to some filthy concentration camp just infuriates me. Eileen and I have decided that if war does come the best thing to do will be to just stay alive and thus add to the number of sane people."[7] In a letter to another friend, written about the same time, Orwell alluded to an antiwar pamphlet which he had written earlier in 1938, but this has not been found.[8]

The complicated maneuvers of the political Left and Right at this time he considered to be contemptible and self-contradictory as well as futile. He was more troubled by what he called "the central evil of modern war—the fact that, as Nietzsche puts it, 'he who fights against dragons becomes a dragon himself.'"[9] He elaborated the possibilities in this way:

> The only apparent alternatives are to smash dwelling houses to powder, blow out human entrails and burn holes in children with lumps of thermite, or to be enslaved by people who are more ready to do these things than you are yourself; as yet no one has suggested a practicable way out.[10]

For years this dilemma intruded upon Orwell's thoughts and actions and in controversy he stressed now one side, now the other.[11] But, as a letter to Richard Rees indicates, he had finally solved it by 1949 and had forgotten his former uncertainty:

> I always disagree, however, when people end up by saying that we can only combat Communism, Fascism or what not if we develop an equal fanaticism. It appears to me that one defeats the fanatic precisely by *not* being a fanatic oneself, but on the contrary by using one's intelligence. In the same way, a man can kill a tiger because he is *not* like a tiger & uses his brain to invent the rifle, which no tiger could ever do.[12]

In 1939, Orwell's war-weariness and suspicion of the Conservative government's intentions led him to adopt two courses of action. One was to press for direct opposition to war. He proposed to Herbert Read that it was time "for those of us who intend to oppose the coming war to start organizing for illegal anti-war activities," and he suggested buying and concealing a printing press and stocks of paper.[13] Read apparently pointed out the absurdity of preparing to go underground without having first clarified one's reasons for doing so, but Orwell was so disgusted with war and rumors of war and so convinced, for the moment, that England would go Fascist that he continued to urge Read to adopt his scheme. After his return to England from Morocco he dropped it.

The second course, an outcome of his belief that another war would be merely a capitalist-imperialist defense of the status quo, was to support for a time the pacifists whom he would soon be attacking. A writer for the *New English Weekly*, to which Orwell was also a fairly regular contributor, had disputed the pacifist claim that the question of war had to be settled before any social advance was possible. To accept such a claim, the writer argued, was to postpone necessary changes until the millennium.

Orwell, in response, denied that the pacifists were at fault. Dissociating pacifism from the intellectuals, he asserted that indeed the "left-wing intelligentsia" as a whole were eager for war and that the pacifist case was not being given a fair hearing. He said that "anyone who helps to put peace on the map is doing useful work" by "mobilising the dislike of war that undoubtedly exists in ordinary decent people, as opposed to the hack-journalists and the pansy left." Supporting the pacifists, he argued that social progress was possible only when the mass of people refused to fight for the mistaken policies of their rulers. "So long as they show themselves willing to fight 'in defence of democracy,' or 'against Fascism,' or for any other fly-blown slogan, the same trick will be played upon them again and again: 'You can't have a rise in wages *now*, because we have got to prepare for war. Guns before butter!' "[14] His conclusion was that "modern war is a racket," and a year later he was sounding the same note. As late as July 1939 he was writing that "nothing is likely to save us except the emergence within the next two years of a real mass party whose first pledges are to refuse war and to right imperial injustice."[15]

These sentiments changed overnight. He had begun with a childish admiration for war heroes. Later he still observed in himself "a faint feeling of sacrilege not to stand to attention during 'God Save the King,' " and he admired the unemployed for chalking up slogans like "Poor but Loyal." Personal experience with war and the insight it gave him into political treachery had turned him against war and in favor of pacifism. Then he had a dream the night before the Russo-German Pact was announced (presumably the night of August 23, 1939), which he did not recount but which revealed to him the real state of his own feelings. "It taught me two things, first, that I should be simply relieved when the long-dreaded war started, secondly, that I was patriotic at heart, would not sabotage or act against my own side, would support the war, would fight in it if possible."[16]

Orwell did not revert to being an eleven-year-old jingo. His patriotism usually was marked by the same reserve that characterized the boys and masters in the chapter of *Stalky and Co.* called "The Flag of Their Country," wherein they ridicule the member of Parliament who makes a chauvinistic speech and presents them with a flag. Ironically, A. K. Chesterton, the nephew of G. K., accused Orwell in 1943 of lacking patriotism. In reply Orwell quoted G. K.'s remark, made when the same charge was brought against him during the Boer War, that "'My Country, right or wrong' was on the same moral level as 'my mother, drunk or sober.'"[17] What his dream had showed him was that "the long drilling in patriotism which the middle classes go through had done its work."[18]

Temperament and education, exerting themselves subconsciously at a critical moment, produced the bias against pacifists. Orwell had more logical reasons, however, for condemning them, the same in essence as those which motivated his attacks on other groups of intellectuals he disagreed with: they did not think, they would not face unpleasant facts, they refused to accept the consequences of their arguments.

One of the unpleasant facts that Orwell wanted pacifists to face was that they were dependent for their well-being and security on the willingness of others to work and fight for them. The way he arrived at this judgment is interesting. Among the beliefs about life in England which colored his thinking and complicated his opinions about war and patriotism was the idea that the British Empire rested on the labor of millions of exploited "natives." Writing about the people he observed working near Marrakech he said:

> When you see how the people live, and still more how easily they die, it is always difficult to believe that you are walking among human beings. All colonial empires are in reality founded upon that fact. . . . Are they really the same flesh as yourself? Do they even have names? Or are they merely a kind of undifferentiated brown stuff, about as individual as bees or coral insects? They rise out of the earth, they sweat and starve for a few years, and then they sink back into the nameless mounds of the graveyard and nobody notices that they are gone.[19]

Julian Symons is a witness to how this idea obsessed Orwell. Symons, Orwell, Malcolm Muggeridge, and Anthony Powell at one time used to lunch together once a week. On these occasions, Symons wrote:

> In a friendly and even affectionate way, Muggeridge and Powell would often lure Orwell away from sensible empiricism to wild flights of political fantasy, like his view that the Labour Government should, in honesty, try to convert the British electorate to the idea that they should accept a lower standard of living in order to get rid of the evils of colonialism. "Freedom for the Colonies,

and a Lower Standard of Living for all," that would have been his election rallying cry.[20]

Fantasy it may have been, but it was rooted in an idea to which Orwell clung. One had to acknowledge also that the exploiting Empire continued to exist only because it was maintained by a strong army and navy. More than once he found fault with the "one-eyed pacifism of the English" and praised Kipling for his willingness to confront the reality disclosed in a phrase like "making mock of uniforms that guard you while you sleep."[21] The English-speaking peoples had a higher standard of living and more security than others, hence there was less violence in their world. Because they felt safe, pacifism could develop among them. He says of a German refugee doctor in Alex Comfort's novel *No Such Liberty:*

> His greatest hope is to get to America, with another three thousand miles of water between himself and the Nazis. He will only get there, you note, if British ships and planes protect him on the way, and having got there he will simply be living under the protection of American ships and planes instead of British ones. If he is lucky he will be able to continue with his work as a pathologist, at the same time keeping up his attitude of moral superiority towards the men who make his work possible. And underlying everything there will still be his position as a research-worker, a favoured person living ultimately on dividends which would cease forthwith if not extorted by the threat of violence.[22]

Orwell argued that what the pacifist refused to admit is that "civilization rests ultimately on coercion. What holds society together is the good will of common men, and yet that good will is powerless unless the policeman is there to back it up."[23]

The pacifist's refusal to acknowledge his dependence on the willingness of others to use violence in his behalf, if necessary, apart from whatever moral discredit accrues from his being a parasite, had the further significance on the eve of World War II that one of this persuasion also failed to distinguish between degrees of violence and their consequences. England and Germany used violence, and yet there were such important differences between them that people fled Germany and found refuge in England; they voted with their feet. The pacifist who maintained that England and Germany were equally bad did so only by ignoring vital differences in the social atmosphere and behavior of the English and Germans; in a word, he had to disregard the evidence and stop thinking in order to remain a pacifist.

For those who argued that Gandhi's nonviolence had worked against the English, Orwell replied that Gandhi's tactics were moral blackmail and that they depended on publicity. Gandhi would have been unsuccessful in the Soviet Union or Germany because he would have been killed or otherwise disposed of without anybody's being the wiser. But Gandhi, he said, was at least honest enough to admit that one must take sides in war because it makes a difference who wins. Orwell also admired Gandhi's willingness to face the consequences of his beliefs; as Orwell remarked, "In relation to the late war, one question that every pacifist had a clear obligation to answer was: 'What about the Jews? Are you prepared to see them exterminated? If not, how do you propose to save them without resorting to war?'" Orwell asserted that no pacifist had ever given him an honest answer to this question, but he approved Gandhi's answer when Louis Fischer asked him the same question. Gandhi had said that the Jews should commit collective suicide. Orwell thought that this showed Gandhi's willingness to accept the extreme consequences of his beliefs.[24]

Orwell also respected even those who found supernatural explanations for opposing the war, believing that Hitler and the Nazis were "doing the dirty work of the Lord." Middleton Murry considered it to be "demonstrable to the imagination that Hitlerism is 'the scourge of the Lord'—the destructive dynamic of this rotten civilization." Orwell noted that these were not exactly the sentiments of a pacifist, but they deserved some credit for being straightforward and courageous.[25]

The uncompromising nature of Orwell's views on pacifism is also evident in his disagreement with those who sought to limit war—to "humanize" it by doing away with indiscriminate bombing or poison gas. He attacked a pamphlet in which Vera Brittain set forth these aims, basing his argument on the grounds that it is better to kill a cross-section of the population than to kill only the young men. But he was more concerned to denounce those who wished to limit war without trying to alter the structure of the society which had caused the war in the first place:

> We must either build a good society or continue to do evil. The "peace" to which Miss Brittain wants to return is ultimately based on the truncheon and the machine-gun. As to war, you cannot at present avoid it, nor can you genuinely humanize it. You can only, like the pacifists, set up a moral alibi for yourself while continuing

to accept the fruits of violence. I would sooner be Air-Marshal Harris than Miss Brittain, because he at least knows what he is doing.[26]

Orwell's review of Alex Comfort's novel and his "London Letters" for *Partisan Review* in 1941 and 1942 led Orwell, Comfort, and others into a controversy marked by sharp words and bad verse. In the *Partisan* "Letters," Orwell intensified and enlarged his attacks on the pacifists by charging that they were "objectively" pro-Fascist—the principle being that he who is not with me is against me. He remarked also on "the interpenetration of the pacifist movement by Fascist ideas, especially antisemitism."[27] Moreover, he observed, the Peace Pledge Union, so recently the focus of pacifist agitation in England, with 133,000 members organized in 725 groups, had appeared to suffer a moral collapse after the death of Canon Dick Sheppard, one of its founders. He assailed the alleged moral force of pacifism, not merely because it was ineffective, but also because it seemed to be easily perverted into fascination with the power and success of the oppressor. Alex Comfort had written in a letter to *Horizon:*

> As far as I can see, no therapy short of complete military defeat has any chance of re-establishing the common stability of literature and of the man in the street. One can imagine the greater the adversity the greater the sudden realization of a stream of imaginative work, and the greater the sudden katharsis of poetry, from the isolated interpretation of war as calamity to the realization of the imaginative and actual tragedy of man. When we have access again to the literature of the war years in France, Poland and Czechoslovakia, I am confident that that is what we shall find.[28]

Orwell ridiculed the "money-sheltered ignorance" that could suppose literary life to be continuing in Poland under the Nazi occupation. He thought such statements justified his saying that English pacifists were tending toward the active support of fascism. But he found this less objectionable than the "dishonest and intellectually disgusting line" that "those who fight fascism go Fascist themselves," the dilemma discussed earlier.

Comfort, D. S. Savage, and George Woodcock, replying to Orwell in the *Partisan Review,* rejected his criticisms. Woodcock, after citing certain mistakes in Orwell's article, rightly commented on the self-contradictions in Orwell's position that we have previously noted and concluded: "It would seem that Orwell himself shows to a surprising degree the overlapping of left-wing, pacifist and reactionary tendencies of which he accuses others!"[29] Comfort, also rebutting Orwell's arguments, claimed that "the artist in occupied territory should protest with all his force, where and when he can, against such evils as he sees." But, he asked, "Can he do this more usefully by temporarily accepting the *status quo*, or by skirmishing in Epping Forest with a pocket full of hand-grenades?"[30]

Comfort showed less composure in his poem "Letter to an American Visitor," written under the pseudonym "Obadiah Hornbooke" and published in *Tribune* in 1943. In it he generally denounced everyone aiding the British fight against the Germans, but he also singled out writers who worked for the Ministry of Information or the B.B.C.:

> The land sprouts orators. No doubt you've heard
>   How every buffer, fool and patrioteer
> Applies the Power of the Spoken Word
>   And shoves his loud posterior in your ear;
> So Monkey Hill competes with Berkeley Square—
>   The BBC as bookie, pimp and vet
>   Presenting Air Vice-Marshals set to cheer
> Our raided towns with vengeance (though I've yet
>   To hear from any man who lost his wife
>   Berlin or Lübeck brought her back to life).

He condemned Churchill's speeches, "those resurrection puddings" as the "dim productions of his bulldog brain," but praised himself and others who thought as he did:

> We wrote our own refusals, and we meant them.
>   Our work is plastered and ourselves resented—
> Our heads are bloody, but we have not bent them.
>   We hold no licences, like ladies' spaniels;
>   We live like lions in this den of Daniels.[31]

Two weeks later Orwell replied to Comfort's attack with a poem entitled "As One Non-Combatant to Another." Besides his initial disagreement with what Comfort had said, Orwell had a more personal motive for answering, since he had been a propagandist for the Home Guard, had served in it himself, and had worked for the B.B.C., directing a program of radio broadcasts to India aimed at influencing Indian intellectuals. His attack on Comfort is personal, for he calls him the "captain of a clique of self-advancers," chides him for not signing his name to his poem, and accuses him of attacking only those who cannot hit back:

> Because your enemies all are dead or muzzled,
> You've never picked on one who might reply.
> You've hogged the limelight and you've aired your virtue,
> While chucking sops to every dangerous faction,
> The Left will cheer you and the Right won't hurt you;
> What did you risk? Not even a libel action.
> If you would show what saintly stuff you're made of,
> Why not attack the cliques you *are* afraid of?
>
> Denounce Joe Stalin, jeer at the Red Army,
> Insult the Pope—you'll get some come-back there;
> It's honourable, even if it's barmy,
> To stamp on corns all round and never care.
> But for the half-way saint and cautious hero,
> Whose head's unbloody even if "unbowed,"
> My admiration's somewhere near to zero;
> So my last words would be: Come off that cloud,
> Unship those wings that hardly dared to flitter,
> And spout your halo for a pint of bitter.[32]

These personal remarks are, of course, less important than Orwell's repetition of charges against the pacifists which he had already made in prose. He says, for example, in another part of the same piece:

> Your hands are clean, and so were Pontius Pilate's,
> But as for "bloody heads," that's just a metaphor;
> The bloody heads are on Pacific islets
> Or Russian steppes or Libyan sands—it's better for
> The health to be a CO than a fighter,
> To chalk a pavement doesn't need much guts,
> It pays to stay at home and be a writer
> While other talents wilt in Nissen huts;
> "We live like lions"—yes, just like a lion
> Pensioned on scraps in a safe cage of iron.
> For while you write the warships ring you round
> And flights of bombers drown the nightingales,
> And every bomb that drops is worth a pound
> To you or someone like you, for your sales
> Are swollen with those of rivals dead or silent,
> Whether in Tunis or the BBC,

> And in the drowzy freedom of this island
> You're free to shout that England isn't free;
> They even chuck you cash, as bears get buns,
> For crying "Peace!" behind a screen of guns.

He charged Comfort with intellectual dishonesty for pretending that
Japan had nothing to do with the war, that the Fascists had not
attacked Ethiopia, Spain, Poland, and Czechoslovakia, that Jews
were not being persecuted—in short, for falsifying reality in order
to be able to say that the war is just another capitalist-imperialist
racket. On the other hand, he defended Churchill, saying that many
a "pink" like Comfort had been very willing to shelter behind
Churchill during the crisis of 1939–40:

> Christ! How they huddled up to one another
> Like day-old chicks about their foster-mother!

Churchill, he said, ought to be paid what was due him, even though
after the war he might have to be shot. In any case, Orwell considered Churchill's sentiments to be superior to Comfort's, telling
him:

> I seldom listen-in to Churchill's speeches,
> But I'd far sooner hear that kind of guff
> Than your remark, a year or so ago,
> That if the Nazis came you'd knuckle under
> And peacably "accept the *status quo*."
> Maybe you would! But I've a right to wonder
> Which will sound better in the days to come,
> "Blood, toil and sweat" or "Kiss the Nazi's bum."

Comfort published another, similar poem in *Tribune* a year later,
but Orwell did not reply to it, for by that time the war was going
much better, and the pacifist threat to morale was negligible.

Ironically, both *Tribune* and Orwell as its literary editor were
criticized for publishing this second poem of Comfort's. Orwell's
response is worth noting. When Comfort's second poem was published, he said, he thought it deserved publication because it had
literary merit and also because freedom of thought was one of the
things the war was being fought for:

> I should be the last to claim that we are morally superior to our
> enemies, and there is quite a strong case for saying that British
> imperialism is actually worse than Nazism. But there does remain
> the difference, not to be explained away, that in Britain you are

relatively free to say and print what you like. Even in the blackest patches of the British Empire, in India, say, there is very much more freedom of expression than in a totalitarian country. I want that to remain true, and by sometimes giving a hearing to unpopular opinions, I think we help it to do so.[33]

The invective and personal abuse marking these exchanges in 1943 and 1944 are missing from Orwell's later attacks on pacifists. His review of the letters of Max Plowman made no criticism at all of Plowman's pacifism, because he admired Plowman's courage, his usefulness in assisting refugees, and his goodness. Even so, reviewing a book by Middleton Murry, he continued to notice that Murry's pacifist communities depended on a tolerance in England which would not continue if the Nazis won the war.

When the passion of controversy at last subsided, Orwell was able to regard the pacifists more coolly; he did not retract his arguments, but they have less edge than they had when England was in danger. He confessed that one feature of political controversy in general was its "extraordinary viciousness and dishonesty. . . . Nobody is searching for the truth, everybody is putting forward a 'case' with complete disregard for fairness or accuracy, and the most plainly obvious facts can be ignored by those who don't want to see them." He considered the Communists, Conservatives, pacifists, and the rest equally guilty. Then, characteristically, he indicts himself. He points out, for example, that some people accuse pacifists of obstructing the war effort and "objectively" aiding the Nazis: "I have been guilty of saying this myself more than once. . . . This is not only dishonest; it also carries a severe penalty with it. If you disregard people's motives, it becomes much harder to foresee their actions."[34] He goes on to show that a pacifist's subjective feelings do make a difference when the question of betraying one's country arises.

Despite this apology, Orwell continued to believe in the principal arguments he had advanced against the pacifists. Later on he placed them in the wider context of what he called "nationalism," the habit of identifying oneself with a larger unit, refusing to acknowledge its real ends, and seeking its aggrandizement beyond any other aim. In this sense, pacifists are nationalists, like communists or Zionists, rather than the patriots whom Orwell valued so highly—those who were devoted to a place and a way of life without wishing to force this view on other people.[35]

The absence of patriotism bred defeatism in the intellectuals, what Orwell called "the mechanically anti-British attitude which is usual on the Left."[36] Reviewing Malcolm Muggeridge's *The Thirties*, which he thought brilliant though gloomy because of its neo-Tory pessimism, Orwell found its despair and defeatism not altogether sincere. Muggeridge, neither believing in God at that time nor trusting in man, still after all believed in something—England—and left the Ministry of Information to join the army; as Orwell says, telescoping Newbolt and Henley, "A time comes when the sand of the desert is sodden red and what have I done for thee, England, my England?"[37]

Sharing this emotion himself, Orwell could not help being offended by the absence of patriotism in the "ex-warmongers of the Left."[38] This subjective response was accentuated by his belief that unpatriotic intellectuals endangered the morale of others. He also considered them poor judges of what was happening in politics. This weakness was a specific instance of the intellectuals' failure to understand the importance of the natural sources of energy that shape the world. Having destroyed any feeling of "racial pride, leader-worship, religious belief, love of war," in themselves, they could not understand that others did have these feelings.[39] Churchill, who could be reached by primitive emotions, understood Hitler and Stalin; the intellectuals did not.

Orwell believed intellectuals to be more prone to disaffection than other people. Some, he said, even went on "being defeatist at a time when the war was quite plainly won—partly because they were better able to visualize the dreary years of warfare that lay ahead:

> Their morale was worse because their imaginations were stronger. The quickest way of ending a war is to lose it, and if one finds the prospect of a long war intolerable, it is natural to disbelieve in the possibility of victory. But there was more to it than that. There was also the disaffection of large numbers of intellectuals, which made it difficult for them not to side with any country hostile to Britain. And deepest of all, there was admiration—though only in a very few cases conscious admiration—for the power, energy, and cruelty of the Nazi régime.[40]

Paradoxically, a few years earlier during the period of the Popular Front it was the unpatriotic intellectuals who had been eager for Britain and France to intervene in Spain, though in Orwell's opinion they expected someone else to do the fighting. "In pre-war days, when the appeasement policy still ruled, it was an ironical thing to read through a membership list of the House of

Commons," he said. "It was Labour and Communist members who clamoured for a 'firm stand against Germany,' but it was Conservative members who were members of the R.N.V.R. and R.A.F.V.R."[41]

The *News-Chronicle*, the *Daily Worker*, *Reynolds*, the *New Statesman*, and the sponsors of the Left Book Club had all taken the line, as Orwell described it, that the British nation "wanted nothing better than a ten-million-dead war in defence of democracy."[42] The *New Statesman* had advocated war between 1935 and 1939 and then "sulked when the war started."[43] Maynard Keynes made almost the same point in a letter to the editor of the *New Statesman*, written in October 1939 and criticizing his publication of a particularly offensive letter from Bernard Shaw:

> Sir,—
> The intelligentsia of the Left were the loudest in demanding that the Nazi aggression should be resisted at all costs. When it comes to a showdown, scarce four weeks have passed before they remember that they are pacifists and write defeatist letters to your columns, leaving the defence of freedom and of civilisation to Colonel Blimp and the Old School Tie, for whom Three Cheers.[44]

Orwell saw the same contradiction in the left-wing press generally: hostile references to the Nazis were greatest in 1937–38 and 1944–45, with a marked diminution in 1939–42, when the Nazis seemed to be winning.[45] The same people who demanded a compromise peace in 1940 were demanding the dismemberment of Germany in 1945.[46]

If the intellectuals were unpatriotic it did not follow, in Orwell's mind, that the masses were jingoistic. He believed the English to be characteristically antiwar and antimilitaristic. Although the Empire had been founded on military strength and sustained by the will to use it, most people ignored or easily forgot this fact. He pointed out that it was always difficult to recruit even a small standing army, for ordinary soldiers were despised. The common attitude toward war was "defensive," the soldiers were not inspired by hate; and their songs, which were sometimes mock-defeatist, were belied by their actions. He quotes the following stanza as an example:

> I don't want to join the bloody Army,
> I don't want to go into the war;
> I want no more to roam,

I'd rather stay at home
Living on the earnings of a whore.[47]

Orwell saw a difference between pacifists and the other intellectuals he criticized for their defeatism. Because he himself had held strong antiwar sentiments, if only briefly, he understood and respected the motives that led genuine pacifists to continue hoping for a solution less drastic than an enormously destructive war. Defeatists, by contrast, had no faith in or admiration for their country; their pacifism was the consequence of believing that the country simply was not worth saving.

What intellectuals thought about the war varied somewhat with time and circumstances, but the defeatist strain was usually there. In 1941 it was fashionable to say in left-wing circles that "this war is entirely meaningless."[48] But at that time the only people Orwell found to be "overtly defeatist" were the followers of Mosley, the Communists, and the pacifists.[49] In June 1942, Orwell noted in his diary:

> There is said to be much disagreement on the staff of the *New Statesman* over the question of the Second Front. Having squealed for a year that we must open a Second Front immediately, Kingsley Martin now has cold feet. He says that the army cannot be trusted, the soldiers will shoot their officers in the back etc.—this after endeavouring throughout the war to make the soldiers mistrust their officers.[50]

In 1944, what Orwell called the belief of the "official left-wing" was that "war is a meaningless massacre brought about by capitalists"; it was said that the soldiers hated their officers and deserted when they could.[51] When the Red Army was in question, however, many of those supporting pacifism reversed their usual opinion: the war became good because it produced desirable results; soldiers liked what they were doing and loved their officers while hating their enemies. These pseudo-pacifists thought it right for the Russians to continue fighting but wrong for the English, though they held this attitude, Orwell thought, rather from fear of dominant left-wing opinion than from pacifist conviction.[52]

The same Russophilia that made it difficult for Orwell to find a publisher for *Animal Farm* appeared when the clamor for a second front was coupled illogically with the demand that the bombing of Germany be stopped on the grounds of material destruction. Among those pressing for an invasion from the West that would relieve the Soviet Union, Orwell detected the defeatists' tendency to hate their own country: "I have also heard people say almost in the same breath (*a*) that we must open a Second Front at once, (*b*) that it is no longer necessary because the Russians can defeat the Germans singlehanded, and (*c*) that it is bound to be a failure."[53] Intellectuals wanted the war to end quickly, yet were pleased when things went wrong in Italy; they approved the plans for a harsh peace and at the same time said that Hitler was preferable to the Tories. Orwell summed them up when he said, "Emotionally, what the Left intelligentsia wish for is that Germany and Japan should be defeated but that Britain and America should not be victorious."[54]

Toward the end of the war in Europe, as he became more aware of the contradictions in his own thinking, Orwell wrote an unusual letter to *Partisan Review* in which he acknowledged the mistakes he had made in his analysis and predictions of coming events. For example, he had said that Churchill would be turned out of office in 1942 (after Singapore) and that Germany and the Soviet Union would continue collaborating. He traced these errors to his belief that the war would be lost if it were not also turned into a revolutionary struggle. Other radicals, he said, citing among them the Trotskyites, had shared this opinion; still others were with him in thinking the war worth winning, though they did not share his belief that a revolution would be necessary for victory. But he and those who held some of the same opinions had not been as badly mistaken as those who thought that (*a*) the war was not worth winning; the revolution was more important; or (*b*) fighting the Fascists meant that Britain would turn Fascist; or (*c*) the Germans and Japanese would win anyway.

In other words, except for those who thought the war worth winning at any price (and Orwell did not regard this aim as a satisfactory guide to political action), the theories and opinions of the rest of the Left (including his own) had all been shown by events to be wrong. And yet, he said, "There is complete shamelessness about past mistakes," which explains, perhaps, why Orwell had chosen to confess his own errors in public. "Particularly on the Left," he said, "political thought is a sort of masturbation fantasy in which the world of facts hardly matters."[55]

Orwell could justifiably claim, however, that since he loved his country he could see things to which many of the intelligentsia were blind. Having destroyed patriotism in themselves, they were "blackly defeatist," especially in 1940 and 1942. In contrast he could see, for example, that the chances of holding on to Egypt in

1942 were good; and he could do this, he said, precisely because he did not "share the average English intellectual's hatred of his own country and [was] not dismayed by a British victory."[56]

He feared at the time that such defeatism might help to destroy British morale and contribute to another Nazi conquest, for he agreed with Hitler's estimate that British acceptance of defeat without resistance would destroy the national spirit.[57] We can now see that his fears were exaggerated; but, with the French example before him, they were understandable enough. Following the collapse of France, the efforts made by the Germans to woo French intellectuals and to maintain the illusion that French intellectual life had survived were frightening. "If the Germans got to England, similar things would happen, and I think I could make out at least a preliminary list of the people who would go over," he wrote.[58] He also noted that defections among the intelligentsia accompanied the Nazi conquest of France, and that defeatism and a willingness to accept bribes, as well as imaginative foresight, all played a part in these defections.[59]

When things were at their worst in 1941, Orwell was saying that what sustained the common people was their belief in bourgeois democracy; it was not illusion and not Marxist superstructure. But he feared that if conditions became bad enough for the working class the groups that wished for a German victory—the Communists, Mosley's Fascists, the pacifists, and some Catholics—might be able to bring about the right emotional conditions for a British defeat. "An army of unemployed led by millionaires quoting the Sermon on the Mount—that is our danger."[60] He believed he saw a different attack on morale coming from the more moderate Left, whose unpatriotic, flabby cynicism created a false picture of actuality and a false ideal of Englishmen. "In spite of all the 'anti-Fascist' heroics of the left-wing press," he asked, "what chance should we have stood when the real struggle with Fascism came, if the average Englishman had been the kind of creature that the *New Statesman*, the *Daily Worker* or even the *News-Chronicle* wished to make him?"[61]

Another, equally sinister, consequence of this defeatism seemed to him possible—the growth of anti-Semitism. Orwell noted after the war that "during the past twenty-five years the activities of what are called 'intellectuals' have been largely mischievous," and he did not think it an exaggeration to say that if they had done their work better Britain would have surrendered in 1940. If Britain had come out of the war in a greatly weakened condition, he thought it possible that some form of British nationalism of an intellectual kind might have revived and that prewar leftism would be attacked for having been defeatist. "In that case," he thought, "the kind of anti-Semitism which flourished among the anti-Dreyfus-ards in France, and which Chesterton and Belloc tried to import into this country, might get a foothold."[62]

Pacifism has no chance to become an issue in *1984*. War is a permanent state of affairs in Oceania, deliberately so because the leaders understand how to exploit its cohesive power by controlling the climate of opinion. A succession of military victories— real or imagined—is the best antidote to disaffection and defeatism. The interesting paradox is that the crowds celebrating the victories of Oceania resemble in their mentality the English pacifists whom Orwell wrote about in the late 1930s and early 1940s: they indulged their sentiments at others' expense; they were so blinded by propaganda that they could shift their positions almost overnight; and the defeatists among them had no love for their country because they had no firm faith in anything.

VIII

THE PRESS

IN *1984* the creation of public opinion through the news media is—together with warfare and the secret police—an essential part of government. Images and commands invade the last vestiges of private life left to people, coercing them to their duties and, above all, conditioning them to be orthodox and enthusiastic about the regime—in Newspeak to be "goodthinkers" and "bellyfeelers." Surveillance being continuous, disaffection is soon uncovered and defection impossible. All the devices for communicating and storing knowledge are thus subverted to the uses of state control, and it is a mark of their importance that Winston Smith works for the Ministry of Truth, the organization responsible for propaganda and the rewriting of history. Intellectuals perform the work of the ministry, but for the most part they are technicians carrying out orders. Orwell feared that a similar development might overtake Britain's writers, and he fought against it long before he wrote *1984*.

For many years he depended for his living on the newspapers and journals which published his reviews and other articles, and his ties with the press were strengthened by his friendships with other writers. Nevertheless, he said he learned early in life that no event was ever correctly reported in a newspaper.[1] His opinion of journalists is epitomized in a verse that he attributed to Hilaire Belloc:

> You cannot hope to bribe or twist
> Thank God! the English journalist:
> But seeing what the man will do
> Unbribed, there is no reason to.[2]

It was seldom necessary, he thought, to attack the capitalist press, because people knew it would distort the truth whenever that seemed useful. Occasionally he would launch an objection to conservative journalists, like Sir William Connor ("Cassandra"), a columnist for the *Daily Mirror*. For instance, he criticized Connor's demagoguery in making a whipping-boy of P. G. Wodehouse, and he pointed out that Wodehouse was an easy victim because he was the "kind of rich man who could be attacked with impunity and without risking damage to the structure of society."[3] Ordinarily, though, his targets were writers rather farther to the Left and journals which were influential even though they did not have a mass circulation. His criticisms were often based on personal experiences, and of these perhaps the most important were the events he lived through in Spain during the Civil War.

Before he went to Spain he accepted, he says, "the *News-Chronicle–New Statesman* version of the war as the defense of civilization against a maniacal outbreak by an army of Colonel Blimps in the pay of Hitler."[4] But if he was naive at the outset he learned rapidly how far he had been misled. The press, Orwell found, lied habitually about events in Spain, exaggerating exchanges of rifle fire into major engagements, and treating atrocities as occasions for propaganda. Commenting in 1942 about the German announcement of the destruction of Lidice he noted how the German pact with Soviet Russia had colored certain people's view of events reported in the news:

> What does impress me, however, is that other people's reaction to such happenings is governed solely by the political fashion of the moment. Thus before the war the pinks believed any and every horror story that came out of Germany or China. Now the pinks no longer believe in German or Japanese atrocities and automatically write off all horror stories as 'propaganda.' In a little while you will be jeered at if you suggest that the story of Lidice could possibly [be] true.[5]

His mistrust of journalistic reporting grew so intense that he had to guard against cynicism. "These things [Japanese and Nazi atrocities] really happened, that is the thing to keep one's eye on. They happened even though Lord Halifax said they happened."[6]

In Spain he felt the soldier's usual anger at the reporters who wrote their stories in safety far from the bullets and mud, and he decided: "One of the dreariest effects of this war has been to teach me that the Left-wing press is every bit as spurious and dishonest as that of the Right." He observed, for example, that as late as October 1937 the *New Statesman* was "spreading tales of Fascist barricades made of the bodies of living children."[7] Earlier in the year, however, writing to Cyril Connolly in February, he had praised the same journal for publishing a report that was not written from the Communist point of view.[8]

Elsewhere, in a passage that foreshadows *1984*, he described his impressions of the extent to which journalism had become irresponsible:

> In Spain, for the first time, I saw newspaper reports which did not bear any relation to the facts, not even the relationship that is implied in an ordinary lie. I saw great battles reported where there had been no fighting, and complete silence where hundreds of men had been killed. I saw troops who had fought bravely denounced as cowards and traitors, and others who had never seen a shot fired hailed as the heroes of imaginary victories; and I saw newspapers in London retailing these lies and eager intellectuals building emotional superstructures over events that had never happened.[9]

Orwell's bitterness arose from two sources: the direct distortions of fact through outright lies and the false impression journalists were able to create by suppressing or attacking the truth when they knew it. The most flagrant example of both forms of misrepresentation that Orwell himself knew about from personal experience was the treatment of the clash in Barcelona in May 1937, when the government forces backed by the Communists fought the Anarchists and the P.O.U.M., in whose military arm Orwell was serving.

In reports of the battle, the Communist and left-wing press represented it as a revolt against the Loyalist government, staged by the Anarchists and P.O.U.M. as part of a Trotskyite conspiracy to benefit the Fascists. The news of the subsequent purge by the victorious government forces was either suppressed or disguised to make their harsh retaliation appear to be a legitimate exercise of the government's authority. Orwell's reports tried to tell the truth as he knew it, but the differences between his accounts and the version generally accepted by the British Left were so great that, as we shall see, he had difficulty finding anyone to print them.

Briefly, his account of the conflict was that he had been in Barcelona at the time on two weeks' leave from the front. After the first week, however, he was caught up in the conflict going on in the city and spent most of the remainder of his leave on sentry duty at P.O.U.M. headquarters. Shortly after returning to the front from Barcelona he was shot in the throat and invalided back there, only to find that his life was now endangered, not by Fascist bullets, but by his P.O.U.M. affiliation. The government had succeeded in forcibly asserting its authority in the city and, with Communist help, had begun the purge of those it considered its enemies, especially those in the P.O.U.M.

Fortunately Orwell, his wife Eileen, and two friends were able to escape to France. By July he could write to his friend Rayner Heppenstall: "It was a queer business. We started off by being heroic defenders of democracy and ended by slipping over the border with the police panting at our heels."[10] This experience was not as easily dismissed from his mind as his statement might suggest. The most obvious proof of its significance is *Homage to Catalonia*. The history of that book bears out Orwell's views about the bias of the press, for Orwell found it difficult to reach the public with his version of what had happened in Barcelona.[11]

Referring to Orwell's account of these events in *Homage to Catalonia*, Lionel Trilling wrote: "It would have been very difficult to learn anything of this in New York and London. Those periodicals which guided the thought of left-liberal intellectuals knew nothing of it, and had no wish to learn. As for the aftermath of the unhappy uprising, they appeared to have no knowledge of that at all."[12]

Before leaving France on his return journey to England, Orwell had wired the editor of the *New Statesman*, Kingsley Martin, asking if he would like an article on the events in Barcelona, and Martin had answered that he would. But when he read what Orwell had written, he refused to publish it, not because he disbelieved what Orwell wrote but because he supposed that the Civil War in Spain was one between fascism and democracy and that obviously democracy had to be supported, even at the expense of truth. As Edward Hyams put it, in his history of the *New Statesman*, "If neither triumphed, but Communism came out victorious over both, even that would be better than a Fascist victory."[13]

Commenting on this rejection in a letter to Rayner Heppenstall, Orwell wrote: "To sugar the pill they sent me to review a very good book which appeared recently, *The Spanish Cockpit*, which blows the gaff pretty well on what has been happening. But once again when they saw my review they couldn't print it as it was 'against editorial policy.' "[14] The *New Statesman* offered to pay Orwell for this review, but he regarded the gesture as "hush money," although Heppenstall said it was common practice.[15]

Orwell did succeed in publishing an account of the events in Catalonia in the August 1937 issue of an obscure journal named *Controversy*. The better-known *New English Weekly* also accepted a longer, two-part article in which he asserted that "there has been a quite deliberate conspiracy (I could give detailed instances) to prevent the Spanish situation from being understood. People who ought to know better have lent themselves to the deception on the ground that if you tell the truth about Spain it will be used as Fascist propaganda."[16] The evil implied in this suppression was evident in his going on to argue that such cowardice prevented people from knowing what fascism really is and hence prepared the way for the next war.

He was also finally able to have a review of Franz Borkenau's *The Spanish Cockpit* accepted. *Time and Tide* was to publish it, and Orwell wrote the editor, observing that a similar review had been refused publication by "another well-known weekly paper." At the same time he forwarded a comment Borkenau had sent him. Although his book had been widely praised, Borkenau had said, Orwell was the sole reviewer to draw attention to one of the book's central themes, "the real part played by the Communist Party in Spain." Orwell also told the editor of *Time and Tide* that the pro-Communist censorship extended even to right-wing newspapers, whose editors were more fearful of Anarchists and Trotskyites than they were of Communists.[17]

This letter was published in *Time and Tide* and provoked a personal reply to Orwell written by Raymond Mortimer, then literary editor of the *New Statesman*. He objected to Orwell's statements and denied that the review had been rejected because it "controverted editorial policy." In answer, Orwell sent Mortimer a copy of Kingsley Martin's original rejection and apologized for saying "editorial policy" when he ought to have said "political policy." He went on to defend his criticism of the *New Statesman;* his principal motive was his desire to assist the 3,000 anti-Fascist political prisoners in Republican jails by arousing people outside Spain to protest against the government's injustice.[18]

In the course of the same letter, he also called Mortimer's attention to another instance of misrepresentation in the *New Statesman*. An article by H. N. Brailsford mistakenly claimed that the P.O.U.M. had attacked the government with guns, tanks, and other weapons. Orwell said that he pointed out the error to Kingsley Martin and questioned Brailsford about the source of the story, only to find that the story had been accepted "on what amounts to no authority whatever." Despite all this, "neither the *New Statesman* nor Brailsford has published any retraction of this statement, which amounts to an accusation of theft and treachery against numbers of innocent people." Responding to these and other revelations, Mortimer apologized handsomely to Orwell for his mistake, and added: "I should be sorry for you not to write for us, and I should like to convince you from past reviews that there is no premium here on Stalinist orthodoxy."[19]

Several years later the editors of Orwell's *Collected Essays* remarked in a footnote: "Orwell did book reviews for the literary pages of the *New Statesman* from July 1940 to August 1943 but, as is recorded in conversations with his friends, he never forgave Kingsley Martin for his 'line' over the Spanish civil war."[20] Martin himself continued to justify his decision. The most he has said in exculpation is that he did not know then how "abominably" the Communists had treated the Anarchists, and that he "probably underestimated the Communist atrocities; it was not an unnatural fault when every day brought me news of tortures and shootings carried out by Franco and his Moors."[21]

Another echo of this affair was heard as late as 1945 in the declaration of editorial policy which Orwell wrote when he was Literary Editor of *Tribune*. Alluding to the variety of political opinions found among the contributors to *Tribune*, he said, "All of them knew, of course, what kind of paper they were writing for and what topics were best left alone, but I think that none of them has ever been asked to modify what he had written on the ground that it was 'not policy.'" Later, in the same statement, he added: "To my knowledge, some periodicals coerce their reviewers into following the political line of the paper, even when they have to falsify their own opinions to do so."[22]

Even more serious trouble with the press attended the publication of *Homage to Catalonia*. Orwell had gone to Spain with the idea of writing a book; from there he wrote to Victor Gollancz, his publisher, about this possibility: "I hope I shall get a chance to write the truth about what I have seen. The stuff appearing in the English papers is largely the most appalling lies—more I can't say, owing to the censorship."[23] In the same letter Orwell also thanked Gollancz for writing a foreword to *The Road to Wigan Pier*. There is a certain irony in his doing so, because his attack on Marxist socialism in that book had upset Gollancz. In fact Gollancz had contracted to publish only Orwell's fiction and further limited the contract to the next three works,[24] presumably because he feared that Orwell would continue writing books offensive to the Communists and fellow travelers who, as members of the Left Book Club, made up much of his clientele.

Of the many Popular Front organizations this club, founded by Gollancz, was the most notable in the literary world and had at one time a membership of about 50,000. There were more than a thousand Left Book Club groups and a Left Book Club Theatre Guild with more than 270 groups. Officially the club was not linked to any party. Harold Laski, who helped Gollancz choose the books to be published, and Gollancz were non-Communist left-wingers; John Strachey, who also had a voice in the selection, though not technically a Communist, was advising others to sign up.[25]

A British correspondent for the *Mercure de France* who had asked about the purposes of the club was told that it existed to fight fascism and promote the cause of peace and a better social order. But, as he went on to say, he asked his question in an office where the only picture on the walls was a framed portrait of Stalin, and he was rather sceptical about the answer he got.[26] Gollancz wistfully pointed out to his members that the Communists sought him out to offer him their manuscripts, whereas he had to rack his brains to invent books to be written by those whose politics were different.[27] On the other hand, Kingsley Martin says of Gollancz that "though occasionally publishing books from such people as Orwell and Attlee, he would, at this period, try to persuade non-Marxist writers to cut out any word that could be offensive to the Soviet Union. In every part of England Left Book Club groups were formed and they came mainly under the influence of Communists or near-Communists."[28] This opinion is corroborated by Julian Symons, who acknowledged Gollancz' good intentions but who believed that the chief function of the Left Book Club was to "serve as a propaganda machine for Communism." He found this most apparent in the long reviews and articles written for *Left News,* the Club periodical.[29]

Douglas Hyde, an ex-Communist, has described how the party used the Left Book Club, although not controlling its operation, and even Gollancz seems to have been disturbed that the local units were being used for political ends instead of for the discussion of the books being published. The club declined as the Popular Front movement lost headway; still, in 1940, it retained 36,000 members, of whom about 6,000 were Communists. In a letter written then, Orwell said:

> Gollancz had grown a beard & fallen out with his Communist pals, partly over Finland, etc., partly over their general dishonesty which he's just become alive to. When I saw him recently, the first time in 3 years, he asked me whether it was really true that the GPU had been active in Spain during the civil war, & told me that when he tied up with the Communists in 1936 he had not known that they had ever had any other policy than the Popular Front one. It's

frightful that people who are so ignorant should have so much influence.[30]

There is in *Coming Up for Air* a memorable account of a Left Book Club group meeting, in which Orwell stresses the message of hate purveyed by the speaker, a "well-known anti-Fascist," and the vision of terror and violence he offers to his peaceable, middle-class audience. The few Communists and the single Trotskyite in the group are already in the proper emotional state; the rest have to be prepared.

Considering the political line that the Left Book Club was following, Orwell could not have been surprised when he discovered, quite soon after his return to England, that Gollancz was not interested in his book about the war in Spain. As he wrote in a letter to Rayner Heppenstall:

> Gollancz is of course part of the Communism-racket, and as soon as he heard I had been associated in the POUM and Anarchists and had seen the inside of the May riots in Barcelona, he said he did not think he would be able to publish my book, though not a word of it was written yet. I think he must have very astutely foreseen that something of the kind would happen, as when I went to Spain he drew up a contract undertaking to publish my fiction but not other books.[31]

It was at this time that Orwell told Geoffrey Gorer that the *Daily Worker* had been abusing him.[32] Gollancz silenced the attackers, but the rupture with Orwell was not mended. A month later Orwell wrote to Jack Common that he had to change his publisher, "Gollancz won't have any more to do with me now I am a Trotskyist."[33]

Homage to Catalonia was finally published in April 1938 by Secker and Warburg, who from then on published most of Orwell's books. It did not sell. According to F. J. Warburg it "barely caused a ripple on the political pond. It was ignored or hectored in failure."[34] Of the 1,500 copies printed, 638 were sold in the first six months. After that the annual sale was fewer than fifty copies, and the balance of the first edition was still unsold when Orwell died in 1950.[35]

The hectoring tone to which Warburg refers is exemplified by an anonymous review in *The Listener*, which begins:

> If Mr. Orwell would stick to his last, which is writing, and would abandon the idea that he understands politics, which he does not,

he could produce a better book about the Spanish civil war than almost anyone who has visited the peninsula since July, 1936. As it is he has produced as muddle-headed and inaccurate a political treatise as the war has yet given birth to.[36]

The reviewer then presented his version of the events in Catalonia, including the usual charge that the P.O.U.M. was a Franco fifth column, and concluded pityingly that Orwell had "spoiled what might have been a splendid book," because of his inadequate perception of political matters. Orwell replied to this unfavorable notice, pointing out some of the contradictions in the review and claiming that he had been misrepresented. Surprisingly enough, the editor of *The Listener* agreed with him and apologized in print.[37]

V. S. Pritchett's review in the *New Statesman* took a similar line. People like Orwell, he said, ought to keep out of politics because they harm the causes they try to help—a point made by Orwell, as we have seen, about some Socialists. He praised Orwell's rendering of the nastiness of the war and approved the idealism which led Orwell to fight for the Republic. But he too thought these virtues were outweighed by Orwell's deficiency in political insight. Pritchett made no effort, however, to discredit the abundant evidence with which Orwell supported his conclusions; he scarcely discussed it. He agreed, in rather ambiguous language, that "the wretched P.O.U.M. got a raw deal," but he accepted without question the story of the Anarchist rising.[38] There is in Pritchett's review no hint that the Communists used the occasion to attack their enemies; nor is Orwell credited with presenting a firsthand account of the events and interpreting them in a way that the press had so far ignored.

Despite such efforts to discount its merits, the book, so John Lehmann thinks, had an important effect. He said that Orwell's "account of what happened in Catalonia and of the fate of the P.O.U.M. broke the last resistance of many who had been desperately holding out against the shock of truth."[39] Against this estimate one must weigh the book's meager sales and the generally damning reviews and acknowledge that the work, one of the best Orwell wrote and one of the most valuable of all those written about the Spanish war, was a failure at the start. And it is a legitimate inference, supported by the book's later acceptance after the political climate had changed, that the early failure was caused by the enmity of those—especially those on the Left—who took care to discredit any story about Spain but their own.

What Orwell had learned about the press, especially the left-wing press, from his experience in Spain was confirmed by a number of incidents during World War II in which journals—anticipating the Ministry of Truth—revised or obscured events to suit their own aims. One was the attempted rising against the Germans in Warsaw that led to the slaughter of many members of the Polish resistance in 1944 at a time when the Russian armies were very close to the city. The facts of the situation were at least as complicated as those which Orwell knew from his firsthand experience in Barcelona; even so, it again seemed clear to him that the version of the left-wing press was biased. Almost unanimously (and, he thought, unfairly) writers of the Left condemned the rising. They said it had been directed against the Russians, and they accepted the story the Russians gave to explain why they failed to help the Poles once the rising began. Such an uncritical acceptance of what he considered Communist exploitation of a confusing story prompted Orwell to direct a "message that he hoped English Left-wing journalists and intellectuals generally would heed":

> Do remember that dishonesty and cowardice always have to be paid for. Don't imagine that for years on end you can make yourself the boot-licking propagandist of the Soviet régime, or any other régime, and then suddenly return to mental decency. Once a whore, always a whore.[40]

Orwell felt all the more strongly about this matter because he was convinced that a satisfactory Anglo-Russian understanding could result only from "free discussion and genuine criticism *now*. There can be no real alliance on the basis of 'Stalin is always right.' "[41] The bitterness of his attack provoked a number of replies, among them letters from Douglas Goldring and Kingsley Martin.[42]

Another example of bias on the part of the press, and one referred to more than once by Orwell, concerned Maurice Thorez, the leader of the Communist party in France. Thorez had been called up for military service in the French army in 1939, but once in the army he had almost immediately deserted and fled to the Soviet Union. After the liberation of France in 1944 the French government granted him amnesty from the sentence for desertion that had been pronounced on him *in absentia*. In reporting this action, at least one London newspaper said that he would now be able to return to France after having lived in exile for six years. The five years' absence had been altered to six, and the reason in Orwell's opinion was "in order to make it appear that Thorez deserted, if he did desert, a year before the war and not after the fighting had started. This is merely one act in the general effort to whitewash the behavior of the French and other Communists during the period of the Russo-German pact. I could name similar falsifications in recent years."[43]

In the same article Orwell also cited the treatment the press had given to Mihailovich, the Yugoslav partisan leader. At first the British government had backed Mihailovich and then dropped him in favor of Tito. Orwell noted that a campaign then began in the press and over the B.B.C. to show that Mihailovich was a German agent. "Reputable British newspapers," he said, connived "at what amounted to forgery in order to discredit the man they had been backing a few months earlier." When the newspapers were shown "very strong evidence" that Mihailovich was not a German agent, they not only refused to print it but advanced the same charges of treachery they had been making all along.[44] Orwell's interpretation of the Mihailovich-Tito story is similar to Evelyn Waugh's in *Sword of Honour*.

After Germany's defeat Orwell visited some of the concentration camps, as well as the prisoner-of-war camps and repatriation centers, while he was serving briefly as a correspondent for the *Observer*. On his return he wrote that many Soviet Russians had changed sides and had fought for the Germans. Furthermore a small though significant number among the Russian prisoners and displaced persons had refused to go back to the Soviet Union and were repatriated against their will. These facts, he said, were "almost unmentioned in the British Press, while at the same time Russophile publicists in England continued to justify the purges and deportations of 1936–38 by claiming that the U.S.S.R. 'had no quislings.' "[45]

He also cited other instances of deception, referring to the "fog of lies and misinformation that surrounds such subjects as the Ukraine famine, the Spanish civil war [and] Russian policy in Poland." His understated conclusion was that a writer or journalist who is a Soviet sympathizer had to "acquiesce in deliberate falsifications on important issues."[46]

Some of the misrepresentation in the press during the war can obviously be laid to immediate political necessity—though Orwell would have hesitated to accept this excuse. But the opposition to *Homage to Catalonia* because it contradicted left-wing orthodoxy in 1937–38 was inexcusable. Nor can he be blamed for resenting the effect of his anti-Soviet opinions on the publishing history of *Animal Farm.* According to their contract Gollancz had the right to issue the book, but he rejected it.[47] Orwell's friend Julian Symons says Orwell told him that the manuscript was refused "primarily on the ground that this was no time for launching an attack on our Soviet ally. But, of course, he added, a time when the Soviet Union was popular in Britain was precisely the moment at which the whole corrupt nature of the Russian State should be exposed, and that such a man as Gollancz should reject the book on this ground seemed to him shameful."[48]

George Woodcock's account of Orwell's difficulties in finding a publisher for *Animal Farm* indicates that more than one faction found the book objectionable. Orwell offered the work to the Freedom Press, with which Woodcock was then associated. "I did my best," he said, "to persuade the editorial committee, but left-wing factionalism prevailed. Orwell called himself a Socialist and supported the war; the owners of Freedom Press were Anarchists and opposed it. Orwell's book was rejected sight unseen." He did not tell Orwell of their attitude, he said, "Since I did not want him to feel conspired against by anti-Communists as well."[49]

This was the fifth in a long series of refusals. Jonathan Cape rejected the story too, apparently after consulting the Ministry of Information.[50] T. S. Eliot, acting for Faber and Faber, also turned it down; a passage from his letter to Orwell is worth quoting for the sense it gives of the atmosphere prevailing then. Eliot wrote that he had consulted another director of the firm, and they were agreed "that it is a distinguished piece of writing; that the fable is very skilfully handled, and that the narrative keeps one's interest on its own plane—and that is something very few authors have achieved since Gulliver." He went on to say, however, "We have no conviction (and I am sure none of the other directors would have) that this is the right point of view from which to criticise the political situation at the present time."[51] Eliot also found fault with the negative quality of the book and discounted what he called its positive point of view (which he called "Trotskyite") as "unconvincing."

Writing to Philip Rahv of *Partisan Review* in 1944, Orwell said of the manuscript:

> I think you will agree that it deserves to be printed, but its "message" is hardly a popular one nowadays. I am having hell and all to find a publisher for it here though normally I have no difficulty in publishing my stuff and in any case all publishers are now clamouring for manuscripts. A few weeks back a newspaper I write

for regularly refused to print a book review of mine because it was anti-Stalin in tone. Comically enough the Stalinists themselves haven't much influence in the press, but Stalin seems to be becoming a figure rather similar to what Franco used to be, a Christian gent whom it is not done to criticise.[52]

Meanwhile the manuscript was, in Orwell's words, "peddled round from publisher to publisher over a period of a year or so."[53] At one point Orwell and his friend Paul Potts considered publishing the book themselves through the Whitman Press, with which Potts was associated. In fact, they even started to print the book, apparently as a two-shilling pamphlet which was to be prefaced by an essay on freedom of the press.[54] But at the last minute, late in 1944, Secker and Warburg again came to the rescue and accepted the manuscript, though it was not finally published until August 1945.[55]

The work had also been submitted to publishers in the United States, with the same lack of success as in England, though perhaps not always for the same political reason, since at least one company turned it down because it thought a book about animals would not interest the American public.[56] According to Warburg, it was declined by almost a dozen American publishers before Harcourt, Brace accepted it.

Nor were publishers the only ones who feared the effect of the book. Orwell temporarily left off writing his column, "As I Please," for *Tribune* because Aneurin Bevan, the Labour politician who was editor, foresaw an adverse response to the book. Orwell wrote to Herbert Read that "Bevan was terrified there might be a row over *Animal Farm*, which might have been embarrassing if the book had come out before the election, as it was at first intended to."[57] Even after the work had appeared in England and America the French publisher, as Orwell explained to Arthur Koestler, "got cold feet and says it is impossible 'for political reasons.'"[58]

Once in print *Animal Farm* was, of course, an immediate success. The Stalinist reviewers in England pretended that it was a satire on Nazi Germany; and, as Spencer Brown has shown, some reviewers in the United States gave it similar treatment.[59] Six different New York newspapers failed to mention the Soviet Union in their reviews. The advertising material on the book jacket did not refer either to the Soviet Union or to communism, nor did the publicity for the filmed version. Even as late as 1954, a literary Communist like Sean O'Casey was writing about *Animal Farm* without saying that it was an anti-Soviet satire.[60]

Orwell summed up what he had learned through personal experience of the ways the press used in its efforts to form and control opinion in this comment on an attack which the Communist writer Raymond Swingler had launched against him:

> Because I committed the crime known in France as *lèse-Staline* I have been obliged at times to change my publisher, to stop writing for papers which represented part of my livelihood, to have my books boycotted in other papers, and to be pursued by insulting letters, articles similar to the one which Mr. Swingler has just written, and even threats of libel action.[61]

Despite all that has been written on the subject and all that will be written, we are never going to be certain of the degree of Communist influence on the intellectuals of the thirties in England, especially those in the literary world. Orwell's own conclusion was that "for about three years, in fact, the central stream of English literature was more or less directly under Communist control."[62] By the "central stream" he meant the same thing as the "main tendency" he identified in "Inside the Whale," that is, such writers as Auden, Isherwood, Spender, Day Lewis, MacNeice, and Edward Upward.

Orwell's statement is not precise; the qualifying phrase, "more or less directly," is his attempt to allow for the fact that party membership, implying party discipline, was not the only means by which writers could be controlled. The influence of satellite and front organizations, the unthinking acceptance of fashionable attitudes, and the power of individuals strategically located in the complicated networks of the worlds of journalism and publishing are also means by which control could be exerted. Kingsley Martin says, for example, that between 1936 and 1939 the influence of the Left Book Clubs, particularly in the universities, was "enormous."[63] Orwell's phrase, "the central stream," may also be questioned. Evelyn Waugh and Roy Campbell, for example, were also young men writing in the thirties, and their work was certainly as important as that done by most of those in the "central stream." But after thirty years the impression remains that Orwell was not altogether mistaken.

His opinion has been challenged, however, notably by Neal Wood in his *Communism and British Intellectuals*, who finds that Orwell's was an "easy generalization" that exaggerated a "socio-political tendency."[64] But Wood himself exaggerates. He appears to think that Orwell had said that the thirties were a "red decade," though Orwell was careful to limit his remark to cover only about three years, roughly the period of the war in Spain and the Popular Front. Nor did Orwell say that the writers in the "central stream" had all joined the party or that they remained under its control. Furthermore, the evidence Wood cites in his book tends to corroborate Orwell's opinion. In his book, *The British Communist Party*, Henry Pelling called the fifth and sixth chapters "The Red Decade: Entry of the Intellectuals," and "The Red Decade: Spain and the Purges." The evidence Pelling adduces supports the belief that Orwell's judgment was not the easy generalization that Wood says it was.

One of Orwell's contemporaries, Wyndham Lewis, thought that he did not go far enough. Moreover he accused Orwell of holding back in his criticism because his career depended on the favorable opinions of Communists and fellow travelers who were, at least nominally, his friends and able to influence the publication and reception of his work. He called Orwell an "ex-fellow-traveller" who did not attack the "conventional Left Wing attitudes of his friends."[65] Since Lewis offered no evidence to support his opinion, to refute it one need only point to Orwell's record of consistent opposition to the Communists and fellow travelers.

But even if one leaves aside the question of Communist influence, in Orwell's opinion a writer who wrote what he believed would find that he had offended virtually every communications agency in the land. One had to pay this price to remain free. In 1945 Orwell attended a symposium at a P.E.N. Club meeting celebrating the tercentenary of Milton's *Areopagitica*. In reviewing the collected speeches, published under the title *Freedom of Expression*, he said the book was depressing because no one at the meeting had dared to speak openly and explicitly in favor of freedom of the press and therefore in favor of freedom of the intellect. He called attention to the subjects which should have been talked about but were ignored:

> The centralized ownership of the British press, with its consequent power to suppress any bit of news that it chooses; the question of who really controls the B.B.C.; the buying up of young writers by film units, the M.O.I. [Ministry of Information], etc.; the methods by which British correspondents in foreign countries are squeezed into telling lies or concealing truths; the corruption of literary criticism by the publishing trade; the vague semi-official pressure

that prevents books on unpopular themes from getting published; the spread of totalitarian ideas, mostly emanating from the U.S.S.R., among English intellectuals.[66]

1984 furnishes ample evidence that Orwell never lost his hatred of those who bent popular opinion to suit the necessities of a totalitarian regime. But his harsh judgments about some journalists may have softened. On at least one occasion during the war years he was able to see the ironic contrast between the work he was doing for the B.B.C. and what he had written earlier. This excerpt is from the diary he kept in 1942:

> Connolly yesterday wanted to quote a passage from *Homage to Catalonia* in his broadcast. I opened the book and came on these sentences: "One of the most horrible features of war is that all war propaganda, all the screaming and lies and hatred, comes invariably from people who are not fighting. . . . It is the same in all wars; the soldiers do the fighting, the journalists do the shouting, and no true patriot ever gets near a front-line trench, except on the briefest of propaganda tours. Sometimes it is a comfort to me to think that the aeroplane is altering the conditions of war. Perhaps when the next great war comes we may see that sight unprecedented in all history, a jingo with a bullethole in him."
>
> Here I am in the BBC, less than 5 years after writing that. I suppose sooner or later we all write our own epitaphs.[67]

PART THREE

The Novels

IX

PREDECESSORS TO *1984*

THE NOVELS Orwell wrote before *1984* have been thoroughly and usefully studied by critics in recent years, and our sense of their quality as works of art is fairly well established. Here the interest taken in them is more parochial; that is, we will be looking back at them from the perspective of *1984*, seeing them as imaginative concepts which find their fullest expression in Orwell's last work. This is, of course, not only a matter of plot and theme or atmosphere, but also of ideas, attitudes, and details which have sometimes been thought to be unique to *1984*.

It is surely a permissible exaggeration to say that from first to last Orwell, like George Eliot, was always writing the same novel.[1] Not simply are his works marked by the same tone and style, but each one represents with variations the same troubled situation which he tries, without ever quite succeeding, to bring to an intellectually and emotionally satisfying outcome. Stated most generally, this central situation is a hidden or overt rebellion against a way of life accepted by most but intolerable to the protagonists. These, as Orwell sees them, are victims of forces they are never strong enough to oppose with any show of equality. Good is defeated by evil; the bully wins. Because of his constancy to this theme we can detect the seeds of *1984* in all Orwell's published fiction, beginning with *Burmese Days*, his first novel.

The particular pattern of *Burmese Days* is one now regarded as commonplace in the history of the novel. It is exemplified by Julien Sorel in *The Red and the Black*—the young man who rebels against what he considers an oppressive and corrupt society. He is seemingly unable to reconcile his ideals with the world as he finds it, yet he can neither change the world nor acquire the cynicism necessary to live comfortably in it.

In *Burmese Days* the society with which the individual is at odds is a British dependency still preserving the forms and attitudes of absolute rule. The essence of what drives John Flory, the central figure in the novel, to suicide is contained in this passage:

123

Each year had been lonelier and more bitter than the last. What was at the center of all his thoughts now, and what poisoned everything, was the ever bitterer hatred of the atmosphere of imperialism. . . .

It is a stifling, stultifying world in which to live. It is a world in which every word and every thought is censored. In England it is hard even to imagine such an atmosphere. Everyone is free in England; we sell our souls in public and buy them back in private, among our friends. But even friendship can hardly exist when every white man is a cog in the wheels of despotism. Free speech is unthinkable. All other kinds of freedom are permitted. You are free to be a drunkard, an idler, a coward, a backbiter, a fornicator; but you are not free to think for yourself. Your opinion on every subject of any conceivable importance is dictated for you by the pukka sahibs' code.

In the end the secrecy of your revolt poisons you like a secret disease. Your whole life is a life of lies. . . . The time comes when you burn with hatred of your own countrymen, when you long for a native rising to drown their Empire in blood. And in this there is nothing honourable, hardly even any sincerity. For, *au fond*, what do you care if the Indian Empire is a despotism, if Indians are bullied and exploited? You only care because the right of free speech is denied you. You are a creature of the despotism, a pukka sahib, tied tighter than a monk or a savage by an unbreakable system of tabus.[2]

Burmese Days was published in 1934, yet here are ideas and attitudes in a familiar constellation which will be transposed with scarcely any change to *1984*. They are worth tracing both to heighten their significance when we meet them in *1984* and to show how closely Orwell's writing is related to his convictions about men and politics. The themes developed in *Burmese Days* are rooted in Orwell's experience in police work in Burma, but it would be a mistake to equate John Flory with Orwell himself. Orwell was tougher-minded.

Flory feels like an alien among his fellow Englishmen because he thinks them insensitive about their exploitation of the Burmese. He grows bitter because, although he recognizes the evil, he is powerless to mitigate it or even to make others aware of it. The self-hatred that comes from robbing the Burmese while pretending to be civilizing them is apparent only in Flory, but he believes that the other members of the community nevertheless have a hidden sense of guilt that shows itself in their constant need to justify themselves. It is bad enough that the exploiters destroy the native culture and impoverish the country, but it is worse that they lie to themselves about their motives. Thus very early in Orwell's work he announces one of his principal themes— a decent man's frustration and rage against lying and pretense and his realization that lying corrupts the liar—a theme that receives its final treatment in the official lies and totalitarian corruption of *1984.*

Another theme that is markedly featured in both novels is the loneliness of the man who believes he sees through the lies and hypocrisy around him and who has no one to whom he can safely confide his insight. "Each year Flory found himself less and less at home in the world of the sahibs, . . . So he had learned to live inwardly, secretly, in books and secret thoughts that could not be uttered. . . . But it is a corrupting thing to live one's real life in secret."[3] This is what destroys him, just as it destroys Winston Smith. In the effort to live with the stream of life, not against it, and to assuage his feelings of guilt for what his country is doing to the Burmese, he tries to establish friendships with them; but they are too alien and too filled with hatred for the British, and his efforts to prove that he is a different kind of Englishman naturally make his compatriots even more hostile. Knowing that he dislikes them and sympathizes with the Burmese, they do not even try to conceal their own suspicion of him.

Here is an early reminder—one that will recur in Orwell's other novels—of Winston Smith's life of secrecy and loneliness as he, like Flory, wanders through the "native quarters," longing to join his life to that of the Proles. Orwell, speaking of Winston Smith, mentions "the interminable restless monologue that had been running through his head, literally for years."[4] This remark also characterizes the state of Flory's mind.

Another way in which Flory attempts to put himself in touch with his fellows and escape from living "silent, alone, consoling oneself in secret sterile worlds," is marriage. He thinks he is in love, but what he really wants is an understanding listener. "My God, how I've longed all these years for somebody to talk to! How I could talk to you interminably! . . . That sounds boring. . . . You see, there's—how shall I say?—a demon inside driving us to talk. We walk about under a load of memories which we long to share and somehow never can."[5] Like Julia in *1984* and George Bowling's wife, Flory's fiancée Elizabeth is too much a part of the system to feel that his complaints are warranted. Bored with the rush of words and what she considers his perversity, she too fails him, just as, in his own way, he fails her.

That Orwell himself outgrew the weaknesses which destroyed Flory—insofar as he shared them—is shown in the following passage, first printed in *Horizon*, July 1942, eight years after *Burmese Days* had appeared. Reviewing *The Sword and the Sickle* by Mulk Raj Anand, he expresses surprise that a novel written by an Indian should have so little bitterness and makes this comparison: "In a novel on the same subject by an English intellectual, what would you expect to find? An endless masochistic denunciation of his own race, and a series of traditional caricatures of Anglo-Indian society, with its unbearable club life, its chota pegs, etc. etc."[6] This is a singularly objective view of what most readers do find in *Burmese Days*, and fairly clear evidence that Orwell thought of himself as an intellectual who, at one time at least, had the faults he was later to denounce.

Although Orwell found a way of leaving Burma, Flory can muster only enough strength to struggle unsuccessfully against a Burmese intrigue, a failure that intensifies his self-hatred. He lives and dies an alien in two worlds. Flory is a timber merchant, not an intellectual, but he shares many traits with the thin-skinned, at least half-educated rebels like Julien Sorel and more recently Lawrence's Paul Morel.

Two physical features in Flory emphasize this theme. One is his white skin, creating an impassable barrier between himself and the Burmese. No matter how much he tries—or thinks he tries—to be their friend and to be one of them, his color prevents such fellowship. Flory is also set apart by a disfigurement which Orwell apparently considered to be a key symbol:

> The first thing that one noticed in Flory was a hideous birthmark stretching in a ragged crescent down his left cheek, from the eye to the corner of the mouth. Seen from the left side, his face had a battered woe-begone look, as though the birthmark had been a bruise—for it was a dark blue in color. He was quite aware of its hideousness. And at all times, when he was not alone, there was a sidelongness about his movements, as he manoeuvered constantly to keep the birthmark out of sight.[7]

At critical moments in the novel, Orwell reminds the reader of this visible mark of Flory's difference from other men, but often the allusion is awkward; and the birthmark, probably because it is so personal, never comes to signify more than itself. It is simply a fact about Flory and his embarrassing narcissism.

Orwell knew, of course, what it meant to be an outsider, not only in Burma but also in England. Writing about what he called the "class racket," he described his own feelings when he confronted laboring men on their own ground; the terms he uses apply almost as well to Flory and his predicament: "You see I was still half afraid of the working class. I wanted to get in touch with them, I even wanted to become one of them, but I still thought of them as alien and dangerous; going into the dark doorway of that common lodging-house seemed to me like going down into some dreadful subterranean place—a sewer full of rats, for instance."[8]

Even in so early a work, Orwell is quite aware of the evil in political and social systems which, in addition to exploiting one class by another, make it forever impossible for people from different classes to be on easy, friendly terms. British imperialism, of course, never approached the degree of control found in Oceania, nor was it even in essence what the members of the Inner Party intended Oceania to be. Still in the themes we have discussed *Burmese Days* is a clear anticipation of Orwell's last work.[9]

Orwell's second novel, *A Clergyman's Daughter*, appears to be outside the line of development being traced. One departure is that the central character is a woman; another is that the subject of the book is the loss of religious faith. Even in the broadest sense this book is not political, as the others are. Despite these differences, the novel cannot be ignored, for it has important connections with the ideas that Orwell was to treat in *Coming Up for Air* and would develop even more comprehensively in *1984*.

A Clergyman's Daughter represents the familiar predicament to Orwell's readers of a character struggling against oppressive authority, in this instance a selfish, domineering father. The chief character, Dorothy, is further weighed down by the suspicion and surveillance characteristic of village life. Her name recalls George Eliot's Dorothea Casaubon, and her exacting father resembles Dorothea's first husband.

The rebellion that characterizes Orwell's chief characters, except those in *Animal Farm*, is never overt; and in Dorothy's case it is a special form of going underground, for she loses her memory and in this state of amnesia wanders away from her home. She is driven by some of the feelings that beset George Bowling, worry over money, overwork and harassment endured for the sake of an unloving family, and an awareness that life ought to be better. She is, moreover, afflicted with religious doubts that make life with her father doubly difficult.

Her loss of religious faith has interesting relations to some of Orwell's ideas, and it is noteworthy that the link between language and consciousness is also raised here, though it is not stressed as it is in *1984* and in "Politics and the English Language." But the most interesting topic, as far as this study is concerned, is Dorothy's amnesia and its effect on her view of the world.

When she first begins to recover the use of her senses she remembers nothing; even the way she perceives her surroundings is affected. Orwell says of her:

> But as yet it could not properly be said that she was *looking*. For the things she saw were not apprehended as men, trams and cars, nor as anything in particular; they were not even apprehended as things moving; not even as *things*. She merely *saw*, as an animal sees, without speculation and almost without consciousness. The noises of the street—the confused din of voices, the hooting of horns and the screams of the trams grinding on their gritty rails—flowed through her head provoking purely physical responses. She had no words, nor any conception of the purpose of such things as words, nor any consciousness of time or place, or of her own body or even of her own existence.[10]

Though the question, "Who am I?" is too sophisticated to be asked, Dorothy slowly discovers that being alive is something more than the experience of sensation. As she learns that she exists, she also realizes that existing implies duration, but the past has no distinctive features she can identify. The destruction of the past, this time through an upsetting of the normal workings of memory, links this novel with *Coming Up for Air* and *1984*.

For the first time, but not the last, Orwell is asking what it is like for an individual to be without a history, and how this divorce from previous experience changes his nature. Dorothy's loss of memory obliterated the reality that had become too painful to face; she has to be born again, this time with a reduced faculty for feeling pain and injustice. Bowling's more deliberate turning away from present reality also destroys the past, because the attempt to recapture it reveals the unacceptable discrepancy between the recollection and the real thing. Winston Smith's past is annihilated by the Party's rewriting of history and by O'Brien's electrical shock treatments, which eliminate portions of his brain and leave him less than human.

After the initial attack of amnesia, Dorothy begins a painful reconstruction of her identity, hampered by the necessitous demands of her life as a hop-picker. Orwell's description of this state reminds us forcefully of Winston Smith's experience:

> In the strange, dirty sub-world into which she was instantly plunged, even five minutes of consecutive thought would have been impossible. The days passed in ceaseless nightmarish activity. Indeed, it was very like a nightmare; a nightmare not of urgent terrors, but of hunger, squalor and fatigue, and of alternating heat and cold. Afterwards, when she looked back upon that time, days and nights merged themselves together so that she could never remember with perfect certainty how many of them there had been.[11]

Amnesia and exhaustion unite to prevent her from attempting to get back into what George Bowling—and earlier, John Flory—had called the main stream. "More and more she had come to take her curious situation for granted, to abandon all thoughts of either yesterday or tomorrow. That was the natural effect of life in the hopfields; it narrowed the range of your consciousness to the passing minute."[12] In Orwell's view physical misery—whether from hunger, fatigue, cold, or illness—could reduce one to this state. In *Down and Out in Paris and London* he described his feelings after going two and a half days without food:

> On the second day I thought of pawning my overcoat, but it seemed too far to walk to the pawnshop, and I spent the day in bed, reading the *Memoirs of Sherlock Holmes*. It was all that I felt equal to, without food. Hunger reduces one to an utterly spineless, brainless condition, more like the after-effects of influenza than anything else.[13]

Regardless of what induces such withdrawal, the return to life and recollection of one's place in the world is not easy. As Dorothy's memory slowly revives she feels much as Winston Smith does when, owing to his dreams or chance events, something in his past struggles to return to his consciousness. "Her memory was coming back to her, that was certain, and some ugly shock was coming with it. She actually feared the moment when she should discover her own identity. Something that she did not want to face was waiting just below the surface of her consciousness."[14]

Like Winston Smith, what she has to face is the truth about herself and her degradation. For her the revelation, ironically, comes through the medium of a lying, sensational newspaper.

Typically, too, the attempt to escape leaves her even worse off. The amnesiac state had been nightmare enough; it was succeeded by the reality of being miserably poor and abandoned in London, first without work and then in prison. Orwell tries, without much success, to communicate the insane quality of this experience in a climactic phantasmagoria imitative of Joyce's nighttown scene, but the real political terror of 1984 is missing; the English policeman has not yet turned into O'Brien.

Orwell's demonstration of a vital tie between an individual and his past is reinforced in *A Clergyman's Daughter* by the episode in which Dorothy, released from prison and beginning to regain some control over her fate, takes a post as a teacher. The school is a wretched private academy, a sort of Dothegirls Hall, where she is sweated and abused along with her young pupils. Nevertheless she comes to take an interest in her broken-spirited, ignorant charges, and at last she even delights in trying to teach them history, of whose meaning they have no notion.

They too—like Dorothy herself and like the Proles in 1984—have known only the miserable present. What little they do take in about history is so falsified that it obscures rather than enlightens; the figures of Columbus and Napoleon, the only historical personages the girls knew anything about, "swelled up in the children's minds, like Tweedledum and Tweedledee, till they blocked out the whole landscape of the past." This distortion is magnified by the kind of textbook a machine civilization—to use Orwell's phrase—would inevitably produce, stuffed with clichés, complacently stressing British superiority, glorifying war. *The Hundred-Page History of Britain,* from which Dorothy has to teach, is "a nasty little book" of which this is a sample:

> After the French Revolution was over, the self-styled Emperor Napoleon Buonaparte attempted to set up his sway, but though he won a few victories against continental troops, he soon found that in the "thin red line" he had more than met his match. Conclusions were tried upon the field of Waterloo, where 50,000 Britons put to flight 70,000 Frenchmen—for the Prussians, our allies, arrived too late for the battle. With a ringing British cheer our men charged down the slope and the enemy broke and fled. We now come on to the great Reform Bill of 1832, the first of those beneficent reforms which have made British liberty what it is and marked us off from the less fortunate nations, etc., etc.[15]

This caricature of truthful history, we should notice, is duplicated in 1984, where Smith comes across a similar passage in a children's history during his subversive but futile researches into the past.

Dorothy's efforts to arouse the children to some sense of history are successful, not so much because they learn anything in the conventional sense but because they become more human and their minds expand as they grow even faintly aware of the continuity of civilization and their place in it. She is indeed beginning to civilize children who have been dulled by their parents' bigotry and stifled under Mrs. Creevy's regime.

But of course Dorothy is put down by authority soon enough. Her attempts to teach the truth about the past are frustrated because she has to obey the Money God, what Orwell here calls "the eleventh commandment which has wiped out all the others: 'Thou shalt not lose thy job.' "[16] Neither the parents nor Mrs. Creevy will allow her to continue teaching unless she will once again parrot the conventional lies. The point of this episode in Dorothy's history is its stressing in a new context the significance of what had earlier happened to her: just as memory is necessary to the individual—making him what he is as a personality—so truthful history is necessary to a nation and to humanity. Winston Smith writes of the Proles in his diary, "Until they become conscious they will never rebel, and until after they have rebelled they cannot become conscious."[17] Without memory the individual is not conscious; he is not a human being but an animal—witness how quickly the past recedes from the thoughts of the beasts in *Animal Farm*. Without history a nation and a race are in the same state.

Related also to Orwell's belief in the importance of continuity is Dorothy's response to the loss of religious faith. She continues to go to church because the atmosphere there is peaceful and because it is a refuge from Mrs. Creevy's spying and nagging. But there is also at church "something of decency, of spiritual comeliness." Even for one without belief, she thought, it was better to go to church than to stay away, "better to follow in the ancient ways, than to drift in rootless freedom."[18] Dorothy clings to the Christian observances because they are an essential part of her life; without this tie she would not be the same person.

One final connection may be drawn between Dorothy's experience and the ideas in *Coming Up for Air* and *1984*. Put at its grandest, it has to do with the nature of reality, a subject at which Orwell worried throughout his career and never quite got straight for himself. When Dorothy reflects on the strange experiences and hardships she has undergone, she finds that they seem irrelevant and accidental. Even though they were extremely difficult to live through, they have ceased to seem important. She decides that "all real happenings are in the mind," and they are what matter.[19] The way to change the aspect of the world is to change one's way of looking at things. In other words, objective reality is a myth.

George Bowling's experience brought him up against the same problem of mentally rejecting external circumstances in a way that upsets natural law. He kept his mother and father alive, so to speak, by guarding his memory of them as they sat at the tea table. Orwell deals with the problem again in a sharper and more extensive way in *1984*, when Winston Smith keeps insisting that the foundation of reality lies in the equation two plus two equals four, yet cannot refute O'Brien's claim that reality is what the Inner Party, the "collective solipsism," says it is.

A Clergyman's Daughter then—though it is not political and to that extent is tangential to the pattern described in the other novels—is yet relevant to the origins of *1984*. It contains what appears to be Orwell's first try at representing the psychological experience which Winston Smith suffers, the alteration of personality through the destruction of memory and the falsification of history. In Dorothy this comes about through natural forces; amnesia is her body's way of setting her free from oppression. But it is no more a genuine escape than Winston's, for she is compelled to acknowledge the official version of history under the threat of punishment—losing the little security she has. The difference between the treatment of these ideas in this earlier and in the later book is that *1984* deals with them more philosophically and more fully, and—an important point—that Winston Smith's amnesia is deliberately induced. His mind is subjected to what has become, in that world, a normal, standard technique of control.

Despite some notable differences between Gordon Comstock and Winston Smith, Orwell's third novel, *Keep the Aspidistra Flying*, is a long step in the direction of *1984* and the way the intellectual is portrayed in that work. Looking backward at the progress from *Burmese Days*, the difference is not so much in theme—a similarly narcissistic young man in a similar state of rebellion—as in the use of symbol, the choices facing the two men, and the ways they decide what to do.

Like Flory's inner debates, Gordon Comstock's "interminable restless monologue" is marked by rage and hatred, but where Flory is disgusted by what British imperialism does to exploiters and exploited, Comstock detests the commercialism, the domestic aspect of imperialism, in which he is immersed like a dish in soapy water.

PREDECESSORS TO *1984* **133**

The poem he so laboriously works on during the novel is an excellent summary of it:

Sharply the menacing wind sweeps over
The bending poplars, newly bare,
And the dark ribbons of the chimneys
Veer downward; flicked by whips of air,

Torn posters flutter; coldly sound
The boom of trams and the rattle of hooves,
And the clerks who hurry to the station
Look, shuddering, over the eastern rooves,

Thinking, each one, "Here comes the winter!"
"Please God, I keep my job this year!"
And bleakly, as the cold strikes through
Their entrails like an icy spear,

They think of rent, rates, season tickets,
Insurance, coal, the skivvy's wages,
Boots, school-bills and the next instalment
Upon the two twin beds from Drage's.

For if in careless summer days
In groves of Ashtaroth we whored,
Repentant now, when winds blow cold,
We kneel before our rightful lord;

The lord of all, the money-god,
Who rules us blood and hand and brain,
Who gives the roof that stops the wind,
And, giving, takes away again;

Who spies with jealous, watchful care,
Our thoughts, our dreams, our secret ways,
Who picks our words and cuts our clothes,
And maps the pattern of our days.

Who chills our anger, curbs our hope,
And buys our lives and pays with toys,
Who claims as tribute broken faith,
Accepted insults, muted joys;

Who binds with chains the poet's wit,
The navvy's strength, the soldier's pride,
And lays the sleek, estranging shield
Between the lover and his bride.[20]

The first thing to notice about the poem is how many things familiar to us in *1984* are expressed here: the wretched weather, the posters, the atmosphere of secrecy and terror, the corruption, the humiliating repentance, and the jealous despotism's oppressive control over thought, sex, language, daily life, and even clothes. Worth noting also, in view of Comstock's sense of isolation, is this poem's remarkable structural resemblance to a much more famous poem about human isolation, Arnold's "To Marguerite—(*continued*)":

> Who order'd, that their longing fire
> Should be, as soon as kindled, cool'd?
> Who renders vain their deep desire?—
> A God, a God their severance ruled!
> And bade betwixt their shores to be
> The unplumb'd, salt, estranging sea.

And finally, we have the fact that when *Keep the Aspidistra Flying* appeared Orwell had already published Comstock's poem in the *Adelphi* under his own name, giving it the title "St. Andrew's Day," that is, November 30, marking the onset of winter. We can thus presume that the sentiments in the poem were those of Orwell himself.

In structure and some other important features Comstock's world of the Money God resembles Oceania. There are two classes, slaves and rulers:

> [Gordon] had a vision of London, of the western world; he saw a thousand million slaves toiling and grovelling about the throne of money. The earth is ploughed, ships sail, miners sweat in dripping tunnels underground, clerks hurry for the eight-fifteen with the fear of the boss eating at their vitals. And even in bed with their wives they tremble and obey. Obey whom? The money-priesthood, the pink-faced masters of the world. The Upper Crust.[21]

The slaves resemble the Proles in not knowing they are slaves: "They were too busy being born, being married, begetting, working, dying." But like Flory and Winston Smith—like Orwell too, according to his friend George Woodcock and his co-worker at the B.B.C. John Morris—Comstock envies the exploited:[22]

> It mightn't be a bad thing, if you could manage it, to feel yourself one of them, one of the ruck of men. Our civilisation is founded on greed and fear, but in the lives of common men the greed and fear

are mysteriously transmuted into something nobler. . . . they lived by the money-code, sure enough, and yet they contrived to keep their decency. . . . Besides, they were *alive*. They were bound up in the bundle of life. They begot children, which is what the saints and soul-savers never by any chance do.[23]

Just how close Orwell was to transcribing reality in this passage may be seen in the reflections of another writer, Christopher Isherwood:

But beneath all my note-taking, my would-be scientific detachment, my hatred, my disgust, there was the old sense of exclusion, the familiar grudging envy. For, however I might sneer, these people *were* evidently enjoying themselves in their own mysterious fashion, and why was it so mysterious to me? Weren't they of my own blood, of my own caste? Why couldn't I—the would-be novelist, the professional observer—understand them? Why didn't I know—not coldly from the outside, but intuitively, sympathetically, from within—what was it made them perform their grave ritual of pleasure. . . ?

People like my friends and myself, I thought, are to be found in little groups in all the larger towns; we form a proudly self-sufficient, consciously declassed minority. We have our jokes, we amuse each other enormously; we are glad, we say, that we are different. But are we really glad? Does anybody ever feel sincerely pleased at the prospect of remaining in permanent opposition, a social mis-fit, for the rest of his life? I knew, at any rate, that I myself didn't. I wanted —however much I might try to persuade myself, in moments of arrogance, to the contrary—to find some place, no matter how humble, in the scheme of society.[24]

This is also a society in which birth control is enforced by circumstances and by submission to the prevailing *mores* in all but the lower classes, as it is in *1984*. There is an embarrassing scene of seduction in the open air, when Rosemary and Gordon, like Winston and Julia, spend Sunday in the country. Their conduct is as effectively supervised as if they were surrounded by microphones. Rosemary is fearful that she might conceive a child, and Gordon reacts with his usual rage: "Even in the most secret action of your life you don't escape it; you've still got to spoil everything with filthy cold-blooded precautions for money's sake. Money, money, always money! Even in the bridal bed, the finger of the money-god intruding. In the heights or in the depths, he is there."[25]

Like that of Oceania, this society is cruel, though for a different reason. Gordon reminds his patron Ravelston of the prologue to *The Man of Lawes Tale:* "Where he talks about poverty. The way it gives everyone the right to stamp on you! The way everyone *wants* to stamp on you!"[26] After leaving Ravelston, Gordon repeats the same words to himself. The metaphor, of course, recurs in *1984,* this time applied to O'Brien and his vision of the unchanging future; and its associations with tyranny reverberated in Orwell's mind because of London's use of it in *The Iron Heel.*

Comstock resembles Winston Smith in another way, for he is a writer in a world where books are turned out "as mechanically as sausages and with much less skill."[27] He has labored honestly over a volume of poems called, ironically, *Mice,* which has no success. Nor will his new attempt at serious writing, another poem with the ironic title of *London Pleasures.* In fact, this one will never be finished. These failures make it all the more irritating that he is a talented writer of advertising copy, clever at turning out "the neat little para. that packs a world of lies into a hundred words," just as Winston Smith is clever at rewriting history in the difficult medium of Newspeak.[28]

Psychologically, Gordon Comstock and Winston Smith follow the same course: dissatisfaction leads to revolt, not an open rebellion, but a secret struggle against superior force. Comstock rebels against the Money God of his poem: "It was a kind of plot that he was nursing. . . . He was as though dedicated to this war against money. But it was still a secret. The people at the office never suspected him of unorthodox ideas."[29] He keeps the manuscript of his poems as a symbol of his private war, just as Winston Smith keeps his diary; but for both men this is only a gesture, and their knowledge of its futility intensifies their distress.

One important difference between their situations is the seriousness of their secret war. For Winston Smith conformity is a condition of his survival; he has a fairly clear idea of what he is risking when he rebels. In contrast, Comstock is free to return to the fold at any time. He is tempted by his inner self to do this. "Sometimes your salvation haunts you down like the Hound of Heaven," he says, foreshadowing the relief he experiences when at last he becomes a convert to what he had once called the "swinish priesthood" of the Money God.[30]

But he does resemble Winston Smith in the hopelessness of his fight. His break with the money world made him miserable, not only because of physical discomforts and humiliations but because he had cut himself off from people in a way that seemed futile and empty of meaning. When he admits that his flight into the sub-world of the very poor has failed, he finds that, like Winston, he has learned to love what he thought he hated.

Comstock is more clearly the representative intellectual than Flory; he is a poet, or tries to be, in a society which finds the best use of poets to be in advertising agencies. His mode of defiance links him to one avatar of the intellectual in the nineteenth century. He is no Prometheus, but rather, like the central personage in Dostoevsky's *Notes from Underground,* he is a mouse, hyper-conscious, cherishing his own spite, taking pleasure in his own humiliation. He will not give in to the system, even though he knows that he is not really strong enough to resist it. He confirms Dostoevsky's belief that man does not act as reason and self-interest tell him to. He prefers the irrationality of what appears to him to be willful, gratuitous conduct. He enjoys suffering, and he likes to smash things. What others think, he pretends, has no effect on how he acts; nor do the ties of affection and duty, which he regards as having been imposed on him by the Money God. Like that of Dostoevsky's hero also, his life is "gloomy, disorganized, and solitary to the point of savagery"; he has "the underground in [his] soul."[31] Furthermore, Comstock wishes to subjugate Rosemary in the same way that Dostoevsky's character confesses he wants to tyrannize over his friend. The resemblance extends even to such specific details as the dinner which becomes the occasion for quarreling, extravagant displays of pride, drunkenness, whoring, and fighting. In both stories, the heroes escape to a solitary underground world, but Dostoevsky's anti-hero stays underground; Comstock returns to the world symbolized by the aspidistra. He goes to work as a writer of copy for the New Albion advertising agency, a job at which he is remarkably successful, marries Rosemary, and buys an aspidistra to help furnish their first flat. The intellectual in Orwell's book is reconciled to the tough, persistent, and healthy world of ordinary, decent men by the thrilling fact that his wife is going to bear his child.

Against this background, we are not surprised when we find in *1984* that Winston Smith wants to enter a different sort of underground, the underground of the resistance to a regime he hates as much as Flory and Comstock hate theirs. Smith bears the same stigmata as Comstock and Flory: sensitivity, loneliness, hatred of the system, a certain amount of talent (again as a writer), self-pity, and weakness. Like them he always has running through his head the same "interminable restless monologue"—part complaint, part exposition, part question—which is their chief means of responding to the rest of the world. Like Flory, but unlike Comstock, Smith is corrupted by his world. Flory sees nothing worth living for; Smith is so helpless against its viciousness, or rather his hatred of its viciousness, that he accepts its code—the end justifies the means—thus dooming his revolt at the start, because he becomes a power-worshipper in order to destroy power.

In *Burmese Days*, Flory's birthmark, too obviously meant as a symbol of his singularity among people who are nothing if not conformists, is not very effective. The aspidistra, however, is a symbol that really works. It is a tough plant commonly found in English homes, and among other associations it evokes the affectionately comic and English overtones summed up in "The Biggest Aspidistra in the World," as it used to be sung by Gracie Fields. The aspidistra can bear the weight of being called the "tree of life," and it is fitting that Gordon should insist, to the point of quarreling about it, on buying an aspidistra when he and Rosemary establish their first home. A similar device is used, as we know, in *1984*, where the coral embedded in crystal takes on such significance that it might seem, on reflection, to sum up the whole book.

As a final point about this novel, there is special meaning in the incident when Gordon, in a familiar burst of self-pity, says to Ravelston that his poems are "dead." Although this was a fashionable term of condemnation in the 1930s, there appears to be more in it than Orwell's usual ironic way of presenting Gordon, for he extends the metaphor: " 'My poems are dead because I'm dead. You're dead. We're all dead. Dead people in a dead world.' "[32]

In *Coming Up for Air*, George Bowling, after his visit to his friend Porteous, thinks that all the decent people are dead; the only live men are those he calls gorillas, with nothing much in between. Next morning, waking up with a hangover, he decides in a fit of gloom that he too is dead. Contrary to his first impression of Lower Binfield and its people, they are alive and he is the ghost, and the idea is, of course, reinforced by the ironic epigraph, "He's dead, but he won't lie down."[33] In *1984*, at the moment when Winston and Julia are trapped by the kind of people George Bowling describes as "stream-lined men who think in slogans and talk in bullets," Winston has been thinking about the woman who symbolizes the Proles for him:

> Out of those mighty loins a race of conscious beings must one day come. You were the dead; theirs was the future. But you could share

in that future if you kept alive the mind as they kept alive the body, and passed on the secret doctrine that two plus two make four.

"We are the dead," he said.

"We are the dead," echoed Julia dutifully.

"You are the dead," said an iron voice behind them.[34]

In this context the cant term is both a metaphor and a sinister prediction.

It perhaps seems contradictory that Orwell should have the intellectuals in his novels think of the Proles of *1984*, the "gorillas" of George Bowling's world, and—at least by implication—the ordinary men and women in *Keep the Aspidistra Flying* as the only people who are alive. Repeatedly in his nonfiction he expresses his belief that at its worst their lot is little better than slavery and that one of its evils is to kill the spirit. Yet he clearly believes that the defeatism of the intellectuals he writes about, expressed in its most extreme form by this conviction that they are dead, is typical of their class.

To some extent he felt the attitude to be a pose, an example of what he viewed as "the proletarian cant from which we now suffer. Everyone knows, or ought to know by this time, how it runs: the bourgeoisie are 'dead' (a favourite word of abuse nowadays and very effective because meaningless)."[35] But there is no doubt that Orwell believed in and admired the toughness and spirit of working men and felt them to be alive in a way that many intellectuals were not.

The answer is that there is more than one kind of slavery, and to Orwell the one the intellectuals were subjected to was probably the most insidious. Living what is called the life of the mind, they often lacked the touchstone of actuality to keep their judgments closer to the common-sense standards of most people. The ivory tower becomes a mausoleum. Then, too, they are enslaved by their own sense of superiority. Since they are cleverer than most, it follows that they and their fellows are always right. The lies and deceptions of one group are thus taken up by others, and they become willing followers of leaders whose chief interest is in establishing their own power.

Throughout *Keep the Aspidistra Flying*, Orwell tried, with only intermittent success, to present Comstock ironically as well as sympathetically. He is much less cold-blooded than Joyce was with Stephen Dedalus. This unevenness probably results from Orwell's inability to subdue his political and social views to his artistic purpose as Joyce could. The sincerity of Comstock's feelings about what the system does to the bodies and spirits of the poor comes through to us colored by his thin-skinned hysteria about himself, so that we rather impatiently sympathize with his metaphorical suicide: "that moneyless existence to which he had condemned himself had thrust him ruthlessly out of the stream of life."[36]

His return to the ordinary world, his grudging acceptance of fatherhood and Rosemary's good sense, has been viewed by Woodcock as perhaps another defeat, this time with Rosemary as the victorious enemy. But perhaps Gordon's earlier version of the life of the mind was insufficiently critical. One can read another meaning into his thrusting his manuscript into a street drain, namely, his recognition of pretentious poetry, and what is worse, pretentious emotions as symptoms of malaise. His return to the life of common men, symbolized by the aspidistra, is a vote for health, a democratic gesture that Winston Smith is not permitted to make.

Outwardly, at least, George Bowling is different from Orwell's other heroes. The kind of world he lives in and his perception of it are remarkably like theirs, however, even though his responses are not. The epigraph, "He's dead, but he won't lie down," tells us that he is tough, and this quality, added to his unpitying self-mockery, makes him brighter and more engaging than the others. John Wain says rightly that *Coming Up for Air* is an important book for the understanding of Orwell, if only because the vision of society it embodies is evoked more concretely than in the earlier books. The novel is also important for an understanding of *1984* because it lays so much stress on the past and the Golden Country, which are central features of Orwell's last novel.

In *Coming Up for Air* the monologue of Flory, Comstock, and Winston Smith becomes the device by which the story is told—a sometimes derisive, sometimes sardonic account of the life and times of George Bowling. For him, as for Gordon Comstock, the modern world is a smash and grab affair, permeated by fear. "Fear! We swim in it. It's our element. Everyone that isn't scared stiff of losing his job is scared stiff of war, or Fascism, or Communism, or something."[37] The shop girl is watched; Bowling is watched. He cannot escape:

> Strictly speaking I was in flight. And what was curious, I was no
> sooner on the Oxford road than I felt perfectly certain that *they*
> knew all about it. When I say *they* I mean all the people who
> wouldn't approve of a trip of this kind and who'd have stopped me

if they could—which, I suppose, would include pretty well every-body.

Bowling knows who they are:

> All the soul-savers and Nosey Parkers, the people whom you've never seen but who rule your destiny all the same, the Home Secretary, Scotland Yard, the Temperance League, the Bank of England, Lord Beaverbrook, Hitler and Stalin on a tandem bicycle, the bench of Bishops, Mussolini, the Pope—they were all of them after me. I could almost hear them shouting:
> "There's a chap who thinks he's going to escape! There's a chap who says he won't be stream-lined! He's going back to Lower Binfield! After him! Stop him!"[38]

In George Bowling's world there are many Big Brothers.

Bowling foresees the war; and, as Comstock does, sometimes he seems to yearn for it to destroy the hateful present. Sometimes, like Flory, he longs for "a native rising to drown their Empire in blood." He compares his fellow citizens to turkeys in November.[39] Their future and his will be terrible:

> The world we're going down into, the kind of hate-world, slogan world. The coloured shirts, the barbed wire, the rubber truncheons. The secret cells where the electric light burns night and day and the detectives watching you while you sleep. And the processions and the posters with enormous faces, and the crowds of a million people all cheering for the Leader till they deafen themselves into thinking that they really worship him, and all the time, underneath, they hate him so that they want to puke. It's all going to happen. Or isn't it? Some days I know it's impossible, other days I know it's inevitable.[40]

Emotionally, it is no great distance from Comstock's poem to this vision and thence to *1984*, but in the poem the cause of the evil was more vaguely conceived as the Money God. Bowling blames the power-seekers, and he has the wit to see that a fresh mutation is occurring in this age-old human species: "Old Hitler's something different. So's Joe Stalin. They aren't like these chaps in the old days who crucified people and chopped their heads off and so forth, just for the fun of it. They're after something quite new—something that's never been heard of before."[41]

The herald of the new order is the speaker addressing the local group of the Left Book Club; his subject, naturally, is "The Menace of Fascism." He has talents like those of the orator of *1984*:

"You know the line of talk," Bowling says. "These chaps can churn it out by the hour. Just like a gramophone. Turn the handle, press the button and it starts. Democracy, Fascism, Democracy." But Bowling does not underestimate the power of this talent:

> The same thing over and over again. Hate, hate, hate. Let's all get together and have a good hate. Over and over. It gives you the feeling that something has got inside your skull and is hammering down on your brain. But for a moment, with my eyes shut, I managed to turn the tables on him. I got inside *his* skull. It was a peculiar sensation.

For, to Bowling, what the speaker feels and sees is a vision of smashing people's faces "with a spanner . . . and the more he thinks of it the more he likes it."[42]

Such is the prospect for himself and society that Bowling tries to evade for a day by returning to Lower Binfield where he was born, retreating into the past, into what he calls "a good world to live in." He realizes the complex nature of the past, but he does not anticipate what will happen when he tries to enter it: "The past is a curious thing," he says. "It's with you all the time":

> I suppose an hour never passes without your thinking of things that happened ten or twenty years ago, and yet most of the time it's got no reality, it's just a set of facts that you've learned, like a lot of stuff in a history book. Then some chance sight or smell, especially smell, sets you going, and the past doesn't merely come back to you, you're actually *in* the past. It was like that at this moment.[43]

As he walks along the Strand it seems to him that his memories are more real than his surroundings; he sees and smells and hears things which appear immutable: "When you look back over a long period you seem to see human beings always fixed in some special place and some characteristic attitude. It seems to you that they were always doing exactly the same thing."[44] Like the piece of coral in Winston Smith's crystal paperweight, the past is motionless, unchanging.

Bowling's evocation of the past shows it to be better than the present and the future. It is always summer, and the unchanging routine of people's lives is "almost like some kind of natural process." In those days people were patriotic, and at the same time they held the "good old English notions that the redcoats are the scum of the earth."[45] They were not afraid of the future; they may not have been secure, but they had a sense of continuity, as though they were

living in an eternity. Bowling remembers feeling as a child that there
was no need to hurry or to be frightened, but he thinks now that
such feelings have vanished.

He has gone to Lower Binfield because the present has become too different from the past to be tolerated. The past—its
solidity, its stability, its slower rhythm and uncomplicated rules—
suits him best; and up to now he has been able to put up with the
present because he could get back into the past almost at will,
through his vision of what in *1984* is called "the Golden Country."
This is how it appears to him:

> It was a wonderful June morning. The buttercups were up to my
> knees. There was a breath of wind just stirring the tops of the elms,
> and the great green clouds of leaves were sort of soft and rich like
> silk. It was nine in the morning and I was eight years old, and all
> round me it was early summer, with great tangled hedges where
> the wild roses were still in bloom, and bits of soft white cloud
> drifting overhead, and in the distance the low hills and the dim
> blue masses of the woods round Upper Binfield. And I didn't give a
> damn for any of it. All I was thinking of was the green pool and
> the carp and the gang with their hooks and lines and bread paste.
> It was as though they were in paradise and I'd got to join them.[46]

All this is just as much a dream (and the same dream) as
Winston Smith's. Bowling is awakened to the terrible reality that
Binfield Hall has been turned into what he calls "a looney bin."
The lovely fields and forest are gone, and in their place he finds a
city of new Tudor houses, inhabited by "food-cranks and spook-
hunters and simple lifers with £600 a year." The hidden pool with
its fabulous fish has been drained for use as a rubbish dump.

His idea of the past, instead of being "real," as it was before
his return, is shattered. The present has become the real thing
now, and he is a ghost, a visitor from the past living in the present.
As he discovers that the terrifying present can destroy the past,
there revives in Bowling a hateful vision of the future, but this too
disappears, and he concludes that past and future are unim-
portant. The present swallows up everything. "Nothing's real in
Ellesmere Road except gas-bills, school-fees, boiled cabbage and
the office on Monday. . . . Why had I bothered about the future
and the past, seeing that the future and the past don't matter?"
In this mood of hard-headed stoicism, Bowling goes back to his
nagging and suspicious wife, to "a vulgar low-down row in a smell of
old mackintoshes."[47]

Orwell himself had more to say on this subject, however, and ten years later he evoked the questions of past and present, dream and reality, progress and conservatism in a new context and with a different significance.

Of all Orwell's fiction, *Animal Farm* expresses most economically the tendencies discussed in Part Two of this book. That is, he wrote the story to propagate his version of the truth about revolutionary politics, thinking thus to counteract what he regarded as the lies and distortions of those intellectuals who had transferred their loyalty to the Soviet Union.

The book is an implicit attack on the myth that a violent revolution is a sure means of improving the wearisome condition of humanity, for this revolt of the animals is a pathetic failure. More specifically, Orwell wanted to destroy the Soviet myth to which so many intellectuals had succumbed during his lifetime. He thought this task essential if the cause of socialism was to be revived, and the theme of *Animal Farm* accords with his criticism in *The Road to Wigan Pier* of certain intellectuals whose activities he believed were a disservice to socialism.

This does not mean that Orwell was on the road to becoming a political quietist, for as he said: "All revolutions are failures, but they are not all the same failure."[48] The implication is rather that "the Revolution" insofar as it is founded on a false understanding of human beings or on a misconception of what can be achieved within a given framework of actuality is bound to overreach itself. It promises more than it can possibly deliver.

It does not follow—quite the contrary—that no revolution should be undertaken until men and conditions are perfect. Some revolutions, on this reading of Orwell's dictum, though outwardly or partly failures, will nevertheless succeed in furthering the ideals of human equality and brotherhood, especially as these are exhibited in the methods employed. In the Russian revolution the means did not accord with the goals.

Not only does *Animal Farm* satirize the Soviet Union's betrayal of socialism; on a broader front it is also an attack on intellectuals in politics, for the intellectuals are both the theoreticians and the leaders of this revolution, and they also become the oppressors and betrayers of the animals whose welfare they pretend to cherish. The old boar Major, in an eloquent manifesto, supplies the rationale for the revolution. Interpreting his own dream, like some impossible combination of Freud and Marx, he perceives the true relations between the animals and the human beings who oppress them. In a paraphrase of Hobbes, he declares that life for the animals is "miserable, laborious, and short"; it can be improved only through the violent overthrow of Man, "the only real enemy we have. Remove Man from the scene, and the root cause of hunger and overwork is abolished forever."[49]

What Major fails to realize is that his solution, though emotionally satisfying, is too simple; nor does he take sufficient account of the power-hunger of his fellow pigs or the impossibility of speedily industrializing an agricultural economy. To him apparently, the abstract goal is everything, time and human nature nothing. As it did in Jeremy Bentham, self-interest in Major somehow always took the form of benevolence. He foresaw the goal, but not the terrible means by which the goal was to be reached, if it was to be reached at all.

Major's teachings, codified as the Seven Commandments, were derived, as Richard Rees has suggested, from Swift's *Tale of a Tub*.[50] They owe something too, as we have seen, to *The Island of Dr. Moreau*. In Swift, the greedy sons deliberately misinterpret their father's will and thus destroy the fine coats he has bequeathed them. In *Animal Farm*, of course, what Jack London called "pig-ethics" causes the Commandments to be perverted into a means of subjugating the other animals.

Under the guise of freeing the others from slavery, these "clever ones" teach and organize the slower-witted. Although the pigs learn to do what is necessary on the farm, they chiefly occupy themselves in making sure that others do the work. Thus, as things turn out, a tiny minority of intellectuals put themselves in control of the rest and exert their will by deceit in most instances—following the best Machiavellian precepts—though they are not above violence to punish dissidents and display their power.

It is important for an understanding of Orwell's thought to recognize that those who consolidate their position as the new ruling class and hence betray the revolution are, to use one of Beatrice Webb's favorite words, "brainworkers." The pigs apply this term to themselves to justify the preferential treatment they demand: "We pigs are brainworkers," says Squealer. "The whole management and organisation of this farm depends on us. Day and night we are watching over your welfare. It is for *your* sake that we drink that milk and eat those apples."[51] In much the same way, we may recall, other clever ones like Shaw and Mrs. Webb expected to impose socialism on the workers from above. There are other clever animals in *Animal Farm,* in particular Moses and Benjamin. But Moses is rather ambiguously identified with another faith, and Benjamin's cynicism has eroded his morale.

And so the dictatorship is established. The Sunday meetings are abolished; an SS is selected and trained to protect Napoleon. Snowball is driven from the Farm. The Commandments are altered to give legitimacy to the increasingly tyrannical acts of the leaders. Significantly, considering Orwell's views about journalists, the task of explaining the regime and persuading the animals that everything is designed for their good falls to Squealer, whom F. R. Fyvel identifies with the "servile press."[52] It is Squealer who, in a moment of genius, reduces all the Commandments to one, whose sophistry turns black into white for the rest of the animals, and who incites them to violence but hides when it breaks out. One by one, in this story, Squealer commits the evil acts that Orwell denounced in the press's reporting of the Spanish Civil War and in the leftist apologies for the Soviet pact with Germany.

Orwell also takes care, through the song "Beasts of England" and the figure of Minimus the poet, to show the uses a totalitarian regime can make of art and the debasement it suffers as a consequence. Major launches the rebellion by his singing of a song heard in childhood and forgotten until it returned to him in a dream. Later on Minimus composes a new anthem much less appealing to the animals than "Beasts of England" but the only one sanctioned by the rulers, just as, in the Soviet Union, a new anthem replaced the "International." Napoleon feared, of course, that if Major's song could stir the animals to rebellion once it might do so again and that it could serve also as a reminder of a hopeful past he would prefer the animals to forget. Minimus also wrote a poem, "Comrade Napoleon," which was displayed on one end of the big barn, as a companion piece to the Seven Commandments on the opposite end. The poem to the leader was "surmounted by a portrait of Napoleon, in profile, executed by Squealer in white paint."[53]

Religious orthodoxy is satirized in the portrayal of Moses the raven. The animals dislike him because he does no work and because he spies and bears tales. Nevertheless he is a "clever talker," and they find some comfort in his tales of Sugarcandy Mountain where all animals go when they die. Moses absents himself from the farm when Mr. Jones is no longer at hand to feed him crusts of bread soaked in beer, but after several years he is permitted to to return and live off the indulgence of others, just as after a time the Orthodox church was granted a measure of toleration in the Soviet Union. Despite their declared contempt for his lies and idleness, many of the animals secretly believed there might be some truth in his tales of a better world, arguing that they deserved some recompense for the hardships of this life.

Orwell knew that the process by which the revolution in *Animal Farm* developed and then failed, if not excusable, was understandable, perhaps even inevitable. Writing in 1948 of the early leaders of the Russian revolution, he said:

> The "dictatorship of the proletariat" had to mean the dictatorship of a handful of intellectuals, ruling through terrorism.
>
> Placed as they were, the Russian Communists necessarily developed into a permanent ruling caste, . . . Since they could not risk the growth of opposition they could not permit genuine criticism, and since they silenced criticism they often made avoidable mistakes: then, because they could not admit that the mistakes were their own, they had to find scapegoats, sometimes on an enormous scale.
>
> The upshot is that the dictatorship has grown tighter as the regime has grown more secure, and that Russia is perhaps farther from egalitarian Socialism today than she was 30 years ago.[54]

The myth of the revolution, conceived and elaborated by intellectuals, led by intellectuals, betrayed by intellectuals, thus ends in a dictatorship of intellectuals. *Animal Farm* traces this course and its consequences with greater concentration than anything else Orwell wrote. It does so with extraordinary economy, considering the place these developments occupied in his thinking.[55]

THE ATMOSPHERE OF *1984*

SO FAR we have been considering *1984* only indirectly as we examined some of the materials that went into its making: books that Orwell read and wrote about; his ideas about intellectuals, their motives and functions, as well as the reasons for their susceptibility to totalitarianism; certain themes and characters of his earlier fiction that reappear in *1984*.

The center of attention in the rest of this book is *1984* itself. To be more exact, we need now to study further certain features of the novel—its atmosphere, its concern for the meaning of history and objective reality, its representation of totalitarianism as a natural development from socialism, fascism, and the Roman Catholic church—against the background of Orwell's personal experience and the considerable body of his reading and writing we have not previously discussed.

The atmosphere of *1984* manifests the quality of life under the dictatorship of Big Brother and the Inner Party. As it does in any good novel, the physical and psychological environment provides symbols, nourishes action, molds character, and thus fulfills its main function of establishing a tone that complements and reinforces everything else in the work. The dreary sordidness and pervasive terror of Airstrip One are evoked as concretely as the machinery of hysteria and insanity in *The Fall of the House of Usher* and with as wide a range of rich implication. Equally important, it has a firm spiritual base, being the consequence—and by no means a minor one—of the tyranny Orwell was satirizing.

The discomfort and fear of *1984* are incompatible with the chromium-plated, hygienic, efficient future imagined by Wells, Huxley, and Zamyatin. One reason, apart from temperament, that Orwell emphasizes the cold, filth, and inefficiency is that he did not believe that applied science necessarily improved the conditions of life—witness air warfare and the V-bombs. But a more important reason was psychological or spiritual. Orwell's predecessors had understood well enough that to realize the materialist dream of affluence implied an abridgement of human liberty and might even lead to a lobotomy performed on the human spirit, but they had not observed that the myth of comfort is inadequately grounded in human nature. Orwell knew better than they did that a utopia characterized by warmth, comfort, and the absence of strain would surely fail. What he once called "shallow gutless hedonism" is too feeble a motive to arouse and sustain the devotion and energy needed to build a lasting society.[1]

Orwell described Zamyatin's world as "rationalized, mechanized, and painless," and was criticized for using the term "painless."[2] It is true there is pain in *We;* there is also pain in *Brave New World.* What Orwell stresses is that in both novels life in utopia is very comfortable for those who conform: the environment is pleasant, food is plentiful, people enjoy themselves in the prescribed ways. Zamyatin and Huxley may try to show that pain is preferable to comfort, but the majority of those who inhabit their worlds do not agree; in a more recent utopia, *Walden Two,* the materialist case for comfort and conformity is regarded as self-evidently true.

For Orwell this view is psychologically false. His diary contains this entry:

> On a wall in South London some Communist or Blackshirt had chalked up "Cheese, not Churchill." What a silly slogan. It sums up the psychological ignorance of these people who even now have not grasped that, whereas some people will die for Churchill, nobody will die for cheese.[3]

Orwell had the Soviet Union and Nazi Germany before him as examples of the truth that human beings willingly sacrifice comfort and everything else, including their lives, if they are persuaded that in so doing they are frustrating their country's enemies or advancing the cause of some ideal they cherish.[4] The discomfort and inefficiency characteristic of the dictatorship are by no means evidence that Big Brother has failed to keep his promises. They are paradoxically the tangible proof of success, proof that present pleasure is being sacrificed to future good.

The immediate cause of privation and fear in 1984 is that Oceania is always at war, and daily life on Airstrip One is very like what Londoners went through for nearly seven years of World War II. Orwell stayed in London almost without a break during this long period. We therefore have in his two diaries, his letters, the "As I Please" column in *Tribune,* and his London letters to *Partisan Review* an ample record of what daily life was like for him and his fellow Londoners, and many of the details of this life have found their way into the atmosphere of *1984.*

The worst effect of the bombing, he said, was that "the disorganization of traffic, frequent difficulty of telephoning, shutting of shops whenever there is a raid on . . . combined with the necessity of getting on with one's ordinary work, wear one out and turn life into a constant scramble to catch up lost time."[5] Each "Letter from London" recorded minor but irritating details of wartime life. The paper shortage continued; one could find enough tobacco, but matches were scarce. "They are watering the beer again, the third time since re-armament," he wrote in March 1942. The scarcity of clothing led to a general shabbiness; the quality of cloth was deteriorating; cosmetics were hard to find. Later in the same year, he reported, "Writing paper gets more and more like toilet paper while toilet paper resembles sheet tin. . . . Buildings everywhere are growing very shabby, not only from air raid damage but from lack of repairs. Plaster peeling off, windows patched with linen or cardboard, empty shops in every street." Several months later he wrote: "The war hits one a succession of blows in unexpected places. For a long time razor blades were unobtainable; now it is boot polish." Again, in 1944, he noted:

> Everything grows shabbier and more rickety. Sixteen people in a railway carriage designed for ten is quite common. The countryside has quite changed its face, the once green meadows having changed into cornfields, and in the remotest places one cannot get away from the roar of airplanes, which has become the normal background noise, drowning the larks.[6]

Orwell did not complain, but he was aware of what had been lost, and Winston Smith voices the same feeling. He remembers the Golden Country, and the time "when there were still privacy, love, and friendship, and when the members of a family stood by one another."[7] The change for him is underlined by the dangers that have come to lurk even in the countryside, but it pervades everything: the wine O'Brien offers him recalls the lighted billboard of his childhood, suggesting a color and gaiety missing from his present life; the chocolate from Julia is so like real chocolate that it eventually brings back the painful sequence of his mother's and sister's disappearance after he had run away with more than his share of the rationed treat. And he recognizes the same disparity between the past and present quality of things which Orwell reported feeling:

It was true that he had no memories of anything greatly different . . . [but] was it not a sign that this was *not* the natural order of things, if one's heart sickened at the discomfort and dirt and scarcity, the interminable winters, the stickiness of one's socks, the lifts that never worked, the cold water, the gritty soap, the cigarettes that came to pieces, the food with its strange evil tastes? Why should one feel it to be intolerable unless one had some kind of ancestral memory that things had once been different?[8]

One of the more obvious ironies of 1984 is that the leaders switch the direction of their warfare at a moment's notice, so that today's enemy becomes tomorrow's ally and the next day's enemy again, as illustrated in actuality by the Soviet-German pact and its dissolution, a series of events that caused equally abrupt reversals in the partisan opinions expressed by the left-wing press. In 1984 the effect of these shifts is to prolong the fighting endlessly.

To Britons as well it seemed that the war would continue for a very long time, if not forever. In 1941, Orwell wrote in his diary, "There is no victory in sight at present. We are in for a long, dreary, exhausting war, with everyone growing poorer all the time."[9] A few months later he commented on the state of mind of the seventeen-year-old, working-class boys entering the Home Guard: "Most of them are quite unpolitical in outlook and when asked their reason for joining say that they want to get some military training against the time when they are called up, three years hence. This reflects the fact that many English people can now hardly imagine a time when there will be no war."[10]

By early 1945, Orwell himself had begun to think that permanent war was possible:

A not-too-distant explosion shakes the house, the windows rattle in their sockets, and in the next room the 1964 class wakes up and lets out a yell or two. Each time this happens I find myself thinking, "Is it possible that human beings can continue with this lunacy very much longer?" You know the answer, of course. Indeed, the difficulty nowadays is to find anyone who thinks that there will *not* be another war in the very near future.

Germany, I suppose, will be defeated this year, and when Germany is out of the way Japan will not be able to stand up to the combined power of Britain and the USA. Then there will be a peace of exhaustion, with only minor and unofficial wars raging all over the place, and perhaps this so-called peace may last for decades. But after that, by the way the world is actually shaping, it may well be that war will *become permanent*. Already, quite visibly and more or less with the acquiescence of all of us, the world is splitting up into the two or three huge super-states forecast in James Burnham's *Managerial Revolution*. One cannot draw their exact boundaries as yet, but one can see more or less what areas they will comprise. And if the world does settle down into this pattern, it is likely that these vast states will be permanently at war with one another, though it will not necessarily be a very intensive or bloody kind of war. Their problems, both economic and psychological, will be a lot simpler if the doodlebugs are more or less constantly whizzing to and fro.[11]

Permanent war in Oceania elicits three principal responses among the inhabitants: apathy, hysteria, and fear. The first of these, or what looked like it, was observed by Orwell among his fellow citizens in Britain. The most striking thing, he found, about British behavior during the war was "the lack of reaction of any kind." People lived "in a sort of twilight sleep" showing neither great enthusiasm for the war nor extraordinary hatred of the enemy. As he said:

> I don't know whether this semi-anesthesia in which the British people contrive to live is a sign of decadence . . . or whether . . . it is a kind of instinctive wisdom. It may well be that it is the best attitude when you live among endless horrors and calamities which you are powerless to prevent. Possibly we shall all have to develop it if war becomes continuous, which seems to me a likely development in the fairly near future.[12]

Among the most benumbing hardships that the people of Oceania suffer in common with the British during their war years is the cold. The opening scene of the novel—indeed the opening sentence—speaks of the cold; and in the final scene between Winston Smith and Julia, the cold plays a part in their defeat as lovers:

> There did not seem to be anything more to say. The wind plastered their thin overalls against their bodies. Almost at once it became embarrassing to sit there in silence; besides, it was too cold to keep still . . .
> He had made up his mind that he would accompany her as far as the Tube station, but suddenly this process of trailing along in the cold seemed pointless and unbearable.[13]

In wartime England the people had begun to feel that the cold, like the war, would continue forever. In Orwell's own house the roof was leaking in a dozen places, the plaster was falling, and at one time there had been no water for three days.[14] In the spring of 1946, which was fortunately beautiful, Orwell found the combination of peace and springtime almost too difficult to accept:

> It comes seeping in everywhere, like one of those new poison gases which pass through all filters. The spring is commonly referred to as "a miracle," and during the past five or six years this worn-out figure of speech has taken a new lease of life. After the sort of winters we have had to endure recently, the spring does seem miraculous, because it has become gradually harder and harder to believe that it is actually going to happen. Every February since 1940 I have found myself thinking that this time Winter is going to be permanent.[15]

A year later after the terrible winter of 1946–47, this idea was still in Orwell's mind: "Spring is coming after all, and recent rumours that this was the beginning of another Ice Age were unfounded."[16]

Like other Londoners, Orwell frequented the Underground and observed the astonishing sights there late at night: "the young married couples . . . tucked up under pink counterpanes. And the large families one sees here and there, father, mother, and several children all laid out in a row like rabbits on a slab."[17] Not everything there had been so comfortably assimilated into domestic routine:

> There are disgusting scenes in the Tube stations at night, sordid piles of bedding cluttering up the passage-ways and hordes of dirty-faced children playing round the platforms at all hours. Two nights ago, about midnight, I came on a little girl of five "minding" her younger sister, aged about two. The tiny child had got hold of a scrubbing brush with which she was scrubbing the filthy stones of the platform, and then sucking the bristles. I took it away from her and told the elder girl not to let her have it. But I had to catch my train, and no doubt the poor little brat would again be eating filth in another couple of minutes. This kind of thing is happening everywhere.[18]

He thus saw at first hand the same scene that Winston Smith recalled when his parents had taken him into a tube station during what he thought might have been the raid "when the atomic bomb had fallen on Colchester."[19]

Anthony West, George Woodcock, John Morris, and Rayner Heppenstall have written about Orwell's toleration of squalor and discomfort and the contempt he showed at times for those who enjoyed good living. Whether or not he actually relished wartime adversity, he was able to be cheerful about it, as Julian Symons testifies:

> "Nobody really knows what rationing is until bread and potatoes are rationed," he said to me once. . . . I remember that when he came to our flat for dinner one night my wife had been able to get only some practically inedible pork chops. Fat and flexible, they bounced away from any but the most determined assault with the knife. Orwell conquered his, however, and ate every possible fragment of it. The range of food available in the Bodega on the wartime five-shilling menu was inevitably limited, but he always chose what seemed to me the most synthetic dish, the Victory Pie, as it may have been. After despatching it he often said with satisfaction: "You won't get anything better than this anywhere."[20]

The same grim humor appears in this remark of Orwell's, "Just about two years ago, as we filed past the menu board in the canteen [in the B.B.C., where Orwell worked], I said to the next person in the queue: 'A year from now you'll see "Rat Soup" on that board, and in 1943 it will be "Mock Rat Soup".' "[21]

The resemblances between the conditions described in these passages and the condition of life on Airstrip One underscore the great difference separating Winston Smith's usual state of mind from Orwell's. An obvious cause was that Smith knew that war was simply a device the Inner Party used in the exercise of its power; whereas for Orwell, however little love he might have for Britain's leaders, there was no question about the need to defeat the Axis powers. Even when the V-bombs began to fall, renewing the horrors of the Blitz after a fairly long interval of freedom from air attacks, he could write this ironic account of their effect on people's daily actions:

> Life in the civilised world.
> (The family are at tea.)
> Zoom-zoom-zoom!
> "Is there an alert on?"
> "No, it's all clear."
> "I thought there was an alert on."
> Zoom-zoom-zoom!
> "There's another one of those things coming!"
> "It's all right, it's miles away."
> Zoom-zoom-ZOOM!
> "Look out, here it comes! Under the table, quick!"

Zoom-zoom-zoom!

"It's all right, it's getting fainter."

Zoom-zoom-ZOOM!

"It's coming back!"

"They seem to kind of circle around and come back again. They've got something on their tails that makes them do it. Like a torpedo."

ZOOM-ZOOM-ZOOM!

"Christ, it's bang overhead!"

Dead silence.

"Now get *right* underneath. Keep your head well down. What a mercy baby isn't here!"

"Look at the cat! He's frightened too."

"Of course animals *know*. They can feel the vibrations."

BOOM!

"It's all right. I told you it was miles away."

(Tea continues.)[22]

Although the people in this scene are not among the downtrodden, in spirit they are closer to the Proles of *1984* than to O'Brien and his kind: "The future belonged to the proles . . . though it might be a thousand years, they would stay alive against all the odds, like birds, passing on from body to body the vitality which the Party did not share and could not kill."[23]

Orwell reported that the ending of the European war made "extraordinarily little difference to anybody." Even V-E day was "decorous." He went on to remark that he had noticed this absence of response to great events before the war:

A thing that has much struck me in recent years is that the most enormous crimes and disasters—purges, deportations, massacres, famines, imprisonment without trial, aggressive wars, broken treaties— not only fail to excite the big public, but can actually escape notice altogether, so long as they do not happen to fit in with the political mood of the moment.[24]

But if the English were still anesthetized in 1945, the French were not. Orwell noted their satisfaction with the ruined condition of Germany and the pleasure they took in knowing that what had happened to them had also happened to the Germans.[25] Far from being decorous, the V-E celebration in Paris was an emotional outburst lasting seventy-two hours. Orwell managed to force his way through the masses of people at the Place de la Concorde to listen to the official announcement over the loudspeakers:

Bands of youths and girls marched to and fro in military formation, chanting "Avec Nous! Avec Nous!" and gradually swelling their numbers until by midday the crowds were so enormous that many of the main streets and squares were quite impassable. They remained for the whole of Tuesday and the whole of Wednesday. Some people did go home for part of Tuesday night, while others subsided onto benches or patches of grass and snatched a few hours sleep.[26]

Powerful emotions found other outlets. Earlier, Orwell had commented on the photographs of French collaborators with their heads shaven; and later on, visiting a liberated concentration camp, he described the savagery with which a young Viennese Jew attached to the American army had been treating some captured Germans.[27]

The quiet British reaction to the end of the war in Europe contrasts sharply with the hysteria of the victory celebration in Paris and the acts of personal revenge which Orwell witnessed. A more institutionalized hysteria is evident in the report in the *Times* (London) describing the Russians' public hanging of some prisoners in Kharkov, an event on which Orwell probably based his account in *1984* of the hanging of Eurasian prisoners as the culminating act of Hate Week.[28] The prisoners were three German members of the Gestapo and their Russian chauffeur, who had been accused of killing Russians in gas vans. Many Russian writers, including Alexei Tolstoy, Ilya Ehrenburg, and Konstantin Simonov, were reporters at the trial, and Moscow newspapers gave great prominence to it. After the open proceedings, which were held in a Kharkov theatre, the prisoners were sentenced to death by hanging. Authorities lifted the curfew so that 6,000 people could remain to hear the sentence, which they greeted with applause. The public execution took place at 11 o'clock in the morning in the Kharkov market place and was witnessed by 40,000 spectators. A few days later the *Times* reported that "a grimly satisfied crowd circled round the dangling bodies."

The correspondent of the *Times* also reported:

The trial itself was an important phase in the educational process. It not only satisfied a burning desire for justice in its sternest form, but revealed to the huge crowds that thronged the market-place—the center of German-inspired speculation and corruption—and to the country people, who for three days after the executions saw the swinging bodies, the vulnerability of the enemy and the fundamental weakness in the Fascist character. . . .

When the vehicles on which the condemned men stood were moved away, causing their bodies to drop slowly and initiating the strangling process, there went up from the great crowd a hoarse, low growl of deep satisfaction. There were some who showed their scorn of the dying men by adding whistles to the sound of their gasps. Others applauded. The crowd was not in a lynching mood, for the majesty of the law deeply impressed them; but for the second time in two years there was joy in Kharkov.[29]

It might be supposed that with the end of the war the miserable conditions of life in London would have eased, but instead they temporarily grew worse. Partly this was owing to the dreadful winter of 1946–47, already alluded to, the worst on record for sixty-six years. Orwell wrote to Geoffrey Gorer:

It is foully cold here and the fuel shortage is just at its worst. We only got a ton of coal for the whole winter and it's almost impossible to get logs. Meanwhile the gas pressure is so low that one can hardly get a gas fire to light, and one can only get about 1½ gallons of lamp oil a week. What I do is light the fires with a little of the coal I have left and keep them damped down all day with blocks of wet peat of which I happen to have a few.[30]

Bread was rationed for the first time in British history. The Ministry of Food tried to interest people in eating whale meat and a fish called "snoek," but without success. In addition to these and other hardships, like the heavy floods in March 1947, there were the inhibitions on freedom implied in the reimposition by the Labour government of the wartime Control of Employment Order and the Supplies and Services Bill, which supplemented the Transitional Powers Act and seemed to presage government by ministerial decree.[31]

One more element in the atmosphere of *1984* has only been touched on so far: the fear that hangs over everyone, making it impossible to relax altogether for a moment or to trust even the children. Orwell described the quality of life in Barcelona in these terms ten years before he wrote *1984:*

It is not easy to convey the nightmare atmosphere of that time—the peculiar uneasiness produced by rumours that were always changing, by censored newspapers and the constant presence of armed men. It is not easy to convey it because, at the moment, the thing essential to such an atmosphere does not exist in England. In England political intolerance is not yet taken for granted. There is political persecution in a petty way; if I were a coal-miner I would not care to be known to the boss as a Communist; but the "good party man," the gangster-gramophone of continental politics, is still a rarity, and the notion of "liquidating" or "eliminating" everyone who happens to disagree with you does not yet seem natural. It seemed only too natural in Barcelona. The "Stalinists" were in the saddle, and therefore it was a matter of course that every "Trotsky-ist" was in danger. The thing everyone feared was a thing which, after all, did not happen—a fresh outbreak of street-fighting, which, as before, would be blamed on the P.O.U.M. and the Anarchists. There were times when I caught my ears listening for the first shots. It was as though some huge evil intelligence were brooding over the town. Everyone noticed it and remarked upon it. And it was queer how everyone expressed it in almost the same words: "The atmosphere of this place—it's horrible. Like being in a lunatic asylum."[32]

The bits of evidence cited here to show the provenance of certain aspects of daily life in Oceania derive largely from Orwell's personal experience in wartime Spain and Britain; his mind was saturated with that atmosphere. In *1984* he has concentrated those terrible years of exhaustion, fear, shortages, unceasing labor, un-certainty, apathy, and hysteria into an essence so powerful as to be almost overwhelming. The tense and abrasive atmosphere of Oceania is shown to be created deliberately by the Inner Party as an instrument of government, a logical consequence of the Party's assumptions.

It is worth bearing in mind, however, that the spiritual signifi-cance of the war years in Britain was different. Leaving aside the fact that the British, except perhaps for a handful of the potentially influential, never suffered from the psychological distress experi-enced by the French—a defeated and divided people—Orwell him-self thought that England was happier during the war than before it. He argued that most of the suffering was endured by about 10 percent of the population and that the rest enjoyed a security and social equality without precedent.[33] Even so, not all that came through the war years into *1984* was gloomy. In the lunatic atmo-sphere of the B.B.C. in 1942 occurred moments of rich humanity which Orwell noted in his diary:

The only time when one hears people singing in the BBC is in the early morning, between 6 and 8. That is the time when the char-women are at work. A huge army of them arrives all at the same time. They sit in the reception hall waiting for their brooms to be issued to them and making as much noise as a parrot house, and then they have wonderful choruses, all singing together as they sweep the passages. The place has a quite different atmosphere at this time from what it has later in the day.[34]

This, or something very much like it in spirit, is transmuted into the valiant figure of the Prole housewife singing "It was only an 'opeless fancy" as she pins up the diapers. She is a symbol of hope from Orwell's experience of wartime reality.

XI

DOUBLETHINK AND NEWSPEAK

AN important feature of *1984*, distinguishing it from other books about the future, is Orwell's preoccupation with the ways the state can control the thoughts and emotions of its subjects without a wasteful expenditure of force. In *Brave New World* scientific breeding and the delights of comfort, especially the essence of comfort called soma, were enough to keep the populace subdued. In *The Iron Heel* the Oligarchs used brute force. In *We* the contrived isolation of the United State, characteristic of previous utopias, works reasonably well; those who, owing to an excess of imagination, persist in being dissatisfied are subjected to a brain operation. Orwell took a different line in showing how human beings could be controlled without recourse to mechanical means. What he did, of course, was to project already existing methods into the future, where those using them would have an improved technique, more latitude to apply it for their own ends, and a more profound awareness of what they were doing. Thoughtcrime, duckspeak, the rewriting of history, and doublethink are features of the induced schizophrenia or "reality control" being aimed at by the leaders.

The ability of the mind to hold contradictory attitudes simultaneously must be as old as humanity. When this occurred among British leaders faced with the growing power of fascism on the Continent, a Frenchman observing their reaction might have thought that it was another example of British hypocrisy rather than naïveté or ignorance. Writing about the inner group of English leaders of the thirties—Baldwin, Chamberlain, Sir John Simon, Geoffrey Dawson—whose policies nearly destroyed England, Orwell says:

> It is doubtful whether there were any *conscious* traitors. The corruption that happens in England is seldom of that kind. Nearly always it is more in the nature of self-deception, of the right hand not knowing what the left doeth. And being unconscious, it is limited.[1]

160

The Biblical allusion testifies to the age of this human trait, and Orwell's word, corruption, indicates his seriousness about the consequences of this ambivalence; but it is the italicized *conscious* that shows what Orwell disapproved of even more. In his earliest books Orwell attacks lying, whether used to hide the real nature of the British Empire or to disguise the poor quality of the food and service in a supposedly first-class French hotel. In his view lying is more innocent as well as more limited in its effects if it is unconscious.

Unconscious lying is characteristic of those who do not want to face what Orwell thought of as reality, or who wish certain things they will not acknowledge. This habit of mind or temperament Orwell called sentimental. He said that Galsworthy, for instance, was a sentimentalist, "a very fine specimen of the thin-skinned, tear-in-the-eye, pre-war humanitarian." Galsworthy was troubled about pit-ponies though not about miners; if he had lived ten years longer, he "would quite probably have arrived at some genteel version of Fascism. This is the inevitable fate of the sentimentalist. All his opinions change into their opposites at the first brush of reality." As an example, he said, if you "scratch the average pacifist . . . you find a jingo."[2]

The left-wing intellectual is, in this sense of the term, also a sentimentalist. He is anti-imperialist as a matter of course, but at the same time no Englishman, "least of all the kind that is witty about Anglo-Indian colonels," wants the Empire to disintegrate, if only because he is dependent on it for his high standard of living. Even this doubleness of thought is unconscious and relatively innocent.

In contrast, the ancient habit of mind, corrupt in itself, becomes more evil when practiced consciously:

His mind slid away into the labyrinthine world of doublethink. To know and not to know, to be conscious of complete truthfulness while telling carefully constructed lies, to hold simultaneously two opinions which canceled out, knowing them to be contradictory and believing in both of them, to use logic against logic, to repudiate morality while laying claim to it, to believe that democracy was impossible and that the Party was the guardian of democracy, to forget whatever it was necessary to forget, then to draw it back into memory again at the moment when it was needed, and then promptly to forget it again, and, above all, to apply the same process to the process itself—that was the ultimate subtlety: consciously to induce unconsciousness, and then, once again, to become unconscious of the act of hypnosis you had just performed. Even to understand the word "doublethink" involved the use of double-think.[3]

Orwell first encountered this deliberate denial of an obligation to the truth—indeed a denial that it existed—on anything like a large scale in Spain, and as he became more sensitive to the phenomenon he found it to be characteristic of all political thinking and writing. In Spain it was at first only a matter of lying propaganda from both sides: battles manufactured for foreign readers out of sporadic exchanges of gunfire, massacres invented and massacres denied. Then it became more serious. The Communists, for example, lied deliberately about their supposed allies on the Left; the P.O.U.M. became "Franco's Fifth Column" and "traitors in the pay of the enemy."[4] This deception was necessary because the non-Communist Left had to be discredited if the Communist party was to gain control of the government and suppress the vestiges of the revolution, as it succeeded in doing.

The late stages in this process of deception and self-deception may be shown by the experiences of Stephen Spender and Arthur Koestler. Spender asked one of his Communist friends in 1938 what he thought of the purge trial of Yagoda, who had been responsible for the investigation that led to the earlier trials, and the friend replied, "What trials? I've given up thinking about such things long ago."[5] Koestler was imprisoned in France with some of the leading functionaries of the German Communist Party, who had participated in the purges in Spain and the U.S.S.R. and had, as he says, "actively supported a policy which . . . served the Nazi's aims, and drawn a monthly salary for it." He found these men corrupt in a sense more subtle than is usually supposed. What they did was to insert "the mental cogwheels of self-deception" between political action and self-interest; this procedure allowed them "to commit the basest infamies and yet enjoy the luxuries of a clean conscience." After recounting an argument with one of these functionaries about a particularly outrageous instance of Communist duplicity, Koestler remarks, "One could almost see the well-oiled cogwheels turn in his brain, grind the words out of their meaning, turn them round and round, until it became self-evident that real anti-Fascism meant support for the Fascist."[6]

To Orwell the abrupt shifts in the Communist party line to make it conform to the upheavals in the Soviet Union were a rich source of evidence that doublethink was becoming more common; it was also apparent among the apologists for Hitler, who had to explain what he meant each time he announced, "This is positively my last territorial demand in Europe." The Communists moved from the "Social Fascist" line of the early thirties, to the "Popular Front against Fascism," thence to the slogan of the "Imperialist War," and finally to the "Great Fatherland War" against the Fascist aggressor. Contrary to all expectations they were able to carry people with them. As Orwell viewed the popular support for Russia:

> One could not have a better example of the moral and emotional shallowness of our time, than the fact that we are all now more or less pro-Stalin. This disgusting murderer is temporarily on our side, and so the purges, etc., are suddenly forgotten. So also with Franco, Mussolini, etc., should they ultimately come over to us."[7]

Writing of the People's Convention, a Communist front, he repeats the well-worn story of the party member who, during a meeting with some comrades on June 22, 1941, went to the lavatory and returned to find that the party line had reversed itself while he was absent.

Doublethink was not, of course, confined to Communists. Reviewing Lionel Fielden's *Beggar My Neighbour*, Orwell wrote in 1943:

> We live in a lunatic world in which opposites are constantly changing into one another, in which pacifists find themselves worshipping Hitler, Socialists become Nationalists, patriots become quislings, Buddhists pray for the success of the Japanese Army, and the Stock Market takes an upward turn when the Russians stage an offensive.[8]

We have already seen that a disproportionate number of intellectuals inhabited the world which Orwell here calls lunatic. David Caute, in his book on the French intellectuals, speaks of the intellectual's desire to "have a coherent, integrated and comprehensive philosophy of political and social life as a praxis." Paradoxically, this worthy aim may explain the intellectual's speed in shifting his position to accommodate changes in the facts. In a notable understatement, Caute remarks, "Some call it self-deception."[9] Orwell called it doublethink—"reality control" was another term that he used—a way of averting the consequences of mistakes and failures.

Orwell thought that the intellectuals' security during the twenties and their freedom from responsibility had put them "in the position of a young man living on an allowance from a father whom he hates. The result is a deep feeling of guilt and resentment, not combined with any genuine desire to escape."[10] To justify these feelings to himself, the disaffected intellectual withdraws his allegiance and love from such traditional institutions as his nation and his family, attaching himself instead to some fashionable cause, and choosing it carefully so that he can reassure himself that he is accepting responsibilities, with little chance that he will be called on to fulfill them:

> These creeds [pacifism, Stalinism, anarchism] have the advantage that they aim at the impossible and therefore in effect demand very little. If you throw in a touch of oriental mysticism and Buchmanite raptures over Gandhi, you have everything that a disaffected intellectual needs. The life of an English gentleman and the moral attitude of a saint can be enjoyed simultaneously. By merely transferring your allegiance from England to India (it used to be Russia), you can indulge to the full in all the chauvinistic sentiments which would be totally impossible if you recognized them for what they were. In the name of pacifism you can compromise with Hitler, and in the name of spirituality you can keep your money. . . . As soon as you have "rejected" industrialism, and hence Socialism, you are in that strange no man's land where the Fascist and the pacifist join forces. There is indeed a sort of apocalyptic truth in the statement of the German radio that the teachings of Hitler and Gandhi are the same. One realizes this when one sees Middleton Murry praising the Japanese invasion of China and Gerald Heard proposing to institute the Hindu caste system in Europe at the same time that the Hindus are abandoning it.[11]

Orwell grew more and more interested in this trait of the intellectual, until one might say that he regarded it as an occupational disease, like silicosis among coal miners. His later writing is full of examples holding up to the reader this self-justifying obscurantism so contrary to the intellectual's love of and pursuit of truth. He noticed it especially in connection with war and militarism. The line was to condemn all war unless the Red Army was involved; then condemnation turned into praise.[12] He associated this schizophrenia with what he believed to be the growing power-worship of intellectuals. As this association grew stronger he was able to put his ideas into some perspective, that is, to see these developments as part of a larger whole which united slavery, power-

worship, and totalitarian government in a single ideology which in
1984 he called Ingsoc.

Doublethink is the characteristic way the totalitarian mind
works:

> Totalitarianism, however, does not so much promise an age of faith
> as an age of schizophrenia. A society becomes totalitarian when its
> structure becomes flagrantly artificial: that is, when the ruling class
> has lost its function but succeeds in clinging to power by force or
> fraud. Such a society, no matter how long it persists, can never afford
> to become either tolerant or intellectually stable. It can never permit
> either the truthful recording of facts, or the emotional sincerity that
> literary creation demands.[13]

This "power of holding simultaneously two beliefs which cancel
out" Orwell considered to be especially evident in politics, since
people's wishes and fears usually determined their political opinions.[14] The best corrective was to keep relating the opinions to what
Orwell calls "the book of arithmetic," a form of reality not altered by wishes. Most people are quite realistic about their weekly
budget, he says. "Two and two invariably make four":

> Politics, on the other hand, is a sort of sub-atomic or non-Euclidean
> world where it is quite easy for the part to be greater than the whole
> or for two objects to be in the same place simultaneously. Hence the
> contradictions and absurdities [are] . . . finally traceable to a secret
> belief that one's political opinions, unlike the weekly budget, will
> not have to be tested against solid reality.[15]

The evidence in this study has shown that these ideas about
politics and truth had been working in Orwell's mind for a long
time; in his "Notes on Nationalism" (1946) he ties them together.
He conceives nationalism to be the identification of the self with
some entity—religion, nation, a specific movement—which places the
individual's actions beyond good and evil because he is submerged
in the totality. In this identification the only acknowledged duty
is service in the chosen cause. In Orwell's words, "Nationalism is
power-hunger tempered by self-deception." To him it was characterized by obsession, instability, and indifference to reality, and it
comprehended the higher reaches of doublethink:

> In nationalist thought there are facts which are both true and untrue,
> known and unknown. A known fact may be so unbearable that it
> is habitually pushed aside and not allowed to enter into logical

processes, or on the other hand it may enter into every calculation and yet never be admitted as a fact, even in one's own mind.[16]

Furthermore, in the same way that history is rewritten in 1984, the past can be affected by this way of looking at the world:

> Every nationalist is haunted by the belief that the past can be altered. He spends part of his time in a fantasy world in which things happen as they should . . . and he will transfer fragments of this world to the history books whenever possible. Much of the propagandist writing of our time amounts to plain forgery. Material facts are suppressed, dates altered, quotations removed from their context and doctored so as to change their meaning.[17]

Contemporary leftist intellectuals were peculiarly in need of doublethink, he said, because so many of their ideas and attitudes were formed at a time when they had "no immediate prospect of attaining power."[18] Moreover their belief in perfectibility and in the idea that truth will prevail led them into "a whole series of contradictions, as a result of successive bumps against reality," as the Left became more powerful and confronted the necessities imposed by the burden of governing. When reality would not give way, the intellectuals had to; that is, they created abstractions and substituted them for the real world they could not control. In their thinking about the Soviet Union, for example, "There has arisen a sort of schizophrenic manner of thinking, in which words like 'democracy' can bear two irreconcilable meanings, and such things as concentration camps and mass deportations can be right and wrong simultaneously." The pacifism and internationalism of leftists were shaken by fascism, yet they made no real effort to reject or alter beliefs that experience had shown to be false.[19]

Doublethink is, finally, a method of coping with the dilemma of totalitarian nations, which demand constant loyalty in the face of inconstant policies: "What is new in totalitarianism is that its doctrines are not only unchallengeable but also unstable. They have to be accepted on pain of damnation, but on the other hand they are always liable to be altered at a moment's notice."[20] The reversals in the party line that an English Communist or fellow traveler had to follow between 1931 and 1941 exemplified for Orwell how doublethink permits a human being to maintain his nationalist obsession. What doublethink aims at is to ensure orthodoxy under any conditions.

Newspeak is the principal intellectual means by which doublethink is transformed into a conditioned reflex. Orwell invented this language partly as a protest against the debasement he thought the English language underwent when it was used for political propaganda: "If you compare commercial advertising with political propaganda, one thing that strikes you is its relative intellectual honesty. The advertiser at least knows what he is aiming at—that is, money—whereas the propagandist, when he is not a lifeless hack, is often a neurotic working off some private grudge and actually desirous of the exact opposite of the thing he advocates."[21]

As he says in "Politics and the English Language":

> In our time it is broadly true that political writing is bad writing. Where it is not true, it will generally be found that the writer is some kind of rebel, expressing his private opinions and not a "party line." Orthodoxy, of whatever colour, seems to demand a lifeless, imitative style.[22]

Since he believed that political speech and writing were largely the "defense of the indefensible" and since they were insincere because they tried to mask the difference between a man's real aim and what he was saying, they were bound to be couched in false and evasive language.

The idea of Newspeak derives from Orwell's love of the English language for its own sake, and from his interest in the possibility that an international language might develop through some such means as Basic English. He wrote about Basic in *Tribune*, stimulated perhaps by his association with William Empson, who worked with Orwell at the B.B.C. and who published an article on Basic in *Tribune* when Orwell was its literary editor.[23] In Orwell's pamphlet collection, now in the British Museum, there is at least one pamphlet on Basic English written in Basic and issued by C. K. Ogden's Orthological Institute. Ogden's *The System of Basic English*, appearing in 1934, gave Orwell the design for a language like Newspeak and, more important, examples of what could be done with its 850 words. One of these is Ogden's "translation" of a part of H. G. Wells's *The Shape of Things to Come*. This section, "Language and Mental Growth" in Book V, "The Modern State in Control of Life," describes the work of a Dictionary Bureau which watches over the development of the language, permitting the invention of new words when necessary or giving older words new shades of meaning. The relation of language to thought is made explicit, and the Dictionary Bureau acts on the belief that mental development has been retarded because in the past the "relation between language and thought [was] so loose and full of error." The possibilities of what the bureau is doing are full of significance:

These changes in the system of thought-connection in the brain, which are now in process, put before us—long before we have any chance of developments in birth selection—the hope that an increase in brain-power may be possible on a scale which at present we have no idea of. For this to come about we will have to take control of events which at present we have no control over at all.[24]

Another interesting feature of the bureau's work, reminding us of Syme's profession in *1984,* is the *Language Discard,* which began by studying words which had gone out of use or were on the verge of doing so and expanded into a "complete unfolding of the simple processes of man's thought."[25]

Orwell was also attracted by the idea of constructing an artificial language. He preserved in his collection a pamphlet on Budao, a form of Esperanto, and he considered Lancelot Hogben's *Interglossa* an important book because it drew attention to "the urgent need for some universal medium of communication, and to the sinister way in which several living languages are being used for imperialist purposes."[26] But he did not think that any purely artificial language could compete with a simplified form of a world language like Basic English.

Orwell believed that the large vocabulary and simple grammar and syntax of English were important assets, and he noted that the language was changing in the direction of even greater simplicity, so that it might turn out to have "more in common with the uninflected languages of East Asia than with the languages of Europe."[27] Even at present the merits of English were considerable:

> The greatest quality of English is its enormous range not only of meaning but of *tone*. It is capable of endless subtleties, and of everything from the most high-flown rhetoric to the most brutal coarseness. On the other hand, its lack of grammar makes it easily compressible. It is the language of lyric poetry and also of headlines. On its lower levels, it is very easy to learn, in spite of its irrational spelling. It can also for international purposes be reduced to very simple pidgin dialects, ranging from Basic to the "Bêche-de-mer" English used in the South Pacific. It is therefore well suited to be a world lingua franca, and it has in fact spread more widely than any other language.[28]

Nevertheless, English has certain weaknesses, and the greatest of these is its vulnerability. "Just because it is so easy to use it is easy to use badly," he said. It is peculiarly subject to jargon, but perhaps its deadliest enemy is standardized English, the dialect of officialdom and those who serve it, the "language of leading articles,

White Papers, political speeches, and B.B.C. news bulletins." It is recognizable by its reliance on ready-made phrases, clichés, and dead metaphors—all mechanical substitutes for thought. "Language ought to be the joint creation of poets and manual workers," Orwell wrote, "and in modern England it is difficult for these two classes to meet." Instead he saw this mandarin English spreading downwards in the social scale and into the spoken language.[29]

American English also contributed to the growing debasement of English, he believed, despite virtues like the vividness of its slang. In it the interchangeability of the parts of speech had been carried even farther than in English itself, and verbs had been burdened with useless prepositions. Moreover, because it showed too sharp a break with the past and with literary tradition, a huge loss had occurred in the vocabulary, such as the native names of insects and the poetic names for wild flowers.

A number of critics have said that Orwell got the idea for Newspeak from "cablese," and so far as they are talking only about form they may be right. The sentence "times 14.2.84 miniplenty malquoted chocolate rectify" is recognizably derived from the language reporters use when they send cables to their newspapers. Eugene Lyons gives an example of this language in *Assignment in Utopia:*

> tomsky oppositionist leader again recanted political errors tiflis yesterweek publicked today wellinformeds consider significant marking collapse antistalin opposition reliquidation kulaks tomsky said quote monolithic party under leadership genius stalin best disciple lenin always right stop right opposition left deviationists tools kulaks kulak agents unquote[30]

Orwell may also have used cablese when he was a foreign correspondent for the *Observer* for a brief period after the war. But this explanation does not do justice to Orwell's long-standing interest in the language, its changes, and their implications, an interest which may be called philosophical in the sense that he saw and tried to understand and describe a relation between language and thought that was more than merely arbitrary. Newspeak, like *1984* itself, is a projection of existing tendencies toward the debasement of English when it is used in politics. Newspeak as a medium for doublethink is thus solidly grounded in Orwell's professional experience as a writer and in his ideas about language as an instrument for attaining power.

XII

OBJECTIVE REALITY IN 1984

DOUBLETHINK is one aspect of the schizophrenia characteristic of the totalitarians who rule Oceania, and Newspeak the most pervasive means by which doublethink is cultivated and institutionalized. But totalitarians must go even further. Anything that might combat schizophrenia, anything that furnishes a standard for measuring the madness, has also to be transformed or suppressed. This explains why the Inner Party must attack the idea of objective reality, the significance of human memory, and the possibility of truthful history; for if these have a life of their own totalitarianism may be judged and opposed. Totalitarianism must be total.

The Inner Party denied "not merely the validity of experience, but the very existence of external reality. . . . The heresy of heresies was common sense."[1] This declaration was not invented by Orwell merely to serve the purpose of his novel; he believed it to be true of contemporary totalitarianism:

> The organized lying practised by totalitarian states is not, as is sometimes claimed, a temporary expedient of the same nature as military deception. It is something integral to totalitarianism, something that would still continue even if concentration camps and secret police forces had ceased to be necessary.[2]

In 1984 the appeal to reason, which in earlier ages was used to attack religion, is now turned against the concept—also a matter of faith—of objective reality. In keeping with the dictum of Marx, this is not done in any purely speculative or philosophical spirit, but in order to change the world. Orwell supposed that there were two safeguards against the spread of totalitarianism. The first was the belief that "however much you deny the truth, the truth goes on existing . . . behind your back, and you consequently can't violate it in ways that impair military efficiency."[3] The other, a variant of the first, is the continued presence somewhere of a state that is not totalitarian, where the liberal tradition of free inquiry is kept alive. In 1984 these safeguards have disappeared, and consequently the Inner Party can prove that objective truth—founded on a belief in external reality—no longer exists. Because the belief is also a matter of faith it can, even so, linger among the Proles, and occasionally elsewhere. Julia has no use for the official attempts at thought control: "One knew that it was all rubbish, so why let oneself be worried by it?"[4] But eventually, when the objective conditions that corroborate the faith have disappeared or can be made to seem absent, the faith is weakened and will also disappear. No belief which is not solipsistic can, by itself, withstand the corrosion of a skeptical reason, unless, of course, skepticism itself be challenged as a form of dogmatism.

Commenting on the difficulty of finding out how many people were killed in World War II, Orwell remarked that after World War I it was possible to use statistics from the opposing sides because both assumed that there existed a "body of neutral fact." But now, in 1943:

> Nazi theory indeed specifically denies that such a thing as "the truth" exists. There is, for instance, no such thing as "Science." There is only "German Science," "Jewish Science," etc. The implied objective of this line of thought is a nightmare world in which the Leader, or some ruling clique, controls not only the future but *the past.* If the Leader says of such and such an event, "It never happened"—well, it never happened. If he says that two and two are five—well, two and two are five.[5]

What is involved here is Orwell's own faith in the existence of objective reality. The touchstone of his faith was the belief that $2 + 2 = 4$; this equation is a self-evident truth from which truthful inferences may be drawn by the use of reason. Paradoxically, a belief in the truthfulness of this abstraction (i.e., its accurate correspondence to external reality) is typical of those who, like Orwell, value common sense.

The use of this particular touchstone goes back a long way in Orwell's career. Writing about Henry Miller in 1936, he said, "The truth is that the written word loses its power if it departs too far, or if it stays away too long, from the ordinary world where two and two make four."[6] In 1939, discussing Bertrand Russell's assumption that dictatorships cannot endure because they have never survived in the past, he wrote:

> Underlying this is the idea that common sense always wins in the end. And yet the peculiar horror of the present moment is that we cannot be sure that this is so. It is quite possible that we are descend-

ing into an age in which two and two will make five when the Leader says so. Mr. Russell points out that the huge system of organised lying upon which the dictators depend keeps their followers out of contact with reality and therefore tends to put them at a disadvantage as against those who know the facts. This is true so far as it goes, but it does not prove that the slave-society at which the dictators are aiming will be unstable. It is quite easy to imagine a state in which the ruling caste deceive their followers without deceiving themselves. Dare anyone be sure that something of the kind is not coming into existence already? One has only to think of the sinister possibilities of the radio, state-controlled education and so forth, to realise that "the truth is great and will prevail" is a prayer rather than an axiom.[7]

What has kept the dictators from, in Burnham's phrase, believing their own myths, what has prevailed even over the demands of ideology, is the need to prepare for war, which in this context is indeed the *ultima ratio*, the final test of reality. "So long as physical reality cannot be altogether ignored, so long as two and two have to make four when you are, for example, drawing the blueprint of an aeroplane, the scientist has his function, and can even be allowed a measure of liberty."[8]

Eugene Lyons offered him a striking example of the misuse of his touchstone. Writing of the first Five-Year Plan, Lyons said:

Optimism ran amuck. Every new statistical success was another justification for the coercive policies by which it was achieved. Every setback was another stimulus to the same policies. The slogan "The Five-Year Plan in Four Years" was advanced, and the magic symbols "5-in-4" and "$2 + 2 = 5$" were posted and shouted throughout the land.

The formula $2 + 2 = 5$ instantly riveted my attention. It seemed to me at once bold and preposterous—the daring and the paradox and the tragic absurdity of the Soviet scene, its mystical simplicity, its defiance of logic, all reduced to nose-thumbing arithmetic. . . . $2 + 2 = 5$: in electric lights on Moscow housefronts, in foot-high letters on billboards, spelled planned error, hyperbole, perverse optimism, something childishly headstrong and stirringly imaginative. . . . $2 + 2 = 5$: a slogan born in premature success, tobogganing toward horror and destined to end up, lamely, as $2 + 2\frac{1}{4} = 5$.

The preliminary triumphs which evoked the slogan $2 + 2 = 5$ were in many ways disastrous. They corroborated the taskmasters' inherited conviction that any miracles could be worked through the sorcery of naked force. At the same time the first triumphs encouraged a costly revision of plans upward beyond the range of reason. Under the pseudo-scientific exterior of charts and blueprints the planners were religious mystics in a trance of ardor. Their optimism was hyperbolic.[9]

Here is detailed evidence of how the self-evident truth has been transformed in the Soviet Union, stated by Lyons in language which places the Communist slogan in a context of religious fervor, if not madness. The equation is used differently by Zamyatin; for him it exemplifies the unhealthy domination of reason over feeling. The citizens in *We* are numbered, not named, and their lives regulated by the minutely detailed schedules of the "Hour Tables," which D-503 calls "the heart and pulse of the United State." The prototype of the Hour Tables is "that greatest of all monuments of ancient literature, the 'Official Railroad Guide'" now, of course, nearly perfected; and D-503 looks forward to the day when "all of the 86,400 seconds will be incorporated in the Tables of Hours."[10] Even poetry is used to celebrate the beauty of numbers. The narrator is pleased, for example, by a poem entitled "Happiness," which he calls "a piece of rare beauty and depth of thought." The first four lines, as he quotes them, are:

> Two times two—eternal lovers;
> Inseparable in passion four . . .
> Most flaming lovers in the world,
> Eternally welded, two times two.

The rest, he says, is in the same vein, celebrating "the wisdom and the eternal happiness of the multiplication table." This moves him to add, "There is but one truth, and there is but one path to it; and that truth is: four, and that path is: two times two."[11]

Zamyatin's novel contains a multitude of ironic variations on the theme that the equation $2 + 2 = 4$ epitomizes the tyranny of reason. To Orwell, on the contrary, it is reason's essence, the secret doctrine which guarantees the existence of objective reality. A number of writers—Chesterton, Dostoevsky, Proust, André Breton— have used this proverbial metaphor for self-evident truth in the context of argument about the superiority of the irrational over the rational. Orwell puts it at the center of the struggle between O'Brien and Winston Smith, and it is therefore interesting to examine Dostoevsky's detailed exposition of the point in *Notes from Underground*, which we know Orwell had read.[12]

The story is about the contrast between "l'homme de la nature et de la vérité"—the man of action and the intellectual. The man of action accepts something as impossible because the laws of nature tell him so, "because two times two is a law of mathematics. Just try refuting it." But the narrator (the spiteful intellectual) says: "What do I care about the laws of nature and arithmetic, when, for some reason, I dislike those laws and the fact that two times two makes four?"[13] The narrator foresees a time when the millennium will have arrived, "the crystal palace will be built," through the strict application of natural laws to every human activity, even to human nature itself, and he argues that two times two is the beginning of death:

> But two times two is, after all, something insufferable. Two times two makes four seems to me merely a piece of insolence. Two times two makes four is a fop standing with arms akimbo barring your path and spitting. I admit that two times two makes four is an excellent thing, but if we are going to praise everything, two times two equals five is sometimes also a very charming little thing.[14]

Dostoevsky's narrator despises rationality and opposes to it the human will or caprice or wish. The will, he says, "is the manifestation of all life." The existence of the human will guarantees the preservation of what is most precious to us, "our personality, our individuality," and he argues that the history of the world is not rational, for in the last extremity men will rebel against reason and even make fools of themselves to prove that "men are still men and not piano keys." He asserts, finally, that more important than anything else to man is what he terms the advantage of suffering, and he finds it "very pleasant to smash things too." He says:

> Man will never renounce real suffering, that is, destruction and chaos. Why, after all, suffering is the sole origin of consciousness. . . . Consciousness, for instance, is infinitely superior to two times two makes four. Once you have two times two makes four, there is nothing left to do or to understand.[15]

In Orwell's experience both the figure of Dostoevsky's narrator and his message were familiar, as we know from what he has written about Baudelaire and Lermontov. The latter's Pechorin is related to the Byronic version of the disappointed intellectual, says Orwell, who is incapable of "behaving with ordinary decency."[16] His mood of splenetic futility, his unworthy emotions, his meanness of spirit are aspects of a character whose willful self has swallowed up everything including respect for reason. When Orwell made the denial of objective reality a theme of *1984*, he was not only writing about one of the important instruments of totalitarianism, he was also consciously digging under the surface of the contemporary world to the roots of the rebellion against reason in the nineteenth century. His "book of arithmetic" and "secret doctrine that two plus two equal four," are signs of his recognizing an opposition that went back as far as Byron.

Related to Orwell's own faith in objective reality is his concern for the truthfulness of history and even the possibility of writing it; he thought that one of the most important of his own motives for writing was the "desire to see things as they are, to find out true facts and store them up for the use of posterity."[17] But even in ordinary circumstances, where one thinks one has firsthand knowledge, it is difficult to find out precisely what is happening. Orwell more than once mentions Sir Walter Raleigh, imprisoned in the Tower, who passed his time trying to write a history of the world but abandoned it when he could not even find out the facts about the death of a workman just outside his cell. "This story has come into my head I do not know how many times during the past ten years," he said, "but always with the reflection that Raleigh was probably wrong." Some uncertainty about Raleigh's decision remained, for he continued, "A Nazi and a non-Nazi version of the present war would have no resemblance to one another, and which of them finally gets into the history books will not be decided by evidential methods but on the battlefield."[18]

He once said to Arthur Koestler, "History stopped in 1936," and Koestler agreed. Both had in mind the rise of totalitarianism, and especially the Spanish Civil War. History had stopped because the possibility of discovering the objective truth had disappeared. Loyalists and Rebels had lied; the records of both were unreliable. "Yet, after all," Orwell wrote, "*some* kind of history will be written, and after those who actually remember the war are dead, it will be universally accepted. So for all practical purposes the lie will have become truth."[19]

Truthful history has always been difficult to write, but when men begin to doubt that it can be written it is not a big step farther to the realization that distorted history can be an instrument of government:

> From the totalitarian point of view history is something to be created rather than learned. A totalitarian state is in effect a theocracy, and its ruling caste, in order to keep its position, has to be thought of as

infallible. But since, in practice, no one is infallible, it is frequently necessary to rearrange past events in order to show that this or that mistake was not made, or that this or that imaginary triumph actually happened. Then, again, every major change in policy demands a corresponding change of doctrine and a revaluation of prominent historical figures. . . . Totalitarianism demands, in fact, the continuous alteration of the past, and in the long run probably demands a disbelief in the very existence of objective truth.[20]

Other instances of this process stayed in Orwell's mind. In the same essay, written in 1946, he cites the perplexity a Communist would face in dealing with a very rare pamphlet written by Maxim Litvinov and published in 1918. The pamphlet outlined events in the early days of the revolution and praised Trotsky, Zinoviev, and Kamenev; it did not mention Stalin. Orwell remarks that "the most intellectually scrupulous Communist," confronted with the pamphlet, could at best take the obscurantist position of saying "it is an undesirable document and better suppressed."[21]

A famous example of falsification after the fact is the one already cited concerning Maurice Thorez, the date of whose desertion from the French Army was altered in newspaper reports in order to give the impression that he had deserted before and not after the fighting started. Lest it be thought that Orwell exaggerated this tendency, the testimony of Alexander Weissberg on the revision of Russian history in 1938 is worth noting:

> Stalin had to make not only Lenin and *Pravda* illegal, but also his own past. For instance, an article written by him appeared in *Pravda* on 6 November 1918 giving the main credit for the victory of the insurrection in Petrograd to the Chairman of the Petrograd Soviet and leader of the Revolutionary War Committee. But the comrade in question was none other than Lev Davidovitch Trotzky. Six years later Stalin wrote that Trotzky had played no important role in the revolution and had really been a very unimportant person—at that time Trotzky had not yet graduated to the role of leader of the counter-revolution. But another seven years after that affairs had ripened, and Stalin announced that Trotzky had always been a Fascist agent in the ranks of the Party. Any reference to the newspapers and the literature of the revolutionary period was now dangerous.[22]

Louis Fischer explains how, when things were going badly in the thirties, the Soviets tried to keep alive the great dream of future success. "Among other things, they ordered all writers, in the middle of the 1930's, to treat the present as though it did not exist and the future as if it had already arrived. This literary device became known as 'Soviet realism.' "[23]

Consider also what happened in the Soviet Union following the purges in 1938. Under Stalin's command a new history of the Communist party was written. Those who did the work made certain that it was falsified in all the usual ways in order to conform to the new conditions created by the purges. They also got rid of the books and documents that might have contradicted the new history and even sought to eliminate those who were in a position to know what had been done: "The directing staff of the Institute of Marx, Engels, and Lenin in Moscow, repository of ideological truth, were removed and the more important people among them imprisoned or shot. The same thing happened in branches of the Institute in various parts of the country."[24]

As already noted, Orwell encountered in *Darkness at Noon* the use of a photograph to illustrate the Communist party's practice of falsifying history. He commented in *Tribune* on another instance of this sort, though it was not, it should be said, the work of the Communist party. The *Daily Herald* of January 1, 1947, carried a story and photographs of two Indians and accused them of collaborating with the Nazis by broadcasting over the German radio during the war. According to Orwell they were not collaborators; they were nationalists who were, however mistakenly, trying to help their own country. The interesting point to Orwell, however, was that one of the men had spoken over the Italian, not the German, radio and that the photograph was captioned incorrectly. One of the names given was that of a man who Orwell knew had been in England throughout the war. Nevertheless he was identified as one of the collaborators: "The caption 'Brijlal Mukerjee' appears under the face of a totally different person." Orwell was willing to concede that all this might have been an honest mistake, but he thought it would have been much less likely to happen had the men not been Indian nationalists. As he observed on the same occasion in commenting on Victor Gollancz' book *In Darkest Germany*, Gollancz had "taken the wise precaution of including himself in a good many [of the photographs]. This at least proves that the photographs are genuine and cuts out the routine charge that they have been obtained from an agency and are 'all propaganda.' "[25]

Orwell's concern for the truth preserved in history and human memory is closely linked to his interest in the past, which he believed to be both a component of personality and a stabilizing external influence in political life. As we saw in discussing *A Clergy-*

man's Daughter, memory is vital to human character. In his review of *Darkness at Noon,* Orwell described Gletkin as one who has grown up in isolation from the outside world: he was a "good party man, an almost perfect specimen of the human gramophone." The source of his strength lay in the "complete severance from the past, which leaves him not only without pity but without imagination or inconvenient knowledge."[26] Furthermore, it seemed to Orwell that the men who deliberately spurned tradition—the scientists and men of the machine exemplified in Wells's books—were really reactionaries, incapable of assisting genuine progress.[27] To him England could never do what Germany had done because their pasts were different:

> Human beings are influenced by their past. England may suffer many degenerative changes as a result of war, but it cannot, except possibly by conquest be turned into a replica of Nazi Germany. . . . The necessary human material is not there. That much we owe to three centuries of security, and to the fact that we were not beaten in the last war.[28]

As he did in *Keep the Aspidistra Flying,* Orwell tries by symbolic means to convey the importance of this theme in *1984.* The nursery rhymes are an obvious example; so is the diary with its paper of a fineness no longer found. But it is the paperweight—the coral embedded in the crystal—which best stands for the unchanging past. Orwell was a connoisseur of junk shops and found good ones in all the shabbier neighborhoods of London. He was careful to distinguish them from the antique shops in the prosperous quarters, clean shops selling high-priced merchandise where one would probably be pressed, however politely, to buy something. On the contrary, he said, in an article for the *Evening Standard,* "A junk shop has a fine film of dust over the window, its stock may include literally anything that is not perishable, and its proprietor, who is usually asleep in a small room at the back, displays no eagerness to make a sale."[29] He valued junk shops as sources of useful and inexpensive objects, and also because they satisfied the jackdaw instinct in every human being. One could, without buying, simply take pleasure in the hoard of objects they contained. Still, they did sometimes offer beautiful things for the diligent searcher: ships in bottles, musical boxes, Jubilee mugs, and glass paperweights with pictures at the bottom. Of these latter, the same article mentions that he was particularly struck by some which had a bit of coral set in the glass, and apparently he would have bought one if they had not been so expensive.

The junk shop in *1984* is almost a replica of those he described in the *Evening Standard*, but richer in significance. It is a trap for the unwary, and a museum of fragments from which Smith chooses two to shore against his ruins. The coral in the crystal is a piece of objective truth testifying beautifully to the existence of a better world in the past and to the fact that even the lowest forms of life may bequeath something to later generations. Its destruction signifies that neither past nor future can be allowed to exist in the harsh present of *1984*, since "all sentiment for the past carries with it a vague smell of heresy," and heresy, like history, comes to an end in Oceania.[30]

Toward the end of his life, Orwell identified the past more and more closely with the individual human personality and with the unique vision a man acquires from living in a particular time and place:

> There is now a widespread idea that nostalgic feelings about the past are inherently vicious. One ought, apparently, to live in a continuous present, a minute-to-minute cancellation of memory, and if one thinks of the past at all it should merely be in order to thank God that we are so much better than we used to be. This seems to me a sort of intellectual face-lifting, the motive behind which is a snobbish terror of growing old. One ought to realize that a human being cannot continue developing indefinitely, and that a writer, in particular, is throwing away his heritage if he repudiates the experience of his early life.[31]

Finally, we may consider whether or not it is possible to withhold anything at all from the "continuous present." If one is cut off from the past as Winston is in Oceania, if one's memory is not sustained by objective evidence, and if one has no recourse to history, can one still preserve from the domination of the environment any part of oneself? This is what Winston and Julia say they will do, but what O'Brien makes impossible by removing the last vestiges of individuality from them. In his first book, *Down and Out in Paris and London*, Orwell had raised this question, noting the extreme contrast between the aspirations of human beings for a decent life and the blighting poverty of his companions. His writings give two contradictory answers: the brutalizing life of a manual worker and the exhaustion caused by long hours of drudgery lead, as is shown in *A Clergyman's Daughter*, to the destruction of human personality. On the other hand, Bozo the screever in *Down and Out in Paris and London* thinks it possible to be free inside himself, in the mind, even if he spends most of the day kneeling on the pavement drawing pictures:

> "You don't *need* to get like that [like Paddy]. If you've got any education, it don't matter to you if you're on the road for the rest of your life."
> "Well, I've found just the contrary," I said. "It seems to me that when you take a man's money away he's fit for nothing from that moment."
> "No, not necessarily. If you set yourself to it, you can live the same life, rich or poor. You can still keep on with your books and your ideas. You just got to say to yourself, 'I'm a free man in here'—he tapped his forehead—and you're all right."[32]

The possibility remains that this core of the mind where freedom lodges may be poisoned from outside, as it is for Winston and Julia. Orwell argued that Tolstoy was trying to do this in his essay on Shakespeare. Even if no outside interference occurs, such an enclave of freedom would be inhuman, for human beings cannot live in isolation. In at least four of the novels the chief character longs to be part of the main stream, and the idea is present in all of them. By 1943, Orwell is clear on the specific point that it is impossible to live under a dictatorship and be free inside:

> The greatest mistake is to imagine that the human being is an autonomous individual. The secret freedom which you can supposedly enjoy under a despotic government is nonsense, because your thoughts are never entirely your own. Philosophers, writers, artists, even scientists, not only need encouragement and an audience, they need constant stimulation from other people. It is almost impossible to think without talking. If Defoe had really lived on a desert island he could not have written *Robinson Crusoe*, nor would he have wanted to.[33]

Orwell here might almost be writing a gloss on the character of Winston Smith. Long before he wrote *1984*, he believed that faith in objective reality and faith in the possibility of writing truthful history are closely related, that memory is an essential part of the self, that.a nation's character and hence its conduct are determined by its history, and that there can be no inner freedom for human beings living in isolation.

XIII

SOURCES AND MANIFESTATIONS OF POWER

WE have seen how Orwell's extensive reading and experience had prepared him for the rise of totalitarianism and the uses that the dictators would make of their power. The Italian example had been there, of course, since 1919, but undergraduates were naming their bull terriers "Musso," and Englishmen, except for some Tory leaders, did not regard Il Duce and the corporate state as a serious threat. In the 1930s, however, the Soviet Union and Germany began to develop in dangerous ways that Orwell believed were foreshadowed by the centuries-old hierarchical absolutism of the Roman Catholic church. He noticed particularly their pyramidal structure and the emergence of a new ruling caste to direct it, and he began to speculate about the possibility that such states would become permanent and universal.

As *The Road to Wigan Pier* shows, Orwell had begun to think that socialism, regarded merely as the common ownership of the means of production, might take a sinister turn. Fashionable left-wing opinion, exemplified by John Strachey's *The Coming Struggle for Power* and Robert Brady's *The Growth and Structure of German Fascism,* held that fascism was a development of capitalism in its last stages, a desperate effort of the old ruling class to hold on to its power by instituting a new tyranny under demagogues whom it controlled. But to Orwell the growth of fascism brought to light its resemblance to socialism, and he saw that industrial civilization was compatible with either political system:

> It is quite easy to imagine a world-society, economically collectivist—
> that is, with the profit principle eliminated—but with all political,
> military and educational power in the hands of a small caste of rulers
> and their bravos. . . . And that, of course, is the slave-state, or rather,
> the slave-world. . . . It is usual to speak of the Fascist objective as
> the "beehive state," which does a grave injustice to bees. A world
> of rabbits ruled by stoats would be nearer the mark.[1]

In 1938, reviewing Eugene Lyons' *Assignment in Utopia,* Orwell made the connection between the Fascist and Communist systems explicit:

181

The system that Mr. Lyons describes does not seem to be very different from Fascism. All real power is concentrated in the hands of two or three million people, the town proletariat, theoretically the heirs of the revolution, having been robbed even of the elementary right to strike; more recently, by the introduction of the internal passport system, they have been reduced to a status resembling serfdom. The GPU are everywhere, everyone lives in constant terror of denunciation, freedom of speech and of the press are obliterated to an extent we can hardly imagine. There are periodical waves of terror, sometimes the "liquidation" of kulaks or Nepmen, sometimes some monstrous state trial at which people who have been in prison for months or years are suddenly dragged forth to make incredible confessions, while their children publish articles in the newspapers saying "I repudiate my father as a Trotskyist serpent." Meanwhile the invisible Stalin is worshipped in terms that would have made Nero blush.[2]

Orwell thought it inevitable that the attempt to establish the dictatorship of the proletariat would end in rule by an elite, enforcing its will through terrorism. "Placed as they were," he said, "the Russian Communists necessarily developed into a permanent ruling caste, or oligarchy, recruited not by birth but by adoption."[3]

A caste system joined to a collectivist economy was what he also saw taking shape in Germany. The intellectuals on the Left and the businessmen on the Right who had supposed that they were witnessing a fresh development of capitalism were wrong:

Then came the eye-opener of the Hitler-Stalin pact. Suddenly the scum of the earth and the blood-stained butcher of the workers (for so they had described one another) were marching arm and arm, their friendship "cemented in blood," as Stalin cheerily expressed it. Thereafter the Strachey-Blimp thesis became untenable. National Socialism *is* a form of Socialism, *is* emphatically revolutionary, *does* crush the propertyowner just as surely as it crushed the worker. The two régimes, having started from opposite ends, are rapidly evolving towards the same system—a form of oligarchical collectivism.[4]

Thus eight years before the publication of *1984*, Orwell had summarized the structure of the totalitarian state as it was to appear in his novel. The reader will recall that the Book in *1984* is entitled "The Theory and Practice of Oligarchical Collectivism."

Several causes—his reading of Burnham, the growth in power of the United States and the Soviet Union, the prolongation of the war and of controls of all sorts after it—sharpened his conception of

what the totalitarian state might be like and strengthened the possibility of its permanence. The worst prospect he envisaged was one
in which the great powers were armed with atomic bombs they
were afraid to use. Writing for *Partisan Review* in 1947, he summarized the power structure that was to appear in *1984:*

> It would mean the division of the world among two or three vast
> super-states, unable to conquer one another and unable to be over-
> thrown by any internal rebellion. In all probability their structure
> would be hierarchic, with a semi-divine caste at the top and out-
> right slavery at the bottom, and the crushing out of liberty would
> exceed anything that the world has yet seen. Within each state the
> necessary psychological atmosphere would be kept up by complete
> severance from the outer world, and by a continuous phony war
> against rival states. Civilisations of this type might remain static
> for thousands of years.[5]

The same idea of the permanent slave state may be discovered
much earlier in Orwell's work, however, quite apart from his repeated references to Belloc and London and his extensive commentary on Burnham. For instance, writing of Hitler and *Mein
Kampf* in 1940 he said:

> When one compares his utterances of a year or so ago with those he
> made fifteen years earlier, a thing that strikes one is the rigidity of his
> mind, the way in which his world-view *doesn't* develop. It is the
> fixed vision of a monomaniac and not likely to be much affected by
> the temporary manoeuvres of power politics.
> What he envisages, a hundred years hence, is a continuous state
> of 250 million Germans with plenty of "living room" (i.e., stretch-
> ing to Afghanistan or thereabouts), a horrible brainless empire in
> which, essentially, nothing ever happens except the training of men
> for war and the endless breeding of fresh cannon-fodder.[6]

Could such a regime be overthrown? As early as 1939 he saw
that men's minds might be so manipulated as to guarantee their
submission:

> The terrifying thing about modern dictatorships is that they are
> something entirely unprecedented. Their end cannot be foreseen.
> In the past every tyranny was sooner or later overthrown, or at least
> resisted, because of "human nature," which as a matter of course
> desired liberty. But we cannot be at all certain that "human nature"
> is constant. It may be just as possible to produce a breed of men
> who do not wish for liberty as to produce a breed of hornless cows.

> The Inquisition failed, but then the Inquisition had not the re-
> sources of the modern state. The radio, press-censorship, standard-
> ized education and the secret police have altered everything. Mass-
> suggestion is a science of the last twenty years, and we do not yet
> know how successful it will be.[7]

The reference to the Inquisition is not accidental. It illustrates
what was said earlier about Orwell's attitude toward religious orthodoxy. One European institution that can lay claim to something like
permanence is the Roman Catholic church, and it has not, perhaps,
been sufficiently remarked that Orwell had it firmly in his mind
when he represented the totalitarian state in *1984*. We have noticed
already some of his feelings about the church in connection with
his attacks on Catholic intellectuals. This dislike, if not hatred, appears as early as 1932 in his praise of a book by a Roman Catholic
on the grounds that unlike most such books it was truthful. Later
he likened the Marxists to the Thomists: "Their real aim is the destruction of liberty, and they consequently argue that any extension
of liberty must lead to slavery."[8] In *1984* this conclusion, epitomized
in the slogan "Freedom Is Slavery," is one of three inscribed on the
facade of the "enormous pyramidal structure" which houses the
Ministry of Truth.

After the war his opinions did not change, for he thought that
the church would oppose every initiative to unify Europe on a
Socialist basis: "Its influence is and always must be against freedom of thought and speech, against human equality, and against
any form of society tending to promote earthly happiness."[9] Given
such convictions it is not surprising that the list of resemblances
between the Catholic church and the totalitarian state of *1984* is
a long one.

The Roman Catholic church is organized in the shape of a
pyramid. At the top is a leader who derives his powers from God,
and beneath him, arranged in a nicely articulated hierarchy, is the
class of intellectuals and bureaucrats. Farther down the pyramid
are the legions of executants of policy—teachers, priests, and nuns.
The rest of the structure is occupied by the faithful who, at least
in theory, obey the orders and instructions announced and transmitted to them by the elite. This society has lasted a long time and
may continue to do so because it is adoptive, not hereditary. As
Orwell says of the ruling class in the U.S.S.R., "If it continues to
co-opt its members from all strata of society, and then train them into

the desired mentality, it might keep its shape almost unaltered from generation to generation."[10]

There are other resemblances. The church has historically forbidden dissent and persecuted heretics when it could. Orwell thought it repressed and distorted the sexual instinct. Details in *1984* are witnesses to Orwell's intention to set up a parallel between the Catholic church and the system in which Winston Smith is enmeshed. O'Brien, for example, calls Julia's torture and confession a classic case of conversion. Winston's pact with O'Brien is symbolized by the drinking of wine. We are told that at the end of the Two Minutes Hate, "the little sandy-haired woman had flung herself forward over the back of the chair in front of her. With a tremulous murmur that sounded like 'My Savior!' she extended her arms toward the screen. Then she buried her face in her hands. It was apparent that she was uttering a prayer."[11] O'Brien's questions are called "a sort of catechism." When O'Brien recruits Winston for service in the Brotherhood he tells him, "Our only true life is in the future," as though he were promising Winston salvation in another world. After Winston has been tortured and his belief in Big Brother restored, "he was back in the Ministry of Love, with everything forgiven, his soul white as snow."[12] The very term "Big Brother" is used ironically to imply a tender concern for the younger children who need a guide and protector.

As early as 1937 Orwell had thus begun to see a new kind of state emerging, in structure and purpose remarkably like those Jack London and Hilaire Belloc had predicted and which Burnham was to elaborate in principle and detail. The Roman Catholic church was proof that such a state had a good chance of becoming permanent. By 1940 Orwell had named the new system "oligarchical collectivism," and when he wrote *1984* he drew on knowledge and speculation stored up over a long time for his picture of the totalitarian system of Oceania.

Certain details in *1984*—the figure of Emmanuel Goldstein, the appearance and appeal of Big Brother, the emotions the dictators stimulate, the image of the boot, the rats, the doctored photograph, and the public display of the guilty—have a special bearing on totalitarianism. Orwell often observed that one of the sources of political power was the personal attractiveness of the leader. When he said that people would fight for Churchill but not for cheese, he meant first of all that Churchill was properly demanding a high sacrifice that transcended commonplace satisfactions. But he must also have had in mind what he later mentioned in his review of *Their Finest Hour,* that the British people were drawn to Churchill despite their disagreement with some of his policies and would follow a man of his courage and large nature.

The dictators also exerted this personal magnetism. Neither Hitler nor Stalin resembled the conventional portrait of a tyrant, according to Orwell, who noted that both Eugene Lyons and H. G. Wells had found Stalin simple and agreeable in their meetings with him. Orwell himself considered that Stalin, at least in the newsreels, had "a likeable face."[13]

Hitler's appeal was different. In his photographs, said Orwell, Hitler resembled Christ and made something of the same impression as Christ crucified: "One feels, as with Napoleon, that he is fighting against destiny, that he *can't* win, and yet that he somehow deserves to. The attraction of such a pose is of course enormous; half the films that one sees turn upon some such theme."[14]

It is a remarkable example of Orwell's talent for rearranging actuality for the purposes of art that he uses both these impressions of the dictator in representing Big Brother and Emmanuel Goldstein. Big Brother's features—the solid face and black mustache— resemble Stalin's, as he was made to seem in the film *Mission to Moscow,* a lovable, rock-like protector, hiding a mysterious, probably compassionate, smile behind the mustache.[15] Despite Winston Smith's hatred of Big Brother at the beginning of the book, this is the vision of the leader which has been imposed on Smith at the end.

In contrast, he sees Goldstein with something of the same pity that Orwell felt Hitler's photograph evoked. In a moment of lucidity when he can shake off the spell of the Two Minutes Hate, his heart goes out to the "lonely, derided heretic on the screen, sole guardian of truth and sanity in a world of lies." The suggestion that Orwell had Hitler in mind when he described Goldstein's appeal cannot be carried too far, however. Deutscher is right in saying that Trotsky is the original of Goldstein, and his opinion is confirmed by T. R. Fyvel, who adds an interesting detail on this point:

> I asked him [Orwell] on one occasion why, in his *Nineteen Eighty-four,* he had given the name "Alexander Goldstein" [*sic*] to the one conceivable rebel left against Big Brother and the Party. Orwell explained that partly his "Goldstein" was, of course, an obvious skit on Trotsky. But he said he also felt that the likely man to stage a hopeless last revolt against a possible totalitarian regime would be some Jewish intellectual.[16]

Had he wished to, Orwell might also have mentioned to Fyvel the similarity of the names, Bronstein and Goldstein.

The emotion the dictators most commonly try to evoke is hatred for the enemy, symbolized by a scapegoat like Goldstein, rather than love for themselves; and it is one more of the system's perversions of truth that the control of law and public safety should be centered in the Ministry of Love. We recall that in Orwell's discussion of Swift's Houyhnhnms he described the limitless tyranny of love acting through public opinion and contrasted it unfavorably with the limited rule of law, which permitted a degree of personal idiosyncrasy and toleration. The Ministry works to arouse citizens to the same sort of indiscriminate rage that sometimes possesses Flory and Gordon Comstock. Orwell had noticed very early the presence of this peculiar emotion in some Socialists. He thought people were mistaken if they assumed that the "book-trained Socialist" was incapable of feeling. It was true enough that the Socialist gave few signs of loving the victims of exploitation, Orwell said, but he believed such a one to be "perfectly capable of displaying hatred—a sort of queer, theoretical, *in vacuo* hatred—against the exploiters."[17] It is this generalized emotion which the dictators make use of:

> As for the hate campaigns in which totalitarian regimes ceaselessly indulge, they are real enough while they last, but are simply dictated by the needs of the moment. Jews, Poles, Trotskyists, English, French, Czechs, Democrats, Fascists, Marxists—almost anyone can figure as Public Enemy No. 1. Hatred can be turned in any direction at a moment's notice, like a plumber's blow-flame.[18]

This passage is almost exactly paralleled in the description of the Two Minutes Hate:

> A hideous ecstasy of fear and vindictiveness, a desire to kill, to torture, to smash faces in with a sledgehammer, seemed to flow through the whole group of people like an electric current, turning one even against one's will into a grimacing, screaming lunatic. And yet the rage that one felt was an abstract, undirected emotion which could be switched from one object to another like the flame of a blowlamp.[19]

The dictator may disguise his power under a benevolent or sorrowful mask as the needs of the moment demand, but the fact of power brutally used is symbolized by a boot in the face. "If you want a picture of the future, imagine a boot stamping on a human face—forever."[20] The source of this image in *The Iron Heel* and its use in *Keep the Aspidistra Flying* have already been mentioned. It is a metaphor that appears again in *England, Your England,* where the context shows Orwell's awareness that even though the use of power is inevitable it does not have to be brutal:

> One rapid but fairly sure guide to the social atmosphere of a country is the parade-step of its army. A military parade is really a kind of ritual dance, something like a ballet, expressing a certain philosophy of life. The goose-step, for instance, is one of the most horrible sights in the world, far more terrifying than a dive-bomber. It is simply an affirmation of naked power; contained in it, quite consciously and intentionally, is the vision of a boot crashing on a face.[21]

George Woodcock has also commented on Orwell's predilection for this image, arguing that it occurred in his writing long before *1984* and therefore was not a peculiar consequence of his illness and low spirits during the time he worked on his last novel. Woodcock quotes from one of Orwell's wartime letters describing how he felt about his work at the B.B.C.: "At present I'm just an orange that's been trodden on by a very dirty boot."[22]

The brutality of the crashing boot heel appears most melodramatically in the use of the rats to make Winston Smith say, "Do it to Julia! Do it to Julia! Not me! Julia!"[23] Some critics have found this scene overwrought, even hysterical, and it may be so; certainly Orwell was dissatisfied with it, though he could think of no way to change it. And yet there is something to be said for the scene. Few people like rats; fewer still would like to be eaten by them. It is well to remind ourselves also that the abominable cruelties practiced at Belsen and Dachau as well as in the prison camps of Asia were still fresh in people's memories when *1984* was written. Like so much else in the novel, the horror was an everyday fact of life.[24]

Possibly Orwell chose to make rats part of the torture because he found them as disagreeable as most of us do. In a passage quoted earlier he compared his descent into a cheap lodging-house to venturing inside "some dreadful subterranean place—a sewer full of rats, for instance."[25] And a loathing almost as strong as Winston Smith's is suggested by this description of life at the front in Spain: "The place was alive with rats. The filthy brutes came swarming out of the ground on every side. If there is one thing I hate more than another it is a rat running over me in the darkness. However, I had the satisfaction of catching one of them a good punch that sent him flying."[26]

Considering his probable wish to reserve the image of the rats for the torture scene, it is understandable that he should compare the typical Party comrades in the canteen of the Ministry of Truth to beetles, but the picture one gets more nearly resembles rats: "It was curious how that beetlelike type proliferated in the Ministries: little dumpy men, growing stout very early in life, with short legs, swift scuttling movements, and fat inscrutable faces with very small eyes."[27]

Many of Orwell's friends have commented on his fondness for animals, but it did not extend to rats. A domestic incident recorded in his notebooks suggests that he might have felt more kindly toward mice, but nevertheless reluctant to be forced to touch them:

> Later in the evening . . . we found a mouse which had slipped down into the sink and could not get up the sides. We went to great pains to make a sort of staircase of boxes of soap flakes, etc, by which it could climb out, but by this time it was so terrified that it fled under the lead strip at the edge of the sink and would not move, even when we left it alone for half an hour or so. In the end E. gently took it out with her fingers and let it go.[28]

Orwell wanted the mouse to live, but it was his wife Eileen who picked it up and set it free.

Finally, the incident concerning Jones, Aaronson, and Rutherford, the traitors whose photograph Winston Smith briefly possesses, has interesting parallels in actuality. As readers will recall, the traitors in *1984* were arrested and eventually executed after having publicly confessed that at the end of a secret flight to Siberia from Canada they had given military information to members of the Eurasian General Staff. Similar charges were a commonplace of the public trials in the Soviet Union, according to Eugene Lyons:

> Always some magnificent lie throws its shadow on the whole texture of eager confessions. In the Ramzin exhibition it was a "conspirator" who had been dead for years before the conspiracy was hatched. In the Menshevik trial the revealing lie was even more startling. One of the leaders of the Second International, Rafael Abramovitch, was supposed to have made a secret visit to Russia on specified dates in the summer of 1928; the whole Menshevik plot centered around that visit, and defendants "confessed" meetings and discussions in detail. Unfortunately for the G.P.U. stage di-

rectors, Abramovitch was attending an International Socialist Congress in Brussels at that very time. Photographs of the delegates made at the very moment he was supposedly plotting in Moscow showed Abramovitch in Brussels.[29]

Orwell, as we saw, knew Lyons' book well. He also wrote two articles on Malcolm Muggeridge's *The Thirties*, in which Muggeridge mentions a former Soviet official who had been apprehended but not immediately killed:

> Sokolnikov, for some years Soviet Ambassador to London, was recalled in 1932; and there were rumours that he had been arrested, and even executed. To counter these rumours, intourists were taken to see him in his Moscow flat, where, though greenish looking, he was indubitably alive. With a noticeably mirthless laugh, he would draw his visitors' attention to this fact, and they would be suitably impressed. He was disposed of in the 1937 batch of Old Bolsheviks, along with Radek, Piatakoff and others.[30]

In *1984* Aaronson, Jones, and Rutherford are also exhibited publicly. Winston Smith, a less important traitor, joins these outcasts in the Chestnut Tree Café.

Isolated and broken by his unequal and self-destroying conflict with the inhumanity of the superstate, this pathetic figure carries us back to Flory, the first such personage in the novels. He symbolizes several themes in Orwell's art. We have seen them emerging from reading, reflection, and punishing actuality, being worked over (even contradicted) more than once, but persisting until they developed into their final statement in *1984*.

PART FOUR

A Judgment of *1984*

XIV

PROPHECY OR WARNING?

THE most notable of those who have found fault with *1984* was Sir Isaac Deutscher, who attacked Orwell and his book with the aim of defusing what he called this "ideological superweapon in the cold war." One can only conjecture how far this criticism is representative and influential, but at least some important issues become clearer if we consider three judgments that helped shape his and perhaps others' interpretations of the work: first, that the purge trials had disoriented Orwell by wrecking his faith in reason and consequently *1984* is the work of a despairing man; second, that Orwell adopted a theory of power which trails away into a "mysticism of cruelty"; and third, that he was disillusioned with "every form and shade of Socialism."[1]

As this book has tried to show, and as other writers have demonstrated in their own ways, there is scarcely anything Orwell wrote that is not assimilated into *1984*. Spender, among others, corroborates this opinion, speaking of *1984* as "the accumulated experience of years"; and Richard Rees remarked that "he succeeds in packing into *1984* nearly all the ideas of his previous books."[2] The sudden break in Orwell's thinking that supposedly took place about 1938, that is, after *Keep the Aspidistra Flying* and *The Road to Wigan Pier* and before *Coming Up for Air*, is not apparent in these works. The momentary flight into pacifism has already been cited, but that was an aberration, not a lasting change.

1984 also is the climax of another kind of continuity present in Orwell's work—the permanent state of mind which shows itself in the characteristic coloring of his own "interminable restless monologue." His tone is not, of course, invariable. It ranges from anger and disgust through disappointment and depression to—but unmistakably—deep affection and love. There are the excitement and elation of the period just before and after Dunkirk, when he thought England was on the verge of revolution, and the frustration and regret accompanying the meager successes of the Labour party in the postwar years. But beneath these crests and troughs runs a current of profound dissatisfaction deriving from his awareness that his cherished vision of human equality was not being realized, especially at the moment when, as the title *Darkness at Noon* implies and as Emmanuel Goldstein says, it had become technically possible.[3] Richard Rees, whose opinion cannot be disregarded, attributes Orwell's feelings to a different cause. "It was not so much man's inhumanity to man but rather his self-absorption and sluggish indifference that was Orwell's permanent nightmare and torment. It stuck in his gizzard. He could not swallow it. And I doubt if he ever succeeded in forgetting it for as much as twenty-four hours in the whole of his adult life."[4]

The point here is not so much why Orwell felt as he did but rather the constancy Rees emphasizes. Neither the 1938 purges, nor the war and its aftermath, nor his illness in the last years changed the characteristic tone of his thinking. Other friends of Orwell's furnish evidence to support this conclusion. Particularly interesting because of the connection with *We* is George Woodcock's statement:

> When Orwell talked in this apocalyptic vein he would paint a horrifying Gothic picture of the fate that might befall us, and here, as some of the more pessimistic parts of *Coming Up for Air* suggest, he was motivated by long-held fears which the reading of *We* merely helped to crystallize. . . . "My God, Orwell is a gloomy bird!" said Herbert Read, himself no lighthearted conversationalist, after one such session. And often, indeed, it seemed as though one had been listening to the voice of Jeremiah.[5]

The usual tone marking his dissatisfaction is controlled anger, though from time to time the control slackened. The anger was a feeling he shared with certain other writers early in his career, and its greater prevalence among writers after the war may be some measure of Orwell's influence. Beverley Nichols, a surprisingly accurate barometer of the between-the-wars generation, writes:

> I used to lie awake at night clenching my fists about armament makers, about *Punch* being cruel to scullery-maids, about the totally damnable condition of the unemployed, about the slobbering apes, who, when they looked at Epstein, were incapable of seeing through the face of the stone to the face of the spirit. Well, there is the link . . . anger. To my surprise I find that the anger persists to this day.[6]

There is a likeness too between Orwell's anger and the bitterness of Jack London in *The People of the Abyss*. One feels that Orwell was enduringly sensitive to the rooted injustice of a social system which he said was like "a family with the wrong members in control," providing the few with power and security and keeping the many subjugated through poverty.[7] The feeling was exacerbated by the knowledge that the injustice could be reduced greatly, if not removed, without recourse to the fantasy of Robin Hood or to the religious communism of a "Digger" like Gerard Winstanley, to whom Orwell has sometimes been compared.

Accompanying Orwell's anger was his suspicion of the conduct and motives of the rulers of the world. We have noted that he was named Cynicus in a diary kept by one of his school fellows.[8] Orwell's suspicion of what Stalin, Churchill, and Roosevelt were doing at Yalta persisted despite efforts to change his opinion. His stubborn assertion, "*They* are all power hungry," impressed Deutscher as an example of "Freudian sublimation of persecution mania."[9] He said nothing of the fact that later events lent support to Orwell's view.

George Bowling knew perfectly well who "they" were and what they would do to interfere with his escapade. F. R. Fyvel tells us how, during the controversy over British policy in Palestine, the intellectuals of the Left were identified with "they" in Orwell's mind:

> He liked thinking in terms of startling paradoxes, and one of his worries was that "They" seemed almost unanimous in support of Zionism. "They" to him were most of the intellectuals of the British left, especially certain contributors to the *New Statesman* and *Manchester Guardian;* together with the fellow-traveler fringe on their left, "They" had become to him dangerous illusionists: "They" had in the 20's supported German demands for Allied evacuation of the Rhineland and Ruhr as a step towards world peace; "They" had in the 30's believed in Communism as merely advanced liberalism; "They" propagated the idea that the Indian Congress movement was genuinely democratic; and now, if "They" equally supported the Palestine Jews against the British government, wasn't that almost a sign that Zionism, too, had its militarist and fascist germ?[10]

The note of exaggeration struck here tends to obscure the measure of truth in what Orwell was saying and makes it easier to believe that Orwell's permanent state of dissatisfaction was irrational, the outgrowth of a warped temperament rather than a justified response to objective conditions. But no facts of modern life are better attested than its anonymity and the growth of bureaucracy. Both provide good reasons for believing that "they" not only exist but are increasing their power, and therefore that the ideas of Orwell (and the man in the street) about them are worth taking seriously. Peter de Mendelssohn, noting the irony of Winston Churchill's being one of the principal creators of the modern English bureaucracy, says:

> The expansion of bureaucracy in England certainly greatly strengthened the staying-power of what is commonly known as "they"; and it is an intriguing question how far it has in fact produced a change in the British character. From about 1906 onwards "they" began to gain a firmer hold of the individual. This was, of course, inevitable. If the State was to assist people in placing their existence on a more secure footing, it must know who, what, and where people were; it required records of their whereabouts and circumstances; and records meant, or at least implied, a measure of supervision. People were no longer callously neglected by their "betters"; but instead they were being "pushed around" and "interfered with," however gently and civilly, by a certain class drawn from their "equals" who owed their own absolute security of tenure to their relative insecurity of existence. The "National Minimum" was administered by a new class of "unsackables"; "they" were indispensable yet unassailable, irksome yet awesome, and the British character, by nature and tradition receptive to fine gradations of class structure, with respectful grumbling took them to its heart. A singular phenomenon produced itself: the anonymous, arbitrary master who signed himself "your obedient servant."[11]

The suspicion intermixed with Orwell's anger was grounded in reality. His gloominess was indeed temperamental, though not merely that, and there is some reason to suppose that it was habitually exaggerated. Cyril Connolly remembered a moment when they were boys at school, passing "under a fig-tree in one of the inland boulevards of the seaside town, Orwell striding beside me and saying in his flat, ageless voice: 'You know, Connolly, there's only one remedy for all diseases.' I felt the usual guilty tremor when sex was mentioned and hazarded, 'You mean going to the lavatory?' 'No—I mean Death!' "[12]

Other testimony to the continuity of Orwell's state of mind comes from Anthony West, to whom Orwell seemed a sick man wanting to punish the whole world for making him so. He attributed Orwell's "sickness" (what Spender called his fantasy) to his early experience at Crossgates, the school described in "Such, Such Were the Joys." According to West, Orwell misunderstood that experience, and was ever afterwards so bitter and angry at the world for having subjected him to it that in *1984* he devised "a fantasy of universal ruin." West cites some details in *1984* and shows their resemblance to events and persons at Orwell's school: "As these parallels fall into place . . . it is possible to see how Orwell's unconscious mind was working. Whether he knew it or not, what he did in '1984' was to send everybody in England to an enormous Crossgates to be as miserable as he had been."[13] Richard Voorhees has, I think, successfully attacked this psychoanalytical explanation of Orwell's work. Whatever the cause, the continuity of Orwell's outlook is accepted as a fact by many critics of diverse schools who have written about him; it thus seems unlikely that the state of mind displayed in *1984* is traceable to some specific event like the purge trials in the Soviet Union or the effect these trials produced in Spain.

Yet it is contended that the Russian purges of 1936–38 and their repercussions in Spain had so traumatic an effect on Orwell as to destroy his faith in rationality, disclosing to him an irrationality which he had to acknowledge as real. The result, according to this view, was that "he found himself bereft of his conscious and unconscious assumptions about life."[14]

As it happens, we have some evidence of Orwell's immediate reaction to the purges. In June 1938 he wrote the following, which I quote in full because of its intrinsic interest as well as its bearing on this question:

> To get the full sense of our ignorance as to what is really happening in the USSR, it is worth trying to translate the most sensational Russian event of the past two years, the Trotskyist trials, into English terms. Make the necessary adjustments, let Left be Right and Right be Left, and you get something like this:
>
> Mr Winston Churchill, now in exile in Portugal, is plotting to overthrow the British Empire and establish Communism in England. By the use of unlimited Russian money he has succeeded in building up a huge Churchillite organisation which includes members of Parliament, factory managers, Roman Catholic bishops and practically the whole of the Primrose League. Almost every day some dastardly act of sabotage is laid bare—sometimes a plot to blow up the House of Lords, sometimes an outbreak of foot and mouth disease in the Royal racing-stables. Eighty percent of the Beefeaters at the Tower are discovered to be agents of the Comintern. A high official of the Post Office admits brazenly to having embezzled postal orders to the tune of £5,000,000 and also to having committed *lèse majesté* by drawing moustaches on postage stamps. Lord Nuffield, after a 7-hour interrogation by Mr Norman Birkett, confesses that ever since 1920 he has been fomenting strikes in his own factories. Casual half-inch paras in every issue of

the newspapers announce that fifty more Churchillite sheep-stealers have been shot in Westmoreland or that the proprietress of a village shop in the Cotswolds has been transported to Australia for sucking the bullseyes and putting them back in the bottle. And meanwhile the Churchillites (or Churchillite-Harmsworthites as they are called after Lord Rothermere's execution) never cease from proclaiming that it is *they* who are the real defenders of capitalism and that Chamberlain and the rest of his gang are no more than a set of Bolsheviks in disguise.[15]

In spirit this is closer to *Animal Farm* than to *1984*, and it does not read like the work of a man whose assumptions about life have suffered a mortal blow. It is also evidence that Orwell did not have to wait until he read *We* seven years later before being able to formulate, in something like fictional terms, some of the important elements of a satire on totalitarianism.

To look more closely at the errors involved in believing that Orwell's faith in reason had been destroyed by the trials it is necessary to consider what Orwell had in mind when he wrote *1984*, and here we are at the heart of the matter. Before the book was published he wrote to Roger Senhouse, one of the directors of Secker and Warburg:

> As to the blurb, I don't think the approach in the draft you sent me is the right one. It makes the book sound as though it were a thriller mixed up with a love story, & I didn't intend it to be primarily that. What it is really meant to do is to discuss the implications of dividing the world up into "Zones of Influence" (I thought of it in 1944 as a result of the Teheran Conference), & in addition to indicate by parodying them the intellectual implications of totalitarianism. It has always seemed to me that people have not faced up to these & that, e.g., the persecution of scientists in Russia, is simply part of a logical process which should have been foreseeable 10–20 years ago.[16]

When *1984* was first published it was widely interpreted as a prophecy about the future; less often it was seen as an attack on socialism or even on the British Labour party. In 1949 Orwell tried to clear up some of the misunderstanding by an explicit statement of what he thought he had done:

> My novel *Nineteen Eighty-four* is *not* intended as an attack on socialism, or on the British Labor party, but as a show-up of the perversions to which a centralized economy is liable, and which

have already been partly realized in Communism and fascism. I do not believe that the kind of society I describe *will* arrive, but I believe (allowing, of course, for the fact that the book is a satire) that something resembling it *could* arrive. I believe also that totalitarian ideas have taken root in the minds of intellectuals everywhere, and I have tried to draw these ideas out to their logical consequences. The scene of the book is laid in Britain in order to emphasize that the English-speaking races are not innately better than anyone else and that totalitarianism, if not fought against, could triumph anywhere.[17]

For the moment the pertinent fact about this statement is Orwell's declaration that he wrote a warning, not a prediction. Rees, Fitzgibbon, Rahv, and Woodcock interpret the book as a warning, and I follow them in doing so. Hollis says that the book is not a definite prophecy. But he then argues that Orwell's failure to explain how the catastrophe was to be avoided justifies the conclusion that the "warning defeats itself because of its underlying boundless despair."[18] This reasoning is curious. Even if we agree, as I do not, that *1984* is a cry of despair, we ought to be grateful for the warning and not find fault with the man who gives it. What Voorhees says in this connection seems fairer: "*Nineteen Eighty-Four*, then, is not a prediction, but an alert. It no more indicates that universal totalitarianism is inevitable than a danger sign on a highway indicates that a wreck is."[19] Orwell is not obliged to provide answers to the perennial questions at the heart of his book, though the revulsion it inspires implies at least negative solutions. Philip Rahv puts it this way:

> To read this novel simply as a flat prediction of what is to come is to misread it. It is not a writ of fatalism to bind our wills. Orwell makes no attempt to persuade us, for instance, that the English-speaking nations will inevitably lose their freedom in spite of their democratic temper and libertarian traditions. "Wave of the future" notions are alien to Orwell. His intention is, rather, to prod the Western world into a more conscious and militant resistance to the totalitarian virus to which it is now exposed.[20]

Did Orwell believe what he wrote in *1984*? He did not believe that what he described was bound to happen. But he certainly believed that in Britain and elsewhere one could discover instrumentalities of government to further totalitarianism—and attitudes of mind indicating a willingness to use them toward that end. He believed also that these needed to be represented so vividly that people would grasp the consequences of letting them flourish and be encouraged to resist them.

One of the curiosities of Deutscher's attack on Orwell and *1984* is that he has little to say about Arthur Koestler's *Darkness at Noon* and little enough about Koestler. The omission contrasts markedly with the belief that Orwell's plunge into the "abyss of despair" was the result of an obsession with the purge trials and a failure to arrive at an explanation of them. He attributes everything in *1984* to *We* (except the Englishness), yet the purges and the trials make no appearance in *We*. How could they? On the other hand, they are the center of interest in Koestler's novel—or, more precisely, its subject is the explanation of the motives behind the trials and the confessions. Furthermore, Orwell and Koestler were friends; Orwell reviewed the novel, calling it brilliant and describing Gletkin in terms that—five years before he read *We*—outline a major theme in *1984*, the race of monsters that totalitarian systems spawn. There are also, as we have seen, several close parallels between *Darkness at Noon* and *1984*. They may be superficial, as Woodcock believes, still it is noteworthy that of all this Deutscher has nothing to say.[21]

If one had to choose a single writer who most profoundly affected the shaping of *1984*, that writer would, I believe, be James Burnham. His arguments about the nature of the changes taking place in modern society as well as the way Orwell responded to them and their development and alteration in Burnham's later work have already been discussed. Some of Burnham's ideas were, as we saw, accepted by Orwell: the concentration of industry and hence of its control, the erosion of capitalist ideology and morale, the rise of a class of managers to replace the owner-capitalists, the emergence of superstates, and the potential perversion of the ideal of socialism. He rejected other ideas: Burnham's theory of power and what Orwell called his "power-worship," as well as many of Burnham's predictions, including his belief that a preventive war against the Soviet Union was inevitable.

What Orwell has done in *1984* is to assume that Burnham's analysis is correct and to work out the consequences. As he said, "James Burnham's theory has been much discussed, but few people have yet considered its ideological implications—that is, the kind of world-view, the kind of beliefs, and the social structure that would probably prevail in a State which was at once *unconquerable* and in a permanent state of war with its neighbours." We know that Orwell disagreed profoundly with many of Burnham's beliefs, but there is no overt sign of this disagreement in the novel and no reason why there should be. Like "A Modest Proposal," *1984* assumes the existence of certain conditions and certain tendencies of mind and attempts to work out their outrageous consequences in order to effect in the reader a revulsion against them.

Emmanuel Goldstein's "The Theory and Practice of Oligarchical Collectivism"—the Book—is in style and content inspired by Burnham's *The Managerial Revolution* and *The Machiavellians*. Deutscher claims, however, that the fragments of the Book "are an obvious, though not very successful, paraphrase of Trotsky's *The Revolution Betrayed*."[22] Presumably this opinion rests on the identification of Goldstein with Trotsky, which Orwell acknowledged, for Deutscher offers no evidence to support it. Trotsky's book describes how, after the death of Lenin, the aims and methods of the revolution were perverted as Stalin gradually consolidated his power. With a wealth of statistics and details it concentrates on Russian developments. It is thus not mainly a theoretical treatise, nor is it, like Burnham's books, a comprehensive study of world politics or human motives. There are indeed similarities in style between Burnham and Trotsky; the tone of authority which they have in common is especially noticeable. But even in its style Goldstein's book has greater similarities to Burnham's, since Burnham is not impeded by the necessity to detail events that have already taken place, and consequently his language and manner can be more sweeping and assured. Furthermore, the Book deals with some subjects treated explicitly by Burnham but not by Trotsky.

There is in this connection a remarkable coincidence. The Book is a forgery carried out by O'Brien and other members of the Inner Party and attributed to Emmanuel Goldstein as a means of waging war against its enemies. Burnham himself in *The Managerial Revolution* cited another document which had a similar origin and aim, *The Brown Book of the Hitler Terror*. He gives a long quotation from this work in support of his argument that social democracy is a means of preserving capitalism and notes that although the article from which he took the quotation appeared in a capitalist journal devoted to Germany's heavy industry, it was in fact Leninist in its analysis. This paradox made Burnham suspicious, and he added this footnote: "I have been unable to verify the authenticity of the quotation. Since *The Brown Book* was a Comintern propaganda document, designed to justify the Stalinist policy in Germany, it is possible that the source of this quotation, as of so many others, is the fertile brain of the GPU."[23]

Burnham was right to suspect the provenance of the quotation, though in fact the book was not the work of the GPU but of Willi Muenzenberg and his staff working behind the facade of the "World Committee for the Relief of the Victims of German Fascism," a Communist front. As Western Propaganda Chief of the Comintern, Muenzenberg had the task of countering the propaganda show trial staged by the Nazis after the burning of the Reichstag. They tried to pin the blame for the fire on the Communists as a pretext for further attacks on the left wing in Germany. The Comintern counterattack in *The Brown Book* (written by Muenzenberg's second-in-command, Otto Katz) took the form of "proving" that the Nazis had themselves destroyed the Reichstag. As Arthur Koestler says in his account of the book:

> But how could we make the naive West believe such a fantastic story? We had no direct proof, no access to witnesses, only underground communications to Germany. We had, in fact, not the faintest idea of the concrete circumstances. We had to rely on guesswork, on bluffing and on the intuitive knowledge of the methods and minds of our opposite numbers in totalitarian conspiracy.[24]

In addition to the "complete inside story" of the fire the book contained reports on German concentration camps, on persecution of the Jews, and on the repression of literature, based on information gathered by the Comintern's intelligence *apparat*. Derived as it was from "isolated scraps of information, deduction, guesswork, and brazen bluff," *The Brown Book* "was a shot in the dark. But it went straight to the target." It was translated into seventeen languages and it became "the bible of the anti-Fascist crusade. It was smuggled into Germany in large quantities, bound in the cover of Reklam's cheap classics series, disguised as Schiller's *Wallenstein* and Goethe's *Hermann und Dorothea*."[25] Orwell may not have known all these details, but his thorough knowledge of Burnham's work and his close friendship with Koestler make it seem probable that he got the idea for the Book from that of Willi Muenzenberg's committee.

Another reason for introducing the Book, only tangentially related to the foregoing, is that each of the authoritarian ideologies satirized in *1984*—Communist, Fascist, Roman Catholic—embodies a personage who incarnates evil: Trotsky, the Jew, the Devil. And each group, from its beginning as a weak and despised sect, had its sacred book: *Das Kapital, Mein Kampf*, the Bible. It is necessary and fitting that the Inner Party, with its superior knowledge of modern administration and methods of mass manipulation, should have created another sacred book, just as it invented Emmanuel Goldstein—and, Edmund Wilson intimates, as Stalin created Trotsky —to focus the emotions of its subjects against the supposed enemy.[26] Three days after Trotsky's assassination Orwell wrote in his diary, "It occurred to me yesterday, how will the Russian state get on without Trotsky? Or the Communists elsewhere? Probably they will be forced to invent a substitute."[27]

The point of greatest difference between Burnham and Orwell lies in their attitude toward power and its use. In *1984* all the questions implicit in this subject are concentrated in the entry Winston Smith makes in his diary: *"I understand HOW; I do not understand WHY."*[28] Later on, when he is being brainwashed and is compelled by O'Brien to speculate about "WHY?" he replies in his old-fashioned way, "You are ruling over us for our own good. . . . You believe that human beings are not fit to govern themselves, and therefore—" a mistake punished by a painful electric shock. O'Brien tells him what he should have said, "The Party seeks power entirely for its own sake. We are not interested in the good of others; we are interested solely in power."[29]

Two questions may be asked about O'Brien's statement. First, did Orwell himself believe this to be a satisfactory explanation of why some men act as they do? And second, is it a reasonable opinion? Orwell did indeed think—and with reason—that some men hunger to have power over others; but, as we know, that is not all he believed. To assume that O'Brien's answer to Winston Smith's implied question is what Orwell himself would have said is to misread *1984*.

O'Brien's answer echoes Burnham's thesis in *The Machiavellians*. The passage in which Orwell himself specifically rejected Burnham's thesis, in an article in the *Manchester Evening News*, is worth repeating: "It would seem that the theory that there is no such thing as a 'good' motive in politics, that nothing counts except force and fraud, has a hole in it somewhere, and that the Machiavellian system fails, even by its own test of material success."[30]

Other evidence can be brought to bear on this point. In 1944, for example, commenting on the asserted immutability of man's nature, an argument which he said was employed by "Christian apologists and by neo-pessimists such as James Burnham," Orwell summarized the case for believing that human greed and sinfulness are incorrigible, and then said:

> The proper answer, it seems to me, is that this argument belongs to the Stone Age. It presupposes that material goods will always be desperately scarce. The power hunger of human beings does indeed present a serious problem, but there is no reason for thinking that the greed for mere wealth is a permanent human characteristic. We are selfish in economic matters because we all live in terror of poverty.[31]

Two years later he again commented directly on this issue:

> The desire for pure power seems to be much more dominant than the desire for wealth. This has often been pointed out, but curiously enough the desire for power seems to be taken for granted as a natural instinct, equally prevalent in all ages, like the desire for food. Actually it is no more natural, in the sense of being biologically necessary, than drunkenness or gambling. And if it has reached new levels of lunacy in our own age, as I think it has, then the question becomes: what is the special quality in modern life that makes a major human motive out of the impulse to bully others? If we could answer that question—seldom asked, never followed up—there might occasionally be a bit of good news on the front page of your morning paper.[32]

In other words, Orwell did not believe that Machiavelli, Burnham, and O'Brien were right. He did not believe that "sadistic power-hunger" is the ultimate motive for human conduct.

XV

THE MYSTICISM OF CRUELTY

SUPPOSE nevertheless that Orwell really did believe the love of power for its own sake was what motivated men, does it follow that he accepted a mysticism of cruelty? O'Brien, it is true, is a priest of this mystical religion, but Machiavelli and Burnham are philosophers, reasonable men who are trying to explain human conduct. Their views, like those of other thinkers, rest on self-evident propositions, axioms whose truth they seek to demonstrate by appealing to logic and experience. Nevertheless, when all the evidence is in, there remains still the famous leap. No philosophy commands universal assent, not only because men differ about what reasonable conduct is but also because they have not been able to accept one another's assumptions; that is, they have not been able to agree about what their experience means. Marx's belief in the class struggle and the dialectic is such an assumption; so is the belief in a developmental struggle for existence; so is Machiavelli's assertion that men are perpetually struggling for power. These are rational beliefs in the sense that men may seek by reason to show that they are true. They are also mystical—to the unbeliever they are not demonstrable assumptions. Marxist faith is to some people as mystical as the visions of St. Theresa and less well grounded in what they conceive to be reality, but they could not fairly call Marxists irrational.

Such abstract considerations apart, however, much informed contemporary opinion favors the idea that at the root of the Fascist and Communist ideologies lies a love of power for its own sake which resists further analysis. Bertrand Russell, for example, wrote an authoritative study of this motive which Orwell reviewed approvingly, all the more so, one may suppose, because Russell linked power to solipsism and lunacy and suggested the pleasure the persecutor takes in persecution, just as Orwell does in *1984*.[1] And one of Hitler's biographers, Alan Bullock, says of him:

> To say that Hitler was ambitious scarcely describes the intensity of the lust for power and the craving to dominate which consumed him.

It was the will to power in its crudest and purest form, not identifying itself with the triumph of a principle as with Lenin or Robes-
pierre—for the only principle of Nazism was power and domination
for its own sake—nor finding satisfaction in the fruits of power, for,
by comparison with other Nazi leaders like Göring, Hitler lived an
ascetic life. For a long time Hitler succeeded in identifying his own
power with the recovery of Germany's old position in the world, and
there were many in the 1930s who spoke of him as a fanatical patriot.
But as soon as the interests of Germany began to diverge from his
own, from the beginning of 1943 onwards, his patriotism was seen
at its true value—Germany, like everything else in the world, was
only a means, a vehicle for his own power, which he would sacrifice with the same indifference as the lives of those he sent to the
Eastern Front. By its nature this was an insatiable appetite, securing
only a temporary gratification by the exercise of power, then rest-
lessly demanding an ever further extension of it.[2]

Bullock's judgment is confirmed with especial force by the
events of the last two years of the war, when Hitler's insane per-
sistence in believing himself infallible and omnipotent caused
Germany's defeat and his own destruction. The same opinion is held
by one of the earliest analysts of the Nazi regime, Hermann
Rauschning. The Nazi ideology, he says, was simply a means of concealing the desire of the elite to keep itself in power: "Force is
applied at all times, for the one purpose of maintaining the elite
in power—and applied ruthlessly, brutally, instantaneously."[3]

He defines the aim of the revolutionary new order as action,
whether revolutionary action on a national or world scale or endless
war, which he believed might become the characteristic state of
future society. Like Winston Smith, Rauschning asks "Why?" and
he always returns to the fact of Nazi irrationality. Nazis are realists
who live in a world of fantasy: "National Socialism has only impulses, no fixed political aims—impulses and a system of tactics.
There is no degree of saturation in the political aims of National
Socialism: there can be none. Thus, nothing can be more irrational
than to ask what are the final demands of its 'dynamic' foreign
policy."[4] In the conclusion of his book, Rauschning stressed his
belief that Nazi aims were indefinite because they were infinite.

Orwell's close friend, Malcolm Muggeridge, was also impressed
by men's seeming pursuit of power for its own sake. In his book
The Thirties which Orwell reviewed, he remarks of the decade:

A great shifting of power has taken place; and when power shifts,
men shift with it. Power is their everlasting pursuit. They follow

it lovingly from place to place, from person to person, from idea to idea, sometimes with resultant confusion. When power shifts rapidly, the most practised power-diviners falter. By the time they have made up their minds to ingratiate themselves with, for instance, the legatees of the Russian Revolution, most of these are shot as spies and traitors; by the time they have accustomed themselves to the idea that Captain Röhm must be counted among the great ones of the earth, he is put to death. Now a Tsar Nicholas is powerful and requires adulation; now a Stalin is powerful, and also requires adulation, largely the same.[5]

Later on Muggeridge comments on the significance of purge trials, using, coincidentally, a phrase similar to Deutscher's "mysticism of cruelty":

> A government based on terrorism requires constantly to demonstrate its might and resolution. Saint George must continually slay his dragon, the dragon ever growing wearier, St. George's thrusts ever more mechanical. This continuous performance heartens the mighty in their seats, and awes the humble and meek, besides providing a convenient means of exterminating actual and potential rebels. It is the mysticism of power, in its technique and temper reminiscent of the Book of Revelation, that terrible expression of the heart's most cruel and destructive appetite, which, being so intense, must be so fantastic in its manifestations.[6]

What Muggeridge says is based in part on observations he made while living in the Soviet Union, and his testimony is corroborated by other qualified observers like Alexander Weissberg, one of the handful of Stalin's victims who lived to bear witness against him. Stalin, said Weissberg, was interested only in power, not in a victory of particular ideas. "He wanted such untrammeled power that when he pressed a button the masses of the Russian people, of the oppressed peoples of Asia and of the revolutionary workers of Europe would swing into movement. . . . He wanted to be absolutely free in all his actions, and the only way open to him was to enslave the Russian people."[7]

It is not essential to my argument that the opinions expressed by these writers be correct, though one must grant that what they say has weight. My point is that these are not irrational opinions. Their stress on the power-hunger implicit in the Fascist and Communist ideologies, and their demonstrations of how this motive works in practice may be old, and in the last analysis, metaphysical; but they are not abstract, banal, or barren. It may even be said that O'Brien himself is like Hitler or Stalin, only without their pretense, or that he conforms to Burnham's model of the new scientific ruler who is without illusion about himself and others. O'Brien's explanation of his conduct and that of the other members of the Inner Party is not irrational; it is the conduct that is irrational, and his creator knew it was. That an insane murderer may understand why he murders neither prevents what he does nor makes the crime less horrifying.

It is too bad that Orwell's beliefs have at times been confused with O'Brien's, for this has prevented some readers from seeing how profoundly Orwell understood totalitarianism, not, to be sure, with a scholar's understanding, like Hannah Arendt's, but also not just with what is usually called an artist's intuition. With Orwell, study and thought habitually reinforced experience and imagination.

The long dialogue between O'Brien and Smith demonstrates Orwell's awareness that implicit in totalitarianism is a desire for expansion—physical, intellectual, spiritual—that, as Rauschning said, recognizes no limits. Oceania will be victorious over Eurasia and Eastasia; and, if it is not, totalitarianism will have conquered anyway. Two plus two will equal five, or three; the human being will be transformed into a model citizen—totalitarian style. O'Brien says to Winston, "Never again will you be capable of ordinary human feeling. Everything will be dead inside you. Never again will you be capable of love, or friendship, or joy of living, or laughter, or curiosity, or courage, or integrity. You will be hollow. We shall squeeze you empty, and then we shall fill you with ourselves."[8]

John Strachey estimates Orwell's achievement justly. Many writers, he says, consider communism to be the "culmination of rationalism . . . they consider that Communism *is* rationalism in its contemporary form. Hence when they depict what they consider to be the ghastly consequences of Communism and cry for its repudiation, they must perforce repudiate rationalism also." But Orwell, he says, shows that communism:

> now indistinguishable from Fascism is . . . patently irrational. It has lost almost all touch with objective reality and pursues psychopathic social objectives. . . . The lesson of his book is *not* that the catastrophe which Communism has suffered proves that reason carried to its logical conclusion leads to horror; that consequently we must retreat from reason into some form of mysticism or supernaturalism. On the contrary, what Orwell is saying is that the catastrophe of our times occurred precisely because the Communists (and, of course, still more the Fascists) deserted reason. He is saying that the Communists, without being aware of it, have lost touch with

reality: that their doctrine has become, precisely, a mysticism, an authoritarian revelation.[9]

Orwell did not abandon rationalism; what he did was to demonstrate the consequences of abandoning reason in favor of a cruel logic applied rigorously and without limit. However one defines reason theoretically, in practice its use means the capacity and will to make discriminations and recognize limits. Paraphrasing Bernard Shaw, we may say that it is unreasonable to put one's grandmother in a bath filled with boiling water in order to find out how much heat she can stand. Reason, in other words, is not the same thing as logical consistency motivated by the desire for knowledge.

Hannah Arendt shows beautifully how the essence of totalitarianism is its unlimited and consistent logic, and it is remarkable how Orwell anticipated her detailed analysis of the destruction of the human person and the manner in which ideology may turn into insanity. She distinguishes three stages by which human beings may be destroyed, and all these occur in *1984*. First, what she calls the juridical person, who exists because laws exist and who has an identity definable by categories accepted by other citizens and by the state, is eliminated by indiscriminate attacks on the population; even the possibility of freely consenting to arrest and imprisonment is denied:

> The aim of an arbitrary system is to destroy the civil rights of the whole population, who ultimately become just as outlawed in their own country as the stateless and the homeless. . . . The arbitrary arrest which chooses among innocent people destroys the validity of free consent, just as torture—as distinguished from death—destroys the possibility of opposition.[10]

Orwell, it is true, retains the idea of crime, but in Oceania this is virtually a fiction expressed in the terms thoughtcrime and facecrime. One could argue that Smith is a kind of criminal, but what are Parsons, Syme, and Ampleforth if not arbitrarily selected victims who are transformed into unpersons because "purges and vaporizations were a necessary part of the mechanics of government."[11]

The second step in what Arendt calls the "preparation of living corpses" is the "murder of the moral person in man." This is done by making martyrdom impossible, which in turn demands the abolition of history. It is part of Winston Smith's anguish in his loneliness that no one will know about him, his thoughts, or his

disaffection. Cut off from past and future, isolated from his contemporaries, any gesture of defiance is deprived of meaning because
it takes place in a social void.[12] O'Brien says to him:

> You must stop imagining that posterity will vindicate you, Winston.
> Posterity will never hear of you. . . . We shall turn you into gas and
> pour you into the stratosphere. Nothing will remain of you: not a
> name in a register, not a memory in a living brain. You will be
> annihilated in the past as well as in the future. You will never have
> existed.[13]

His own conscience might confer value on him, but this possibility
is dimmed by his isolation and finally extinguished when he cries,
"Do it to Julia! Do it to Julia! Not me! Julia! I don't care what you
do to her!"[14]

The third stage Arendt analyzes is one in which the uniqueness
of the human person is nullified by degrading and tormenting the
body in order to kill the self. Thus Winston is bullied, beaten,
tortured—systematically reduced below the status of an animal.
When this process is almost at an end, O'Brien compels him to look
at himself in a mirror. He sees a "bowed, gray-colored, skeleton-
like thing," of frightening aspect, filthy, scarred, emaciated. "At a
guess he would have said that it was the body of a man of sixty,
suffering from some malignant disease." O'Brien asks him, "What
are you? A bag of filth. Now turn round and look into that mirror
again. Do you see that thing facing you? That is the last man. If
you are human, that is humanity."[15] Winston has reached the
stage Hannah Arendt describes as "the human specimen reduced
to the most elementary reactions, the bundle of reactions that can
always be liquidated and replaced by other bundles of reactions that
behave in exactly the same way . . . the model 'citizen' of a totalitarian state."[16]

Once again, lest it be thought that the argument is weakened
because the evidence is drawn from fiction or abstract discussion,
one may cite an example from actuality. Writing of the first trial
of those who conspired to assassinate Hitler, William Shirer remarked how Goebbels succeeded in degrading the accused:

> They were outfitted in nondescript clothes, old coats and sweaters,
> and they entered the courtroom unshaven, collarless, without neck-
> ties and deprived of suspenders and belts to keep their trousers
> hitched up. The once proud Field Marshal [von Witzleben],
> especially, looked like a terribly broken, toothless old man. His false
> teeth had been taken from him and as he stood in the dock, badgered

unmercifully by the venomous chief judge, he kept grasping at his trousers to keep them from falling down.

"You dirty old man," Freisler shouted at him, "why do you keep fiddling with your trousers?"[17]

Why should Oceania (or any totalitarian state) wish to produce such model citizens? The answers that Orwell and Arendt give to this question are not identical, but they have in common their emphasis on the importance of ideology to the totalitarian mind, and especially the importance of the inner and detailed logical consistency of the ideology. As Arendt says about ideologies:

> Once their claim to total validity is taken literally they become the nuclei of logical systems in which, as in the systems of paranoiacs, everything follows comprehensibly and even compulsorily once the first premise is accepted. The insanity of such systems lies not only in their first premise but in the very logicality with which they are constructed. . . .
>
> What makes a truly totalitarian device out of the Bolshevik claim that the present Russian system is superior to all others is the fact that the totalitarian ruler draws from this claim the logically impeccable conclusion that without this system people never could have built such a wonderful thing as, let us say, a subway; from this, he again draws the logical conclusion that anyone who knows of the existence of the Paris subway is a suspect because he may cause people to doubt that one can do things only in the Bolshevik way. This leads to the final conclusion that in order to remain a loyal Bolshevik, you have to destroy the Paris subway. Nothing matters but consistency.[18]

This invented illustration is not merely fanciful. The same inhuman obsession with consistency appears in the story Koestler tells of a Writer's Congress in Moscow at which there were countless speeches "promising universal happiness in a brave new world." Then, as he tells it, "André Malraux asked suddenly: 'And what about the child run over by a tram car?' There was a pained silence; then somebody said, amidst general approbation: 'In a perfect, planned socialist transport system there will be no accidents.' "[19] Of all the remarkable things in *1984*, none is more absorbing than the intellectual and moral struggle between Winston and O'Brien which enacts the bewilderment Arendt describes when the human being who is trying to remain sane amid inhuman conditions is face to face with the power of ideological supersense "driven by the motor of logicality."[20] Given O'Brien's axioms and his power to enforce their truth through terror and logic, no one could fend off his arguments. Winston Smith's effort to comprehend and yet to survive is full of pathos which moves us in the same way that we are moved by the puzzled efforts of the victims of real totalitarians to preserve their beliefs, their values, and their lives in the disorienting environment of the concentration camps.[21] The logic of the Inner Party is inexorable: "You are a flaw in the pattern, Winston. You are a stain that must be wiped out. . . . It is intolerable to us that an erroneous thought should exist anywhere in the world, however secret and powerless it may be."[22]

Finally, in this interpretation of 1984, it remains to show that Orwell's hatred of Soviet totalitarianism did not poison his mind against socialism.[23] Disillusion may be a form of enlightenment rather than a cause of disbelief or disgust. Even in his earliest work we have found signs that he knew socialism was no panacea. In Down and Out in Paris and London, for example, commenting on the acquiescence of intelligent and cultivated people in the continued exploitation of the poor, he says, "Foreseeing some dismal Marxist Utopia as the alternative, the educated man prefers to keep things as they are."[24]

Gordon Comstock in Keep the Aspidistra Flying had been a member of the small self-conscious intelligentsia to be found in any public school who after World War I expressed their impatience with their elders by adopting beliefs that were bound to irritate them: "For a whole year they ran an unofficial monthly paper called the Bolshevik. . . . It advocated Socialism, free love, the dismemberment of the British Empire, the abolition of the Army and Navy. . . . It was great fun. Every intelligent boy of sixteen is a Socialist. At that age one does not see the hook sticking out of the rather stodgy bait."[25]

Rather later, acting as the devil's advocate in The Road to Wigan Pier, Orwell presented the case against socialism with the same powerful advocacy that led some readers to misunderstand 1984. Indeed one might suppose, as Victor Gollancz did, that he agreed with some of his own arguments. He thought it unfortunate that socialism was so closely linked with progress and machine civilization, since there were many like himself who accepted the machine "as one accepts a drug—that is, grudgingly and suspiciously."[26] We have already described the crankiness and snobbishness he found common among Socialists, and power-hunger was there too. According to Richard Rees, Orwell had a stock answer for those who said that under socialism people would not feel at the mercy of unpredictable and irresponsible powers: "I notice people always say *'under* Socialism.' They look forward to being on top— with all the others underneath, being told what is good for them."[27]

Along with his criticisms of socialism Orwell was justifiably gloomy about the prospects for Great Britain after the war. He thought that the Soviet Union and the United States would be hostile to the Labour party, and his fears were intensified by the feeling that its leaders would not be sufficiently courageous to face the contradiction between the long-term need to balance imports with exports and the short-term desire of the people for a higher standard of living. In 1948, he wrote:

> One sees here the still unresolved contradiction that dwells at the heart of the Socialist movement. Socialism, a creed which grew up in the industrialized western countries, means better material conditions for the white proletariat; it also means liberation for the exploited colored peoples. But the two aims, at least temporarily, are incompatible. The leaders of the Socialist movement have never said this, or never said it loudly enough, and they are now paying for their timidity.[28]

The evidence shows that Orwell was dubious about certain features of the Socialist movement before going to Spain, but it does not substantiate the claim that the purge trials disillusioned him with socialism. Orwell was not a Marxist, and we have seen that his socialism was always moral in character, much closer to what he called the "ethical, quasi-religious tradition, deriving ultimately from evangelical Protestantism," than to doctrinaire Marxism.[29] He says of his own political ideas: "On the whole up to 1930 I didn't consider myself a Socialist. By nature I had as yet no clearly defined political views. I became a Socialist more out of disgust with the oppressed and neglected life of the poorer section of the industrial workers than out of any theoretical understanding of a planned society."[30]

By 1941 his feelings and ideas had crystallized. At the time of Dunkirk and for a short period thereafter he was alarmed by the possibility of military defeat and enraged by the feebleness of English leadership, which he traced to the archaic class and social structure: "A generation of the unteachable is hanging upon us like a necklace of corpses." To save England was not simply, he wrote, a matter of introducing a planned war economy superior to that of the Fascists, but of speeding up the English revolution which had started several years earlier: "Obviously there is also needed a complete shift of power. New blood, new men, new ideas—in the true sense of the word, a revolution." The coincidence in 1941 of the historical moment of near defeat and people's eagerness for thoroughgoing change had made war and revolution seem inseparable. Street fighting and bloodshed might be avoided, but if not he was ready to take part in "a conscious, open revolt by ordinary people against inefficiency, class privilege and the rule of the old" in order to establish a "classless, ownerless society."[31]

The frustration of these hopes did not lead to disillusionment. In 1945, for example, Orwell was saying that the middle-class *rentier*, the Communist, and the fellow-traveler were all, for different reasons, in agreement that a "collectivist society would destroy human individuality." But they were mistaken. "It does not occur to them that the so-called collectivist systems now existing only try to wipe out the individual because they are *not* really collectivist and certainly not egalitarian—because, in fact, they are a sham covering a new form of class privilege. If one can see this, one can defy the insect-men with a good conscience."[32] And we find the gloomy pessimist Orwell also praising Wilde and Morris, despite their errors and outdated ideas, because "they do at least look beyond the era of food queues and party squabbles, and remind the Socialist movement of its original, half-forgotten objective of human brotherhood."[33]

We may also note that in March 1947 and again in October 1948 Orwell was writing seriously about a Socialist United States of Europe as a feasible alternative to preventive war against the Soviet Union (advocated under certain conditions by Burnham and Bertrand Russell) or fusion with the United States of America. This alternative meant an effort "somewhere or other—not in Norway or New Zealand, but over a large area—to make democratic Socialism work":

> If one could somewhere present the spectacle of economic security without concentration camps, the pretext for the Russian dictatorship would disappear and Communism would lose much of its appeal. But the only feasible area is western Europe plus Africa. The idea of forming this vast territory into a Socialist United States has as yet hardly gained any ground, and the practical and psychological difficulties in the way are enormous. Still, it is a *possible* project if people really wanted it, and if there were ten or twenty years of assured peace in which to bring it about. And since the initiative would have to come in the first place from Britain, the im-

portant thing is that this idea should take root among British Socialists.[34]

Orwell acknowledged that the idea did not as yet have much "magnetism," and he found fault with Burnham's book *The Struggle for the World* because he felt that the pessimistic world-view of Burnham and others like him might prevail at the cost of the idea he was advocating. A writer who proposes the extension of social democracy on this scale and who criticizes those whose work weakens its chances for success cannot properly be said to be disillusioned "with every form and shade of Socialism."

On the contrary, the varied evidence we have reviewed on this point supports Orwell's categorical denial that 1984 was an attack on socialism or the British Labour party. The evidence also refutes the claim that Orwell had succumbed to a mysticism of cruelty or that the purge trials had destroyed his faith in reason and in so doing had reduced him to despair. It strengthens the argument for interpreting 1984 as a warning against the "perversions to which a centralized economy is liable" and the totalitarian ideas that had taken root among the intellectuals.

XVI

THE VISION OF UTOPIA

FROM the perspective of literary and intellectual history *Animal Farm* and *1984* mark the close of an era that has lasted since the end of the eighteenth century. "All animals are equal, but some animals are more equal than others" and the summary adjective "Orwellian" now resonate significantly even in minds not otherwise aware that the books memorialize a false vision of human beings and their prospects—the vision of Utopia. As late as 1914 it was still possible to believe, despite the brutality of early industrialism, that human society and human beings were perfectible, if not through the Christian change of heart, then as the consequence of material progress animated by humanitarian zeal.[1]

Socialism and anarchism are permeated with this belief. Man is naturally good; once the state has been improved or abolished, once men have been freed from the mind- and soul-destroying burden of manual labor and have leisure to cultivate their innate talents, something like a Golden Age will begin—this is the general line of thought. World War I put an end to this dream in its more naive forms, but many continued to believe that a secular faith like Marxism, embodied with such seeming vitality in the Soviet Union, was still credible. The great purges, World War II, and the continued repression in Central and Eastern Europe have made it virtually impossible to accept any longer that version of the materialist ideal or the moral passion that once inspired it.

Utopian literature in the nineteenth century had incorporated this ideal. In Wells's *When the Sleeper Wakes* (1899) the dominant theme is still that the masses, awakening to their own strength, can themselves through a salutary and justifiable violence create a new and better order. By 1935, however, even Wells was writing, in *The Shape of Things to Come*, of the need for a puritan elite, his samurai in a new form, to seize power and compel human beings to do what was good for them. He imagined a conflict between his World Council and the Roman Catholic church in which the council is victorious, thus ending "a practical truce that had endured nearly three centuries in the matter of moral teaching, in the organization of motive. . . . The new government meant not only to rule the planet but the human will."[2]

The new elite in this society believe that "there can be only one right way of looking at the world for a normal human being," and their duty is to carry out the "mental reconstruction of the race." The Puritan Tyranny purges from the mind of the race the malign influence of tradition. It does away with eccentric types of humanity and disinfects literature. After its task is completed it is somehow peacefully replaced by the "Department of General Psychology" and the Age of Frustration is brought to a close. Wells sees nothing evil in these developments. He is ingenuous, not malicious, logical and not satirical. A few years later he gave up even this trust in the cleansing effect of a new tyranny, having concluded that humanity was done for.

Wells's books are a reliable graph of the decline of confidence in this version of human progress, and Orwell was the first of his successors to see that the hedonistic utopia was finished as an ideal and, except for satire, as a literary mode. It is true that Huxley had reached the same conclusion, though neither Huxley nor Zamyatin was able to imagine the new state of affairs with sufficient rigor or comprehensiveness. In their books the world created by scientific, humanitarian progress still flourishes; they see some of its dangers, but they do not represent the ideal itself as having turned into its opposite. Those who accept the tyranny can still lead comfortable lives. Only unusual persons, those susceptible to love, for instance, get into trouble.

Orwell looks at things from a different point of view. In *We* and *Brave New World* there still lingers something of the Benthamite ideal of maximizing pleasure and minimizing pain. In *1984* the ideal has been inverted. For most people in Huxley's world the worst thing is to be deprived of soma; in *We* the worst thing is to die. But the worst punishment in *1984* is to be compelled to live. Pain is everything to materialists like O'Brien and Winston Smith. Smith can be transformed by pain, recreated by pain—that is, in fact, what happens to him. The distinctive way in which Orwell views the materialistic utopia is vividly expressed by George Bowling after he bites into what is supposed to be a sausage and finds it filled with fish:

> It gave me the feeling that I'd bitten into the modern world and discovered what it is really made of. . . . Everything slick and

streamlined, everything made out of something else. Celluloid, rubber, chromium-steel everywhere, arc-lamps blazing all night, glass roofs over your head, radios all playing the same tune, no vegetation left, everything cemented over, mock-turtles grazing under the neutral fruit trees. But when you come down to brass tacks and get your teeth into something solid, a sausage, for instance, that's what you get. Rotten fish in a rubber skin. Bombs of filth bursting inside your mouth.[3]

The inner nature of this world is what Orwell has penetrated in *1984*, showing the transformation of pleasure into pain and developing the corrupt nature of the ideal itself. In 1942 Orwell wrote a short review of another "Utopia book" called *An Unknown Land* by H. L. Samuel. He remarks there that in trying to depict a utopia favorably it fails, as other books of its sort do, because it cannot "describe a society which is anywhere near perfection and which any normal human being would want to live in." He lists the pleasant features of the society described in the book—the labor-saving machines, the absence of war, crime, poverty, and other ills, and then asks: "Why is it that such 'ideal' conditions as these are always so profoundly unappetizing to read about? One is driven to conclude that fully human life is not thinkable without a considerable mixture of evil."[4]

In a world without evil, humor and fun cannot exist, and the inhabitants of this utopia are characteristically smug. Commenting on their artificially enlarged skulls, he says: "It is noticeable that a 'perfect' society only becomes thinkable if the human mind and even human physiology are somehow got rid of." A like defect can be found, he said, even in the fourth book of *Gulliver's Travels*. To represent an ideal good, Swift turned from men to horses, with the result that "where Swift is describing as best he can the way in which reasonable beings would live . . . a note of melancholy intrudes and the narrative even becomes boring."[5]

Viscount Samuel, in other words, has with perfect good will described a world unfit for human beings to live in. The tendency latent in the materialist ideal of perfection is to regard human beings as objects and to treat them as such. If one begins with the materialist assumptions, there is no reason to exclude human beings from their application, and the Inner Party, quite logically, does not. Bentham supposed that life's possibilities could be measured by the calculus of pleasure and pain, but why should he have assumed that pleasure is good and pain evil? The reverse may be true. If human beings are thought of as material, they will be treated like material—molded, destroyed, transformed—as Winston Smith is. From Butler to Zamyatin writers had foreseen the possibility that eagerness to achieve the utopian ideal through the increasing use of machines might lead to the subjugation of men. Others had warned of the evils of pleasure, which could seduce the reformer or the revolutionary from his task of perfecting human beings and society. Orwell alone represented the ideal carried as far as it could go, and in so doing he revealed that it was inhuman.[6]

Orwell's preoccupation with the intellectuals over a considerable part of his career as a writer shaped, as we have seen, many of the ideas that culminated in *1984*. Intellectuals are also, however, an important feature of the book itself. It is rather surprising that more critics have not asked the question: Who rules the world of *1984*? In Huxley's utopia the intelligent are in control, but apart from his emphasis on the mental abilities needed to maintain a stable society and their use of science to obtain the benefits of a hedonistically conceived common good, they are not otherwise characterized. In *We* also the question of who rules and why is left vague. The Benefactor is in charge, assisted by technicians; but neither his nature nor his interests are elaborated by Zamyatin.

With Orwell it is different. The reader is already familiar with Orwell's statement of his intention in writing *1984*, but one sentence of it bears repeating: "I believe also that totalitarian ideas have taken root in the minds of intellectuals everywhere, and I have tried to draw these ideas out to their logical consequences." In recent times intellectuals as a class have grown far more powerful than they used to be, not only because they are creators and purveyors of ideas but also because they are managers. Orwell had before him the examples of Germany and the Soviet Union where intellectuals occupied places of great power. He was also familiar with Burnham's demonstration of the change taking place less obviously in other countries.

The new elite is composed of executives and technicians of all sorts—bureaucrats, military men, publicists—the experts needed for the efficient operation of a complex industrial civilization.[7] Intellectual pursuits have multiplied, and they have begun to coincide on an ever larger scale with the practical needs of society. Burnham's managers are intellectuals, and this is the way Orwell was beginning to see them. Rees noticed this comprehension growing in Orwell's mind:

Sometime between 1941 and 1947 the main burden of his political animosity seems to have subtly shifted. In *Inside the Whale* (1940) the unpatriotic, deracinated intellectual was one of his principal *bêtes noires*. The "Communism" of the English intellectual, he said, was simply the patriotism of the deracinated. The other big *bête noire* was, of course, the capitalist boss. But already by 1943, in *Poetry and the Microphone*, the bureaucrat with his "genteel throaty voice" begins to subsume in his own person both the boss and the delinquent intellectual. This proves, I think, that Orwell was both prescient and realistic. He worked in broadcasting during the war, and he was already beginning to see where the real danger lay—the enormous power of a technological bureaucracy.[8]

The intellectuals, more and more commonly enrolled in the service of industry and the state, are also the bureaucrats whose talents are not merely those of technicians but also those of manipulators and directors of people. Orwell's political animosity did not shift; it is directed at the same group, now vastly enlarged and much more powerful.

We have studied in detail what Orwell meant by the growth of totalitarian ideas in the minds of intellectuals. He believed they were taking over the direction of a muddled world because their sense of order was offended by the disorganization and loose ends, as well as the sheer waste, of modern life. To achieve their aims they were willing to abandon the liberal tradition in which they had been reared, where individualism and the ideal of political freedom had been so important. At the same time the worship of power expanded among them, stimulated by their success in the Soviet Union and Nazi Germany. They encouraged the emphasis on doctrine and ideology in movements of a quasi-political nature, so that their own talents might have a wider field to work in.

Seeking to explain the intellectuals' fascination with Hitler, Stephen Spender touched on another aspect of this complex development, one which Orwell was also quite aware of, as we know from our discussion of *Notes from Underground:*

> The intelligentsia also had more sinister reasons for underrating Hitler. These were the elements of pure destructiveness, of attraction to evil for its own sake, and of a search for spiritual damnation, which had been present in some European literature for the past century, and which were fulfilled in Nazi politics. European literature had diagnosed, without purging itself of, the evil of nihilism. In Hitlerism the nightmares of Dostoevsky's *The Possessed*, of Nietzsche, and of Wagner, were made real. The cultured Europeans recognized in this political movement some of their most hidden fantasies. Hatred of it was deeply involved with a sense of their own

guilt. As though to demonstrate this to the utmost, certain writers in the occupied countries were actually to welcome Hitler as a destructive force which their art had prophesied.[9]

Spender might well have cited some writers from unoccupied countries, for they too regarded Hitler as a necessary "scourge of the Lord." Orwell at one point was, he said, prepared to draw up a list of intellectuals who would be willing to collaborate with the Nazis if they succeeded in invading England.

When Orwell wrote *1984* as a means of drawing out the logical consequences of the totalitarian ideas which had taken root in the minds of intellectuals, he discarded the traditional rulers of Utopia, the benevolent despots, and chose instead the class of ambitious and disaffected intellectuals he was so familiar with. O'Brien is the only member of the Inner Party who has an important place in the book, and he might very well be Big Brother. O'Brien concentrates in himself the aims and talents of the new ruling class, which are those of the intellectual. As a matter of scientific technique, O'Brien consciously uses argument and force to make Winston Smith obey him, and what he is aiming at is an intellectual achievement—he wants to change Smith's mind. All the issues they consider together lie in the intellectual's special province: the relation between the knower and the known, the reasons for action, the nature and use of history, language, ethics, metaphysics—there is scarcely an important philosophical question they do not examine. The circumstances and spirit of their discourse are so disagreeable that it abuses language to speak of their Socratic dialogue, yet it is nevertheless a dialogue between teacher and pupil.

O'Brien's object is what was once one of philosophy's most comforting goals: "an ideal clarity illuminating an ideal stasis." For the state he envisions a perverted Marxism in which history comes to an end, perfection having been attained. For the individual he seeks perfect unity of thought, feeling, and action—the love of Big Brother. Winston Smith's mind is occupied with the same problems that interest O'Brien. Both exhibit the destructive strain dramatized by Dostoevsky, and it is Smith's principal misfortune that having, like O'Brien, abandoned traditional morality he remains too decent, too human, to accept the consequences of what this means in practice. No wonder Orwell thought of calling his book *The Last Man in Europe*. As followers of Machiavelli, the chief difference between them is that Smith fails and O'Brien succeeds. Ironically, we find in Oceania the same characteristics of the perfect state that Plato laid down in *The Republic* and that are repeated with variations in the nineteenth-century utopias: total organization of the lives of the citizens, perfect justice for each man according to the laws of love, the rule of the philosopher king. It is, I think, significant that his essay "Second Thoughts on James Burnham" sums up Orwell's belief that the new and growing class of intellectual-bureaucrats secretly wished "to destroy the old, equalitarian version of Socialism and usher in a hierarchical society where the intellectual can at last get his hands on the whip."[10]

Whether or not *1984* is an ideological superweapon, one can say that it changed the world by representing the past and present so as to modify people's expectations of the future. Owing to his talent for assimilating the work of his predecessors and his power to concentrate life's intellectual and spiritual experiences so intensely, Orwell was able to show readers that the ideal of the hedonistic utopia had been shattered. Momentous events in the actual world were, of course, the cause, but these are so remarkably crystallized in *1984* that literature and the world since then have been different. We are compelled to think again about what it means to create a society deserving to be called decent.

NOTES

CHAPTER I

1. Richard Rees, "George Orwell," *Scots Chronicle* [*Burns Chronicle and Club Directory*], [26] (1951), 7–14. The magazine referred to was the *Adelphi,* edited by Rees. See Peter Stansky and William Abrahams, *The Unknown Orwell* (London: Constable and Co., 1972), pp. 172 and 261 n.
2. Letter to Francis A. Henson, 16 June 1949, in *The Collected Essays, Journalism and Letters of George Orwell,* ed. by Sonia Orwell and Ian Angus, IV: *In Front of Your Nose 1945–1950* (London: Secker and Warburg, 1968), 30.
3. *The Unknown Orwell* by Stansky and Abrahams deals only with the first thirty years of Orwell's life. At the time of this writing Mrs. Sonia Orwell had just announced in the press that Professor Bernard Crick of Birkbeck College had been authorized to write the life of her husband.
4. George Orwell, "Politics vs. Literature: an Examination of 'Gulliver's Travels,' " in *Shooting an Elephant* (New York: Harcourt, Brace and Co., 1950), p. 62.
5. George Orwell, "Wells, Hitler and the World State," in *Dickens, Dali and Others* (New York: Harcourt, Brace and Co., 1946), p. 122.
6. George Orwell, "The Male Byronic," *Tribune* (London), 21 June 1940.
7. George Orwell, *Nineteen Eighty-Four* (New York: Harcourt, Brace and Co., 1949), p. 189.
8. Orwell, "Male Byronic," p. 21.
9. H. G. Wells, *When the Sleeper Wakes* (New York: Ace Books, n.d.), p. 102.
10. H. G. Wells, *The New Machiavelli* (New York: Duffield and Co., 1910), pp. 114–15.
11. Ibid.
12. Ibid., p. 199.
13. Ibid., p. 320.

14. Ibid., p. 9.
15. George Orwell, *The Road to Wigan Pier* (New York: Harcourt, Brace and World, 1958), p. 235.
16. Ibid., p. 234.
17. George Orwell, "Prophecies of Fascism," *Tribune* (London), 12 July 1940, in *Collected Essays*, II: *My Country Right or Left 1940–1943*, 30.
18. Wells, *When the Sleeper Wakes*, p. 229.
19. Ibid., p. 147.
20. Orwell, "Male Byronic," p. 21.
21. Orwell, "Wells, Hitler and the World State," p. 123.
22. H. G. Wells, *The Island of Dr. Moreau* (Garden City, N.Y.: Garden City Publishing Co., 1896), pp. 107–8.
23. Ibid., p. 144.
24. George Orwell, "Vessel of Wrath," *Observer* (London), 21 May 1944.
25. Orwell, "Prophecies of Fascism," p. 30.
26. Jack London, *The Iron Heel* (New York: Grayson Publishing Corp., 1948), pp. x–xi.
27. Orwell, "Prophecies of Fascism," p. 30.
28. George Orwell, "Jack London," BBC broadcast, 8 October 1945. Script No. 37 in Orwell Archive.
29. George Orwell, "Introduction to *Love of Life and Other Stories* by Jack London," in *Collected Essays*, IV, 24.
30. London, *Iron Heel*, p. 96.
31. Ibid., p. 97.
32. Ibid., pp. 98–99.
33. Ibid., n. 1, pp. 79–80.
34. Orwell, "Introduction to *Love of Life*," p. 24.
35. William L. Shirer, *The Rise and Fall of the Third Reich: A History of Nazi Germany* (New York: Simon and Schuster, 1959), pp. 957–58.
36. London, *Iron Heel*, n. 1, p. 303.
37. Ibid., n. 1, p. 33; George Orwell, "As I Please," *Tribune* (London), 17 March 1944, in *Collected Essays*, III: *As I Please 1943–1945*, 110.
38. Orwell, *Nineteen Eighty-Four*, p. 271.
39. Orwell, "Introduction to *Love of Life*," p. 28.
40. Orwell, "Prophecies of Fascism," p. 31.
41. George Orwell, "The Re-Discovery of Europe," in *Talking to India*, ed. by George Orwell (London: Allen and Unwin, 1943), p. 50.
42. Orwell, *Road to Wigan Pier*, p. 235.
43. Geoffrey Ashe, "Second Thoughts on *Nineteen Eighty-Four*," *The Month*, 4 (November 1950), 286–87.
44. Irving Howe, *Orwell's* Nineteen Eighty-Four: *Text, Sources, Criticism* (New York: Harcourt, Brace and World, 1963), p. 169.

45. Cyril Connolly, "Year Nine," *New Statesman and Nation,* 29 January 1938. Reprinted in Cyril Connolly, *The Condemned Playground; Essays: 1927–1944* (New York: Macmillan Co., 1946), pp. 154–59.
46. George Orwell, "A Nipping Air," *Observer* (London), 2 December 1945.
47. Orwell, "Politics vs. Literature," p. 72.
48. Ibid., p. 73.
49. Ibid., pp. 62–63.
50. Ibid., p. 63.
51. Ibid., p. 64.
52. Ibid., p. 60.
53. Ibid., pp. 65–66.
54. Ibid., p. 66.
55. Ibid.
56. G. K. Chesterton, *The Napoleon of Notting Hill* (London: John Lane, 1904), p. 15.
57. Ibid., p. 208.
58. George Orwell, "The Scientist Takes Over," *Manchester Evening News,* 16 August 1945.
59. George Orwell, "James Burnham and the Managerial Revolution," in *Collected Essays,* IV, 163.
60. G. K. Chesterton, *The Man Who Was Thursday* (New York: Modern Library, n.d.), pp. 61–62.
61. Ibid., p. 91.
62. Ibid., p. 126.
63. Ibid., pp. 188–89.
64. Rudyard Kipling, *A Diversity of Creatures* (London: Macmillan and Co., 1917), pp. 43–44.
65. George Orwell, "As I Please," *Tribune* (London), 3 December 1943.
66. George Orwell, "New Novels," *New Statesman and Nation,* 4 June 1941.
67. John Mair, *Never Come Back* (London: Victor Gollancz, 1941), p. 174.
68. Ibid., p. 69.
69. Ibid., p. 187.
70. Ibid., p. 234.
71. Ibid., p. 240.
72. Isaac Deutscher, " '1984'—The Mysticism of Cruelty," in Deutscher, *Russia in Transition* (rev. ed.; New York: Grove Press, 1960), p. 252.
73. George Woodcock, *The Crystal Spirit: A Study of George Orwell* (Boston: Little, Brown and Co., 1966), pp. 209–16.
74. George Orwell, "Freedom and Happiness," *Tribune,* 4 January 1946, in *Collected Essays,* IV, 75. I have not been able to establish with certainty the date when Orwell first read *We.* Deutscher cites Orwell's comments on *We* as these appeared in *Tribune* of January 4,

1946, but one must question his statement that these are "a conclusive piece of evidence, supplied by Orwell himself, on the origin
of *1984*." He does not explain why the article is "conclusive" evidence, and he makes no further point about the date; his implication
is that Orwell read the book toward the end of 1945. This may be
true, for in Orwell's article he says, "Several years after hearing of its
existence, I have at last got my hands on a copy of Zamiatin's *We*";
later in the same article he says, "The English translation was published in the United States, and I have never been able to procure
a copy; but copies of the French translation (the title is *Nous Autres*)
do exist, and I have at last succeeded in borrowing one" (*Tribune*,
4 January 1946). The repetition of "at last" in these passages appears to imply a date close to the writing of the *Tribune* article,
i.e., late 1945.

Some evidence exists, however, that Orwell read *We* before this.
George Woodcock says, "He first read *We* several years before
starting work on *1984*, and my own introduction to Zamiatin's book
came in 1943 when Orwell lent me a French translation, which he
later made the subject of one of his weekly literary pieces in the
London *Tribune* (George Woodcock, "Utopias in Negative," *Sewanee
Review*, Winter 1956, p. 90). The date specified by Woodcock raises
the question of what Orwell meant by "at last." Further evidence
bearing on the point is in a letter written to Ian Angus, the Deputy
Librarian of University College, London, by another friend of Orwell, Alan Murray Williams, who says he lent *Nous Autres* to
Orwell some time after June 1944. He believes that the loan must
have been after this date, and hence a year later than the date cited
by Woodcock, because he published an article in *Tribune* in June
1944 entitled "What is Socialist Realism?"; and it was after this
article appeared that he lent his copy of the book to Orwell. One
more source of information may be mentioned, a letter dated
February 17, 1944, from Orwell to Gleb Struve thanking him for a
copy of his book *25 Years of Russian Literature*. In the letter Orwell
says, "It has already roused my interest in Zamyatin's *We*, which
I had not heard of before. I am interested in that kind of book, and
even keep making notes for one myself that may get written sooner
or later" (see *Collected Essays*, III, 95). Orwell wrote to Frederic
Warburg that he first thought of the book that was to be his last
work in 1943, and to Roger Senhouse he wrote: "I thought of it in
1944 as a result of the Teheran Conference." These two statements
are not as contradictory as they may at first appear, since the Teheran
Conference took place from November 28 to December 1, 1943
(*Collected Essays*, IV, 448, 460).

From this conflicting evidence I conclude that Mr. Woodcock's
memory may be faulty and that 1943 is too early a date for Orwell
to have read *We*. His "at last" has to be interpreted elastically enough

to cover the period between June 1944 and the latter part of 1945.

75. George Orwell, "As I Please," *Tribune* (London), 24 January 1947.
76. George Orwell, Letter to Gleb Struve, 21 April 1948, in *Collected Essays*, IV, 417.
77. George Orwell, Letter to F. J. Warburg, 30 March 1949, in *Collected Essays*, IV, 486.
78. Orwell, "Freedom and Happiness," IV, 74.
79. Woodcock, *Crystal Spirit*, pp. 215–16.
80. Orwell, "Freedom and Happiness," IV, 75.
81. Eugene Zamiatin, *We* (New York: E. P. Dutton and Co., [1959]), p. 32.
82. George Orwell, "Return Journey," *Observer* (London), 9 July 1944.
83. Orwell, "Freedom and Happiness," IV, 75.
84. Orwell, *Nineteen Eighty-Four*, p. 265.
85. For a useful analysis of the rational-irrational opposition, see D. Richards, "Four Utopias," *Slavonic and East European Review*, 40 (1961–62), 220–28.
86. Stephen Spender, *The Creative Element* (New York: British Book Center, 1954), p. 130.

CHAPTER II

1. Arthur Koestler, *Darkness at Noon* (New York: Macmillan Co., 1941); Boris Souvarine, "Cauchemar en U.R.S.S.," *Revue de Paris*, 1 July 1937. Orwell refers to this latter work as a pamphlet, but it can more easily be found in the source cited here.
2. George Orwell, "Notes on the Way," *Time and Tide*, 6 April 1940, in *Collected Essays*, II, 16.
3. George Orwell, "James Burnham and the Managerial Revolution," in *Collected Essays*, IV, 160.
4. George Orwell, "Revolt in the Urban Desert," *Observer* (London), 10 October 1943.
5. George Orwell, *Down and Out in Paris and London* (Garden City, N.Y.: Doubleday and Co., Permabooks, 1954), p. 130.
6. George Orwell, "Review of *The British Way in Warfare* by B. H. Liddell Hart," *New Statesman and Nation*, 21 November 1942, in *Collected Essays*, II, 248.
7. George Orwell, "Vessel of Wrath," *Observer* (London), 21 May 1944.
8. George Orwell, *Nineteen Eighty-Four* (New York: Harcourt, Brace and Co., 1949), p. 191.
9. Hilaire Belloc, *The Servile State* (London: T. N. Foulis, 1912), p. 6.
10. Ibid., p. 101.
11. George Orwell, "The Christian Reformers," *Manchester Evening News*, 7 February 1946.

12. George Orwell, "As I Please," *Tribune* (London), 31 March 1944, in *Collected Essays*, III, 118.

13. George Orwell, "New Novels," *New Statesman and Nation*, 4 January 1941.

14. "Jadis, Galilée dut avouer à genoux, sous la menace du boucher, que la terre ne tournait pas. Les prisonniers de Moscou avouent des choses non moins énormes." Souvarine, "Cauchemar en U.R.S.S.," p. 137.

15. "Personne ne se souci de vérité, ni les juges, ni les accusateurs, ni les accusés, ni la presse, mais tout le monde s'applique à glorifier un certain Staline et à couvrir d'opprobre un nommé Trotski." Ibid., p. 142.

16. ". . . l'immuable accusé, éternel coupable." Ibid.

17. Ibid., p. 156.

18. "Les tortures morales dispensent de recourir aux tortures physiques. La Guépéou a acquis dans ce domaine une science raffinée dont les effets sont tangibles. Elle égale ou surpasse l'Inquisition, à laquelle nombre de commentateurs se sont référés spontanément à ce propos. Lors du 'procès des menchéviks' Léon Blum a écrit une page magistrale sur 'l'exhibitionisme de l'aveu,' montrant 'qu'à la perversion morale, la terreur Stalinienne ajoute une sorte de décomposition mentale.' Un autre éminent leader socialiste, F. Adler, a comparé avec raison le procès Zinoviev aux procès de sorcellerie du moyen-âge. Ici, Trotski remplace le diable." Ibid., p. 167.

19. "Un accusé avoue être allé de Berlin à Copenhague, en compagnie de Sédov, pour y rencontrer l'exilé [Trotsky] à l'hôtel Bristol. Il est établi et prouvé que l'hôtel n'existe plus depuis vingt ans, que Sédov n'a jamais mis les pieds à Copenhague, que l'entrevue est de pure invention." Ibid., p. 160.

20. Orwell, "New Novels."

21. George Orwell, *Homage to Catalonia* (Boston: Beacon Press, 1952), p. 211.

22. Orwell, "New Novels."

23. Ibid.

24. Koestler, *Darkness at Noon*, p. 185.

25. Ibid., p. 228.

26. Orwell, "New Novels."

27. Koestler, *Darkness at Noon*, pp. 97–98.

28. Ibid., pp. 174–75.

29. George Orwell, "As I Please," *Tribune* (London), 29 November 1946, in *Collected Essays*, IV, 249. This passage is quoted also by Milovan Djilas in *The New Class: An Analysis of the Communist System* (New York: Frederick A. Praeger, 1958), p. 150.

30. Koestler, *Darkness at Noon*, p. 95.

31. Ibid., p. 99.

32. Ibid., pp. 176–77.

33. Ibid., pp. 257–58.
34. Ibid., pp. 6–7.
35. Ibid., p. 9.
36. Ibid., pp. 58–59.
37. Ibid., p. 81.
38. Ibid., p. 199.
39. For an interesting study of the relation between *1984* and *Darkness at Noon*, see R. G. Geering, " 'Darkness at Noon' and '1984'—A Comparative Study," *Australian Quarterly*, 30 (September 1958), 90–96.
40. Sir Paul Dukes, *An Epic of the Gestapo* (London: Cassell and Co., 1940), p. 50.
41. Ibid., p. 76.
42. Ibid., p. 151.
43. Ibid., p. 249.
44. "Wer Hitler dient, dient Deutschland;/ Wer Deutschland dient, dient Gott." Ibid., p. 269.
45. George Orwell, "Propaganda in Novels," *Tribune* (London), 31 September 1940.
46. Erika Mann, *The Lights Go Down* (London: Secker and Warburg, 1940), p. 36.
47. George Orwell, "Life in London's Underworld," *Tribune* (London), 23 August 1940.
48. Julia de Beausobre, *The Woman Who Could Not Die* (London: Chatto and Windus, 1938), p. 32.
49. Ibid., p. 85.
50. Ibid., p. 53.
51. Ibid., p. 168.
52. Ibid., p. 253.

CHAPTER III

1. James H. Meisel, *Counterrevolution: How Revolutions Die* (New York: Atherton Press, 1966), p. 112.
2. Christopher Hollis, *A Study of George Orwell: The Man and His Works* (London: Hollis and Carter, 1956), p. 196; Michael Maddison, "1984: A Burnhamite Fantasy," *Political Quarterly*, 32 (January–March, 1961), 71–79; Frank Wadsworth, "Orwell as a Novelist: The Early Work," *University of Kansas City Review*, 22 (Winter 1955), 93–99, "Orwell as a Novelist: The Middle Period," ibid. (Spring 1956), 189–94, "Orwell's Later Work," ibid. (Summer 1956), 285–90; John Mander, "George Orwell's Politics," *Contemporary Review*, January 1960, pp. 32–36, and February 1960, pp. 113–19; Adrian Cunningham, Review of Orwell's *Down and Out in Paris and London*, *Granta*, 15 February 1964. [*Granta* is the

Cambridge University literary magazine. A later issue of the magazine contained a letter of comment on the review by Howard Fink,
dated April 4, 1964, with a rejoinder by Adrian Cunningham.]

3. James Burnham, *The Managerial Revolution: What Is Happening
in the World* (New York: John Day Co., 1941), p. 29.
4. George Orwell, "James Burnham and the Managerial Revolution," in
Collected Essays, IV, 162.
5. Burnham, *Managerial Revolution*, p. 54.
6. Ibid., p. 216.
7. Ibid., p. 73.
8. Ibid., p. 122.
9. Ibid.
10. Ibid., p. 198.
11. Ibid., p. 126.
12. Ibid., pp. 123–24.
13. Ibid., p. 75.
14. Ibid., p. 132.
15. Ibid., pp. 181–82.
16. Ibid.
17. Ibid., pp. 175–76.
18. Ibid., p. 178.
19. Ibid., pp. 178–80.
20. Ibid., p. 137.
21. Ibid.
22. Ibid., p. 228.
23. Ibid., p. 132.
24. Ibid., p. 152.
25. As evidence of this latter point, Orwell cited an essay in *Horizon*
whose author subscribed to Burnham's "main thesis . . . almost without examination." George Orwell, "As I Please," *Tribune* (London),
14 January 1944, in *Collected Essays*, III, 74. Orwell does not
identify this writer, but he was probably Dennis Routh, whose review of *The Managerial Revolution* appeared in *Horizon* 6 (September 1942), 151–67.
26. George Orwell, "As I Please," *Tribune* (London), 14 January 1944.
27. Letters to the Editor, *Tribune* (London), 24 March 1944.
28. James Burnham, *The Machiavellians* (New York: John Day Co.,
1943), p. 41.
29. Ibid., p. 225.
30. George Orwell, "Why Machiavellis of Today Fall Down," *Manchester Evening News*, 20 January 1944.
31. Burnham, *Machiavellians*, p. 265.
32. Ibid., p. 269.
33. Orwell, "Why Machiavellis of Today Fall Down."
34. Orwell, *Collected Essays*, I: *An Age Like This 1920–1940*, 336.
35. Orwell, "Why Machiavellis of Today Fall Down."

36. Ibid.
37. George Orwell, "You and the Atom Bomb," *Tribune* (London), 19 October 1945, in *Collected Essays,* IV, 8–9.
38. Orwell, "James Burnham and the Managerial Revolution," IV, 165.
39. Ibid., p. 176.
40. Ibid., p. 173.
41. Ibid., p. 174.
42. George Orwell, "Burnham's View of the Contemporary World Struggle," *New Leader* (New York), 29 March 1947, in *Collected Essays,* IV, 313–26.
43. Ibid.

CHAPTER IV

1. D. S. Savage, George Woodcock, Alex Comfort, George Orwell, "Pacifism and the War: A Controversy," *Partisan Review,* September–October 1942, in *Collected Essays,* II, 224.
2. Ibid., p. 229.
3. Conor Cruise O'Brien, *Writers and Politics* (New York: Random House, 1964), p. 33.
4. John Mander, *Great Britain or Little England* (London: Penguin Books, 1963), p. 67.
5. George Orwell, "Raffles and Miss Blandish" in *Dickens, Dali and Others,* p. 218.
6. George Orwell, Letter to Richard Rees, *Encounter,* January 1962, in *Collected Essays,* IV, 478–79.
7. George Orwell, *The English People* (London: Collins, 1947), p. 14.
8. Orwell, "Raffles and Miss Blandish," p. 218. See also note by Dwight Macdonald, *Politics,* November 1944, p. 296.
9. George Orwell, "Who Are the War Criminals?" *Tribune* (London), 22 October 1943, in *Collected Essays,* II, 322.
10. Orwell, "Raffles and Miss Blandish," p. 220.
11. George Orwell, "Marx and Russia," *Observer* (London), 15 February 1948.
12. George Orwell, "James Burnham and the Managerial Revolution," in *Collected Essays,* IV, 179.
13. George Orwell, "As I Please," *Tribune* (London), 1 September 1944, in *Collected Essays,* III, 226–27.
14. George Orwell, "Burnham's View of the Contemporary World Struggle," in *Collected Essays,* IV, 16; "As I Please," *Tribune* (London), 14 January 1944, in *Collected Essays,* III, 73–74. Only part of the original column for this date is reprinted in *Collected Essays.*
15. George Orwell, "Notes on the Way," *Time and Tide,* 6 April 1940, in *Collected Essays,* II, 18.
16. George Orwell, "Catastrophic Gradualism," *C*[ommon] *W*[ealth] *Review,* November 1945, in *Collected Essays,* IV, 15–16.

17. Ibid., 16.
18. Ibid., 18.
19. See Mander, *Great Britain or Little England,* pp. 73–74.
20. George Orwell, "Arthur Koestler," in *Dickens, Dali and Others,* p. 189.
21. See Edward Thomas, *Orwell* (London: Oliver and Boyd, 1965), p. 93.

CHAPTER V

1. George Orwell, *The English People* (London: Collins, 1947), p. 14.
2. George Orwell, "Editorial to Polemic," *Polemic* 3 (May 1946), in *Collected Essays,* IV, 154, 156.
3. George Orwell, "Charles Dickens," in *Dickens, Dali and Others,* p. 73.
4. George Orwell, "As I Please," *Tribune* (London), 25 February 1944, in *Collected Essays,* III, 98.
5. George Orwell, "Raffles and Miss Blandish," in *Dickens, Dali and Others,* p. 219.
6. Orwell, *English People,* p. 14.
7. Ibid., pp. 18–19.
8. John Lehmann, *The Whispering Gallery* (New York: Harcourt, Brace and Co., 1954), p. 275.
9. George Orwell, "Notes on the Way," *Time and Tide,* 6 April 1940, in *Collected Essays,* II, 15.
10. Ibid.
11. Ibid., p. 16.
12. George Orwell, "Inside the Whale," in *Such, Such Were the Joys* (New York: Harcourt, Brace and Co., 1953), pp. 189–90.
13. George Orwell, Review of *Burnt Norton, East Coker, The Dry Salvages* by T. S. Eliot, *Poetry* (London), October–November 1942, in *Collected Essays,* II, 239.
14. Ibid.
15. Orwell, "Inside the Whale," pp. 190.
16. George Orwell, "Culture and Democracy," in *Victory or Vested Interest,* G. D. H. Cole et al. (London: Routledge, 1942), p. 85.
17. Ibid., p. 86.
18. George Orwell, "England Your England," in *Such, Such Were the Joys,* p. 224. This is Part I of *The Lion and the Unicorn, Collected Essays,* II, 56–78.
19. Orwell, "Culture and Democracy," p. 83.
20. George Orwell, "Britain's Struggle for Survival: The Labor Government after Three Years," *Commentary,* 6 (October 1948), 348–49.
21. Cecil Day-Lewis, *Starting Point* (New York: Harper and Bros., 1938), pp. 157, 216.
22. George Orwell, Review of *Great Morning* by Osbert Sitwell, *Adelphi,* July–September 1948, in *Collected Essays,* IV, 446.
23. George Orwell, "Going Down," *Observer* (London), 14 January 1945.

24. George Orwell, "The Christian Reformers," *Manchester Evening News*, 7 February 1944.

25. George Orwell, Review of *The Spirit of Catholicism* by Karl Adam, *New English Weekly*, 9 June 1932, in *Collected Essays*, I, 79–81.

26. George Orwell, "The Prevention of Literature," in *Shooting an Elephant*, pp. 106, 107, 110.

27. George Eliot, *Silas Marner* (New York: A. L. Burt, n.d.), chap. 10, p. 87.

28. Orwell, *English People*, p. 25.

29. Orwell, "Prevention of Literature," p. 117.

30. George Orwell, "As I Please," *Tribune* (London), 3 March 1944, in *Collected Essays*, III, 102.

31. Ibid., p. 103.

32. Orwell, "Shopkeepers at War," in *Collected Essays*, II, 88.

33. George Orwell, "London Letter," *Partisan Review*, November–December 1941, in *Collected Essays*, II, 148.

34. Ibid., p. 149.

35. George Orwell, "As I Please," *Tribune* (London), 23 June 1944, in *Collected Essays*, III, 174.

36. George Orwell, "The Meaning of a Poem," *The Listener*, 12 June 1941, in *Collected Essays*, II, 132–33; "Poet and Priest," *Observer* (London), 12 November 1944.

37. George Orwell, "As I Please," *Tribune* (London), 24 December 1943, in *Collected Essays*, III, 65; "Anti-Semitism in Britain," in *Such, Such Were the Joys*, pp. 105–6.

38. Orwell, Review of *Burnt Norton*, II, 240.

CHAPTER VI

1. C. S. Lewis, "Notes on the Way: George Orwell," *Time and Tide*, 8 January 1955, p. 43.

2. Neal Wood, *Communism and British Intellectuals* (New York: Columbia University Press, 1959), p. 28, n. 1.

3. Randall Swingler, "The Right to Free Expression (Annotated by George Orwell)," *Polemic* 5 (September–October 1946), 45–53.

4. Frederic Warburg, *An Occupation for Gentlemen* (London: Hutchinson, 1959), p. 232. See also John McNair, "George Orwell," *Socialist Leader*, 28 January 1950.

5. George Orwell, "Autobiographical Note," in *Collected Essays*, II, 23.

6. George Orwell, *New Statesman and Nation*, 24 August 1940.

7. George Orwell, Review of *The Novel Today* by Philip Henderson, *New English Weekly*, 31 December 1936, in *Collected Essays*, I, 258.

8. Orwell, *New Statesman and Nation*, 24 August 1940.

9. Ibid.
10. Victor Kravchenko, *I Chose Freedom* (New York: Charles Scribner's Sons, 1946), pp. 107–9.
11. Leslie Paul, *Angry Young Man* (London: Faber and Faber, 1951), p. 202.
12. Kingsley Martin, *Editor: A Second Volume of Autobiography* (London: Hutchinson of London, 1968), p. 207.
13. George Orwell, "The Faith of Thomas Mann," *Tribune* (London), 10 September 1943.
14. Cyril Connolly, *Enemies of Promise* (rev. ed., New York: Macmillan Co., 1948), pp. 164, 207.
15. George Orwell, *The Road to Wigan Pier* (New York: Harcourt, Brace and World, 1958), pp. 172–73.
16. Ibid., p. 180.
17. George Orwell, *The Lion and the Unicorn*, Part III: "The English Revolution," in *Collected Essays*, II, 96.
18. Orwell, *Road to Wigan Pier*, p. 246.
19. Orwell, "The English Revolution," II, 106. See also *Lion and Unicorn*, Part II: "Shopkeepers at War," in *Collected Essays*, II, 80–81.
20. Ibid., 79.
21. Orwell, *Road to Wigan Pier*, p. 206.
22. George Orwell, "Inside the Whale," in *Such, Such Were the Joys*, p. 176.
23. Stephen Spender, *World Within World* (New York: Harcourt, Brace and Co., 1948), p. 133.
24. Ibid., p. 128.
25. John Lehmann, *The Whispering Gallery* (New York: Harcourt, Brace and Co., 1954), p. 176.
26. Orwell, "Inside the Whale," p. 177.
27. John Strachey, *The Coming Struggle for Power* (New York: Modern Library, 1935), p. 358.
28. Philip Toynbee, *Friends Apart* (London: MacGibbon and Kee, 1954), pp. 18, 87.
29. Orwell, "Inside the Whale," p. 183.
30. Arthur Koestler, in *The God That Failed*, ed. by Richard Crossman (New York: Bantam Books, 1952), p. 61.
31. George Orwell, "Notes on Nationalism," in *Such, Such Were the Joys*, p. 83.
32. Ronald Blythe, *The Age of Illusion: England in the Twenties and Thirties 1919–1940* (London: Hamish Hamilton, 1963), p. 221.
33. Orwell, "Inside the Whale," p. 186.
34. Julian Symons, *The Thirties* (London: Cresset Press, 1960), p. 42.
35. Orwell, "English Revolution," II, 93–94.
36. Orwell, *Road to Wigan Pier*, p. 210.

37. Ibid., p. 167.
38. Ibid., p. 211.
39. Ibid., pp. 211–12.
40. Ibid.
41. Ibid., p. 212.
42. Franz Borkenau, *European Communism* (New York: Harper and Bros., 1953), p. 54.
43. Roger Fulford, *Votes for Women* (London: Faber and Faber, 1957), p. 36.
44. Swingler, "The Right to Free Expression," p. 53.
45. Orwell, *Road to Wigan Pier*, p. 214.
46. Orwell, "English Revolution," II, 92.
47. Ibid., II, 102.
48. George Orwell, Preface to the Ukrainian edition of *Animal Farm*, in *Collected Essays*, III, 402.
49. George Orwell and Desmond Hawkins, "The Proletarian Writer," *The Listener*, 19 December 1940, pp. 878–79.
50. Henry Pelling, *The British Communist Party* (New York: Macmillan Co., 1958), p. 106.
51. George Orwell, "London Letter," *Partisan Review*, November–December 1941, in *Collected Essays*, II, 147.
52. *Tribune* (London), 17 December 1943.
53. Correspondence columns, *Tribune* (London), 31 December 1943.
54. George Orwell, "London Letter," *Partisan Review*, Summer 1946, in *Collected Essays*, IV, 188.
55. Konni Zilliacus, Correspondence columns, *Tribune* (London), 17 January 1947, in *Collected Essays*, IV, 191–92.
56. George Orwell, Correspondence columns, *Tribune* (London), 17 January 1947, in *Collected Essays*, IV, 192–94.
57. Paul Winterton, Correspondence columns, *Tribune* (London), 24 January 1947.
58. Konni Zilliacus, Correspondence columns, *Tribune* (London), 24 January 1947.
59. George Orwell, Correspondence columns, *Tribune* (London), 31 January 1947.
60. Orwell, *Road to Wigan Pier*, pp. 235, 229–30.
61. George Orwell, Review in *Horizon* 4 (August 1941), 135.
62. George Orwell, Review of *Mein Kampf*, *New English Weekly*, 21 March 1940, in *Collected Essays*, II, 14.
63. Ibid.
64. George Orwell, "My Country Right or Left," *Folios of New Writing*, Autumn 1940, in *Collected Essays*, I, 540.
65. George Orwell, "Literature and Totalitarianism," *The Listener*, 19 June 1941, p. 882.

CHAPTER VII

1. A. L. Rowse, *All Souls and Appeasement* (London: Macmillan Co., 1961), pp. 52, 20.
2. Ronald Blythe, *The Age of Illusion: England in the Twenties and Thirties 1919–1940* (London: Hamish Hamilton, 1963), p. 257.
3. Eric Blair (George Orwell), "Awake! Young Men of England," *Henley and South Oxfordshire Standard*, 2 October 1914.
4. George Orwell, "As I Please," *Tribune* (London), 19 May 1944, in *Collected Essays*, III, 150–52, 199.
5. George Orwell, *Homage to Catalonia* (Boston: Beacon Press, 1952), p. 192.
6. George Orwell, Review of *The Men I Killed* by Brig.-Gen. F. P. Crozier, *New Statesman and Nation*, 28 August 1937, in *Collected Essays*, I, 283.
7. George Orwell, Letter to Jack Common, 29 September 1938, in *Collected Essays*, I, 354.
8. George Orwell, Letter to Jack Common, 12 October 1938, ibid., 355, 355 n. 2.
9. George Orwell, Review of *Spanish Testament* by Arthur Koestler, *Time and Tide*, 5 February 1938, in *Collected Essays*, I, 295.
10. Ibid., 296.
11. See George Orwell, *The Lion and the Unicorn*, Part III: "The English Revolution," in *Collected Essays*, II, 102; "No, Not One," *Adelphi*, October 1941, in *Collected Essays*, II, 169.
12. George Orwell, Letter to Richard Rees, 3 March 1949, in *Collected Essays*, IV, 478.
13. George Orwell, Letter to Herbert Read, 4 January 1939, in *Collected Essays*, I, 377–78.
14. George Orwell, Letter to the Editor of the *New English Weekly*, 26 May 1938, in *Collected Essays*, I, 331–32.
15. George Orwell, "Not Counting Niggers," *Adelphi*, July 1939, in *Collected Essays*, I, 398.
16. George Orwell, "My Country Right or Left," *Folios of New Writing*, Autumn 1940, in *Collected Essays*, I, 539.
17. George Orwell, "As I Please," *Tribune* (London), 24 December 1943, in *Collected Essays*, III, 65.
18. Orwell, "My Country Right or Left," I, 539.
19. George Orwell, "Marrakech," *New Writing*, Christmas 1939, in *Collected Essays*, I, 388.
20. Julian Symons, "Orwell, a Reminiscence," *London Magazine* 3 (September 1963), 35.
21. George Orwell, "Rudyard Kipling," *Horizon* (February 1942), in *Collected Essays*, II, 187.

22. Orwell, "No, Not One," II, 168.
23. Ibid., 166.
24. George Orwell, "Reflections on Gandhi," in *Shooting an Elephant*, p. 100.
25. Orwell, "No, Not One," II, 170.
26. George Orwell, "As I Please," *Tribune* (London), 23 June 1944, in *Collected Essays*, III, 172–75. The whole of the article is not reprinted in *Collected Essays*.
27. George Orwell, "London Letter," *Partisan Review*, March–April 1941, in *Collected Letters*, II, 55.
28. D. S. Savage, George Woodcock, Alex Comfort, George Orwell, "A Controversy," *Partisan Review*, September–October 1942, in *Collected Essays*, II, 227.
29. Ibid., 224.
30. Ibid., 225.
31. Obadiah Hornbooke (Alex Comfort), "Letter to an American Visitor," *Tribune* (London), 4 June 1943, in *Collected Essays*, II, 294–98.
32. George Orwell, "As One Non-Combatant to Another (A Letter to 'Obadiah Hornbooke')," *Tribune* (London), 18 June 1943, in *Collected Essays*, II, 299–303.
33. George Orwell, "As I Please," *Tribune* (London), 28 July 1944, in *Collected Essays*, III, 199.
34. Orwell, ibid., 8 December 1944, in *Collected Essays*, III, 288–89.
35. George Orwell, "Notes on Nationalism," in *Such, Such Were the Joys*, p. 74.
36. Orwell, "The English Revolution," II, 105.
37. George Orwell, "The Limit to Pessimism," *New English Weekly*, 25 April 1940.
38. Ibid.
39. George Orwell, "Wells, Hitler and the World State," in *Dickens, Dali and Others*, p. 118.
40. George Orwell, "James Burnham and the Managerial Revolution," in *Collected Essays*, IV, 173.
41. George Orwell, "Patriots and Revolutionaries," in *The Betrayal of the Left*," ed. by Victor Gollancz (London: Victor Gollancz, 1941), pp. 242–43.
42. George Orwell, "Political Reflections on the Crisis," *Adelphi* 15 (December 1938), 108.
43. George Orwell, "London Letter," *Partisan Review*, March–April 1942, in *Collected Essays*, II, 179.
44. J. M. Keynes, Letter to the editor, *New Statesman and Nation*, 14 October 1939, p. 520.
45. Orwell, "James Burnham and the Managerial Revolution," IV, 173.

46. Ibid.
47. George Orwell, *The Lion and the Unicorn*, Part I: "England Your England," in *Collected Essays*, II, 60 n.
48. George Orwell, "English Writing in Total War," *New Republic*, 14 July 1941, p. 58.
49. George Orwell, "London Letter," *Partisan Review*, March–April 1941, in *Collected Essays*, II, 50.
50. George Orwell, "War-time Diary," 6 June 1942, in *Collected Essays*, II, 428.
51. George Orwell, "London Letter," *Partisan Review*, Summer 1944, in *Collected Essays*, III, 126.
52. Ibid., 126–27.
53. Ibid., 126.
54. Ibid.
55. George Orwell, "London Letter," *Partisan Review* 12 (Winter 1945), 79.
56. Ibid., 80.
57. Orwell, "The English Revolution," II, 108.
58. Orwell, "London Letter," *Partisan Review*, March–April 1942, in *Collected Essays*, II, 183.
59. George Orwell, "Looking Back on the Spanish War," in *Such, Such Were the Joys*, pp. 144–45.
60. Orwell, "The English Revolution," II, 90.
61. Ibid., 104.
62. George Orwell, "Anti-Semitism in Britain," in *Such, Such Were the Joys*, p. 107.

CHAPTER VIII

1. George Orwell, "Looking Back on the Spanish War," in *Such, Such Were the Joys*, p. 139.
2. Quoted in George Orwell, "As I Please," *Tribune* (London), 7 July 1944, in *Collected Essays*, III, 180.
3. George Orwell, "In Defence of P. G. Wodehouse," in *Dickens, Dali and Others*, p. 241.
4. George Orwell, *Homage to Catalonia* (Boston: Beacon Press, 1952), p. 47.
5. George Orwell, "War-time Diary," 10 June 1942, in *Collected Essays*, II, 430.
6. Orwell, "Looking Back on the Spanish War," p. 253.
7. Orwell, *Homage to Catalonia*, p. 65.
8. George Orwell, Letter to Cyril Connolly, 8 June 1937, in *Collected Essays*, I, 268–69.
9. Orwell, "Looking Back on the Spanish War," pp. 256–57.
10. George Orwell, "Letter to Rayner Heppenstall," 31 July 1937, in

Collected Essays, I, 279. See also Richard Rees, *George Orwell: Fugitive from the Camp of Victory* (London: Secker and Warburg, 1961), chap. V.

11. George Orwell, Letter to the editor of *Time and Tide,* 5 February 1938, in *Collected Essays,* I, 297–98.
12. Lionel Trilling, "Introduction," *Homage to Catalonia,* xii. In this connection see also Lionel Trilling, "Was Orwell Shrewd . . ." *Nation,* 24 January 1953, p. 88; Herbert Matthews, "Homage to Orwell," ibid., 27 December 1952, pp. 597–99; Lionel Trilling, "George Orwell and the Politics of Truth," in *The Opposing Self* (New York: Viking Press, 1955), pp. 151–72, n. 3, p. 171.
13. Edward Hyams, *The New Statesman: The History of the First Fifty Years 1913–1963* (London: Longmans, Green and Co., 1963), p. 199.
14. Orwell, Letter to Rayner Heppenstall, 31 July 1937, I, 279.
15. Ibid.; Rayner Heppenstall, *Four Absentees* (London: Barrie and Rockliff, 1960), p. 140. For another account of the same incident see Orwell's letter to Geoffrey Gorer in *Collected Essays,* I, 280–82.
16. George Orwell, Review of *The Spanish Cockpit* by Franz Borkenau, *Time and Tide,* 31 July 1937, in *Collected Essays,* I, 276.
17. George Orwell, Letter to the editor of *Time and Tide,* pp. 297–98.
18. George Orwell, Letter to Raymond Mortimer, 9 February 1938, in *Collected Essays,* I, 299–302.
19. Ibid., 299 n. 1.
20. Ibid., 299.
21. Kingsley Martin, *Editor: A Second Volume of Autobiography* (London: Hutchinson of London, 1968), p. 216.
22. George Orwell, "As I Please," *Tribune* (London), 5 January 1945, in *Collected Essays,* III, 313.
23. George Orwell, Letter to Victor Gollancz, 9 May 1937, in *Collected Essays,* I, 267.
24. See ibid., IV, 307–8 for a letter to Gollancz about this contract.
25. Henry Pelling, *The British Communist Party* (New York: Macmillan Co., 1958), p. 96.
26. T. L. W. Hubbard, "Les Book-Clubs en Angleterre," *Mercure de France* 290 (March, 1939), 349.
27. Pelling, *British Communist Party,* p. 97.
28. Martin, *Editor,* pp. 205–6.
29. Julian Symons, *The Thirties* (London: Cresset Press, 1960), pp. 102–3.
30. George Orwell, Letter to Geoffrey Gorer, 3 April 1940, in *Collected Essays,* I, 529.
31. Orwell, Letter to Rayner Heppenstall, 31 July 1937, I, 279.
32. George Orwell, Letter to Geoffrey Gorer, 15 September 1937, in *Collected Essays,* I, 285.

33. George Orwell, Letter to Jack Common [October ?] 1937, in *Collected Essays*, I, 289. Orwell was never a follower of Trotsky, but in view of the confusion arising from his affiliation with the P.O.U.M. it seems advisable to say that in the context the remark is ironic.

34. Frederic Warburg, *An Occupation for Gentlemen* (London: Hutchinson, 1959), p. 236.

35. Ibid., p. 237. For a different account of these events, see Stanley Weintraub, *The Last Great Cause* (New York: Weybright and Talley, 1968), chap. 3.

36. *The Listener*, 25 May 1938, p. 1142.

37. Ibid., 16 June 1938, p. 1295.

38. V. S. Pritchett, "The Spanish Tragedy," *New Statesman and Nation*, 30 April 1938, pp. 734, 736.

39. John Lehmann, *The Whispering Gallery* (New York: Harcourt, Brace and Co., 1954), p. 333.

40. George Orwell, "As I Please," *Tribune* (London), 1 September 1944, in *Collected Essays*, III, 227.

41. Ibid.

42. Correspondence columns, *Tribune* (London), 8 September 1944.

43. George Orwell, "As I Please," *Tribune* (London), 17 November 1944, in *Collected Essays*, III, 275; Randall Swingler, "The Right to Free Expression (Annotated by George Orwell)," *Polemic* 5 (September–October 1946).

44. George Orwell, "As I Please," *Tribune* (London), 12 January 1945, in *Collected Essays*, III, 317–18.

45. George Orwell, "The Prevention of Literature," in *Shooting an Elephant*, pp. 108–9.

46. Ibid., p. 109.

47. Warburg, *Occupation for Gentlemen*, p. 231.

48. Julian Symons, "Orwell, A Reminiscence," *London Magazine* 3 (September 1963), 42.

49. George Woodcock, *The Crystal Spirit: A Study of George Orwell* (Boston: Little, Brown and Co., 1966), pp. 14, 15.

50. George Orwell, "As I Please," *Tribune* (London), 30 June 1944, in *Collected Essays*, III, 176.

51. T. S. Eliot, Letter to George Orwell, quoted in a letter from Mrs. T. S. Eliot to the *Times* (London), 6 January 1969.

52. George Orwell, Letter to Philip Rahv, 1 May 1944, in *Collected Essays*, III, 141–42. See also the comment by Dwight Macdonald, ibid., 141, n. 2.

53. Swingler, "Right to Free Expression."

54. Paul Potts, *Dante Called You Beatrice* (London: Eyre and Spottiswoode, 1960), pp. 76–77; George Orwell, "As I Please," *Tribune* (London), 21 July 1944, in *Collected Essays*, III, 187.

55. Orwell describes his difficulties in finding a publisher in an introduction to *Animal Farm* that was discovered in 1971. It was published in the *Times* (London) *Literary Supplement,* 15 September 1972 under the title "Freedom of the Press," with an explanation by Bernard Crick of how the essay came to be written.

56. Dwight Macdonald, "Politicking," *Politics* 3 (March 1946), 96.

57. George Orwell, Letter to Herbert Read, 18 August 1945, in *Collected Essays,* III, 401.

58. George Orwell, Letter to Arthur Koestler, 10 January 1946, in *Collected Essays,* IV, 76–77.

59. Spencer Brown, "Strange Doings at Animal Farm," *Commentary* 19 (February 1955), 155–61.

60. Sean O'Casey, *Sunset and Evening Star* (New York: Macmillan Co., 1954), pp. 139–40.

61. Swingler, "Right to Free Expression."

62. George Orwell, "Inside the Whale," in *Such, Such Were the Joys,* p. 180.

63. Martin, *Editor,* pp. 205–6.

64. Neal Wood, *Communism and British Intellectuals* (New York: Columbia University Press, 1959), p. 74.

65. Wyndham Lewis, *The Writer and the Absolute* (London: Methuen and Co., 1952), pp. 182–83, 189.

66. George Orwell, "Milton in Striped Trousers," *Tribune* (London), 12 October 1945.

67. George Orwell, "War-time Diary," 1 April 1942, in *Collected Essays,* II, 415–16.

CHAPTER IX

1. Tom Hopkinson, *"George Orwell* (London: Longmans, Green and Co., 1953), p. 8; George Woodcock, *The Crystal Spirit: A Study of George Orwell* (Boston: Little, Brown and Co., 1966), p. 140.

2. George Orwell, *Burmese Days* (New York: Popular Library, 1958), pp. 60–61.

3. Ibid., pp. 61–62.

4. George Orwell, *Nineteen Eighty-Four* (New York: Harcourt, Brace and Co., 1949), p. 9.

5. Orwell, *Burmese Days,* p. 156.

6. George Orwell, Review of *The Sword and the Sickle* by Mulk Raj Anand, *Horizon,* July 1942, in *Collected Essays,* II, 217.

7. Orwell, *Burmese Days,* pp. 15–16.

8. George Orwell, *The Road to Wigan Pier* (New York: Harcourt, Brace and World, 1958), p. 183.

9. Donald Barr, "The Answer to George Orwell," *Saturday Review,* 30 March 1957, p. 21.

10. George Orwell, *A Clergyman's Daughter* (New York: Avon Books, n.d.), p. 68.
11. Ibid., p. 75.
12. Ibid., p. 94.
13. George Orwell, *Down and Out in Paris and London* (Garden City, N.Y.: Doubleday and Co., Permabooks, 1954), p. 46.
14. Orwell, *Clergyman's Daughter*, p. 99.
15. Ibid., p. 159.
16. Ibid., pp. 179-80.
17. Orwell, *Nineteen Eighty-Four*, p. 70.
18. Orwell, *Clergyman's Daughter*, p. 187.
19. Ibid., p. 205.
20. George Orwell, *Keep the Aspidistra Flying* (New York: Harcourt, Brace and Co., 1956), pp. 150-51; "St. Andrew's Day," *Adelphi*, n.s. 11 (November 1935), 86.
21. Orwell, *Keep the Aspidistra Flying*, p. 150.
22. John Morris, "Some Are More Equal than Others: A note on George Orwell," in *Pleasures of New Writing*, ed. by John Lehmann (London: John Lehmann, 1952), pp. 423-29; George Woodcock, *The Crystal Spirit: A Study of George Orwell* (Boston: Little, Brown and Co., 1966), pp. 116-17, 121-22.
23. Orwell, *Keep the Aspidistra Flying*, p. 239.
24. Christopher Isherwood, *Lions and Shadows: An Education in the Twenties* (Norfolk, Conn.: New Directions, 1947), pp. 246-47.
25. Orwell, *Keep the Aspidistra Flying*, p. 142.
26. Ibid., p. 91.
27. Ibid., p. 202.
28. Ibid., p. 53.
29. Ibid., p. 48.
30. Ibid., pp. 219, 45.
31. Fyodor Dostoevsky, *Notes from Underground and The Grand Inquisitor*, trans. by Ralph E. Matlaw (New York: E. P. Dutton and Co., 1960), pp. 37, 42.
32. Orwell, *Keep the Aspidistra Flying*, p. 83.
33. George Orwell, *Coming Up for Air* (New York: Harcourt, Brace and Co., 1950), pp. 188, 233.
34. Orwell, *Nineteen Eighty-Four*, p. 222.
35. Orwell, *Road to Wigan Pier*, p. 198.
36. Orwell, *Keep the Aspidistra Flying*, p. 237. See also Edward M. Thomas, *Orwell* (London: Oliver and Boyd, 1965), p. 27.
37. Orwell, *Coming Up for Air*, p. 18.
38. Ibid., pp. 204-5, 206.
39. Ibid., p. 30.
40. Ibid., p. 176.

41. Ibid., p. 185.
42. Ibid., pp. 171, 175.
43. Ibid., pp. 31, 36.
44. Ibid., p. 54.
45. Ibid., pp. 57, 48.
46. Ibid., p. 68.
47. Ibid., pp. 277–78.
48. George Orwell, "Arthur Koestler," in *Dickens, Dali and Others*, p. 201.
49. George Orwell, *Animal Farm* (New York: Harcourt, Brace and Co., 1946), p. 7.
50. Richard Rees, *George Orwell: Fugitive from the Camp of Victory* (London: Secker and Warburg, 1961), pp. 89–90.
51. Orwell, *Animal Farm*, p. 30.
52. T. R. Fyvel, *Tribune* (London), 24 August 1945.
53. Orwell, *Animal Farm*, pp. 78–79.
54. George Orwell, "Marx and Russia," *Observer* (London), 15 February 1948.
55. For a different view of *Animal Farm* see Kingsley Martin, "Soviet Satire," *New Statesman and Nation*, 8 September 1945, pp. 165–66.

CHAPTER X

1. George Orwell, *The Road to Wigan Pier* (New York: Harcourt, Brace and World, 1958), p. 234.
2. Isaac Deutscher, *Russia in Transition* (rev. ed.; New York: Grove Press, 1960), pp. 250–65.
3. George Orwell, Review of *Mein Kampf* by Adolf Hitler, *New English Weekly*, 21 March 1940, in *Collected Essays*, II, 14.
4. Ibid.
5. George Orwell, "War-time Diary," 10 September 1940, in *Collected Essays*, II, 371.
6. George Orwell, "London Letter," *Partisan Review*, March–April 1942, in *Collected Essays*, II, 175–83; "London Letter," *Partisan Review*, November–December 1942, II, 230–36; "London Letter," *Partisan Review*, Fall 1944, III, 191–96.
7. George Orwell, *Nineteen Eighty-Four* (New York: Harcourt, Brace and Co., 1949), p. 31.
8. Ibid., p. 60.
9. Orwell, "War-time Diary," 28 August 1941, II, 409.
10. Orwell, "London Letter," *Partisan Review*, November–December 1941, II, 152.
11. George Orwell, "As I Please," *Tribune* (London), 2 February 1945, in *Collected Essays*, III, 328.

12. Orwell, "London Letter," *Partisan Review*, Summer 1945, III, 385.

13. Orwell, *Nineteen Eighty-Four*, p. 295.

14. George Orwell, "As I Please," *Tribune* (London), 9 February 1945, in *Collected Essays*, III, 330.

15. George Orwell, "Some Thoughts on the Common Toad," *Tribune* (London), 12 April 1946, in *Collected Essays*, IV, 143.

16. George Orwell, "As I Please," *Tribune* (London), 28 March 1947, in *Collected Essays*, IV, 312.

17. Orwell, "War-time Diary," 6 May 1941, II, 399.

18. Orwell, "London Letter," *Partisan Review*, Fall 1944, III, 196.

19. Orwell, *Nineteen Eighty-Four*, p. 33.

20. Julian Symons, "Orwell, A Reminiscence," *London Magazine* 3 (September 1963), 41.

21. George Orwell, "As I Please," *Tribune* (London), 31 December 1943.

22. George Orwell, "As I Please," *Tribune* (London), 7 July 1944, in *Collected Essays*, III, 179–80.

23. Orwell, *Nineteen Eighty-Four*, pp. 221–23.

24. Orwell, "London Letter," *Partisan Review*, Summer 1945, III, 382.

25. George Orwell, "The Germans Still Doubt Our Unity," *Observer* (London), 29 April 1945.

26. George Orwell, "Freed Politicians Return to Paris," ibid., 13 May 1945.

27. George Orwell, "Revenge Is Sour," *Tribune* (London), 9 November 1945, in *Collected Essays*, IV, 3–6.

28. Orwell protested the chaining of German prisoners of war in retaliation against the German treatment of British prisoners. See George Orwell, "An Unpublished Letter to the Editor of *The Times*," 12 October 1942, in *Collected Essays*, II, 243–44.

29. *Times* (London), "Kharkov Delivered," 31 December 1943; "Death Sentences at Kharkov," 20 December 1943; "German Atrocities in Russia," 17 December 1943. For other references to these trials and to the Communist use of planned hysteria, see George Orwell, "As I Please," *Tribune* (London), 31 December 1943; in *Collected Essays*, III, 66; "London Letter," *Partisan Review*, Spring 1944, III, 76; "As I Please," *Tribune* (London), 8 September 1944, III, 230. See also Arthur Koestler, *The Yogi and the Commissar* (New York: Macmillan Co., 1945), p. 176; Eugene Lyons, *Assignment in Utopia* (New York: Harcourt, Brace and Co., 1937), pp. 370–72.

30. George Orwell, Letter to Geoffrey Gorer, 22 January 1946, in *Collected Essays*, IV, 86.

31. John Wheeler-Bennet, *King George VI: His Life and Reign* (New York: St. Martin's Press, 1958), pp. 661–62. See also Michael Sissons and Philip French, eds. *Age of Austerity* (London: Hodder and Stoughton, 1963).

32. George Orwell, *Homage to Catalonia* (Boston: Beacon Press, 1952), pp. 198–99.
33. Orwell, "London Letter," *Partisan Review*, Summer 1945, III, 384.
34. Orwell, "War-time Diary," II, 430.

CHAPTER XI

1. George Orwell, "England Your England," in *Collected Essays*, II, 68.
2. George Orwell, *The Road to Wigan Pier* (New York: Harcourt, Brace and World, 1958), pp. 190, 195.
3. George Orwell, *Nineteen Eighty-Four* (New York: Harcourt, Brace and Co., 1949), p. 36.
4. George Orwell, *Homage to Catalonia* (Boston: Beacon Press, 1952), p. 64.
5. Julian Symons, *The Thirties* (London: Cresset Press, 1960), p. 142.
6. Arthur Koestler, *The Scum of the Earth* (New York: Macmillan Co., 1941), pp. 124–26.
7. George Orwell, "War-time Diary," 30 June 1941, *Collected Essays*, II, 407.
8. George Orwell, Review of *Beggar My Neighbour* by Lionel Fielden, *Horizon*, September 1943, in *Collected Essays*, II, 314.
9. David Caute, *Communism and the French Intellectuals 1914–1960* (London: Andre Deutsch, 1964), p. 124.
10. Orwell, Review of *Beggar My Neighbour*, II, 314.
11. Ibid., 314–15.
12. George Orwell, "London Letter," *Partisan Review*, Summer 1944, in *Collected Essays*, III, 126.
13. Orwell, "Prevention of Literature," in *Shooting an Elephant*, pp. 114–15.
14. George Orwell, "In Front of Your Nose," *Tribune* (London), 22 March 1946, in *Collected Essays*, IV, 123, 125.
15. Ibid., 125.
16. George Orwell, "Notes on Nationalism," in *Such, Such Were the Joys*, pp. 74, 75, 84.
17. Ibid., pp. 84–85.
18. George Orwell, "Writers and Leviathan," in *Such, Such Were the Joys*, p. 67.
19. Ibid., pp. 67–68.
20. Orwell, "Prevention of Literature," p. 113.
21. Orwell, Review of *Beggar My Neighbour*, II, 306.
22. George Orwell, "Politics and the English Language," in *Shooting an Elephant*, p. 87.
23. George Orwell, "As I Please," *Tribune* (London), 18 August 1944, in *Collected Essays*, III, 210; "As I Please," *Tribune* (London), 28

January 1944, in *Collected Essays*, III, 86.

24. C. K. Ogden, *The System of Basic English* (New York: Harcourt, Brace and Co., 1934), pp. 301, 303.

25. Ibid., pp. 301–2.

26. George Orwell, "Interglossa—Make Do and Talk with 750 Words," *Manchester Evening News*, 23 December 1943.

27. George Orwell, *The English People* (London: Collins, 1947), p. 33.

28. Ibid.

29. Ibid., pp. 33, 34, 39.

30. Eugene Lyons, *Assignment in Utopia* (New York: Harcourt, Brace and Co., 1937), p. 338.

CHAPTER XII

1. George Orwell, *Nineteen Eighty-Four* (New York: Harcourt, Brace and Co., 1949), p. 80.

2. George Orwell, "Prevention of Literature," in *Shooting an Elephant*, pp. 109–10.

3. George Orwell, "Looking Back on the Spanish War," in *Such, Such Were the Joys*, p. 142.

4. Orwell, *Nineteen Eighty-Four*, p. 157.

5. Orwell, "Looking Back on the Spanish War," p. 142.

6. George Orwell, "Some Recent Novels," *New English Weekly*, 24 September 1936.

7. George Orwell, Review of *Power: A New Social Analysis* by Bertrand Russell, *Adelphi*, January 1939, in *Collected Essays*, I, 375–76.

8. Orwell, "Prevention of Literature," p. 120.

9. Eugene Lyons, *Assignment in Utopia* (New York: Harcourt, Brace and Co., 1937), pp. 240–41. See also M. Jennifer McDowell, "*1984* and Soviet Reality," *University of California Graduate Journal* 1 (Fall, 1962), 12–19; Louis Fischer, *Men and Politics* (New York: Duell, Sloan and Pearce, 1941).

10. Eugene Zamiatin, *We* (New York: E. P. Dutton and Co. [1959]), pp. 12, 13.

11. Ibid., 63, 64.

12. George Orwell, "How Long Is a Short Story?" *Manchester Evening News*, 7 September 1944.

13. Fyodor Dostoevsky, *Notes from Underground and The Grand Inquisitor*, trans. by Ralph E. Matlaw (New York: E. P. Dutton and Co., 1960), p. 12.

14. Ibid., p. 30.

15. Ibid., pp. 25–27, 31.

16. George Orwell, "The Male Byronic," *Tribune* (London), 21 June 1940.

17. George Orwell, "Why I Write," in *Collected Essays*, I, 4.
18. George Orwell, "As I Please," *Tribune* (London), 4 February 1944, in *Collected Essays*, III, 87.
19. Orwell, "Looking Back on the Spanish War," p. 141.
20. Orwell, "Prevention of Literature," pp. 109–10.
21. Ibid., p. 109.
22. Alexander Weissberg, *Conspiracy of Silence* (London: Hamish Hamilton, 1952), pp. 472–73; George Orwell, "As I Please," *Tribune* (London), 17 November 1944, in *Collected Essays*, III, 275.
23. Louis Fischer, in *The God That Failed*, ed. by Richard Crossman (New York: Bantam Books, 1952), p. 208.
24. Victor Kravchenko, *I Chose Freedom* (New York: Scribner's, 1946), p. 304.
25. George Orwell, "As I Please," 17 January 1947, in *Collected Essays*, IV, 271. See also the doctored photograph of Trotsky, *Sunday Times* (London), 25 April 1965.
26. George Orwell, "New Novels," *New Statesman and Nation*, 4 January 1941.
27. Orwell, "The Male Byronic."
28. George Orwell, "Fascism and Democracy," in *The Betrayal of the Left*, pp. 210–11.
29. George Orwell, "Just Junk—but who could resist it?" *Evening Standard*, 5 January 1946.
30. George Orwell, *The Road to Wigan Pier* (New York: Harcourt, Brace and World, 1958), p. 234. For a discussion of this and other glass objects given symbolic value in *1984*, see John O. Lyons, "George Orwell's Opaque Glass in *1984*," *Wisconsin Studies in Contemporary Literature* 2 (Fall 1961), 39–46.
31. George Orwell, Review of *Great Morning* by Osbert Sitwell, in *Adelphi*, July–September 1948, in *Collected Essays*, IV, 445–46.
32. George Orwell, *Down and Out in Paris and London* (Garden City, N.Y.: Doubleday and Co., Permabooks, 1954), p. 182.
33. George Orwell, "As I Please," *Tribune* (London), 28 April 1944, in *Collected Essays*, III, 133.

CHAPTER XIII

1. George Orwell, *The Road to Wigan Pier* (New York: Harcourt, Brace and World, 1958), pp. 247–48.
2. George Orwell, "Impenetrable Mystery," Review of *Assignment in Utopia* by Eugene Lyons, *New English Weekly*, 9 June 1938, in *Collected Essays*, I, 334.
3. George Orwell, "Marx and Russia," *Observer* (London), 15 February 1948.

4. George Orwell, "Red, White and Brown," Review of *The Totalitarian Enemy* by Franz Borkenau, *Time and Tide*, 4 May 1940, in *Collected Essays*, II, 25.
5. George Orwell, "Toward European Unity," *Partisan Review*, July–August 1947, in *Collected Essays*, IV, 371.
6. George Orwell, Review of *Mein Kampf* by Adolf Hitler, *New English Weekly*, 21 March 1940, in *Collected Essays*, II, 13.
7. George Orwell, "The Russian Regime," Review of *Russia Under Soviet Rule* by N. de Basily, *New English Weekly*, 12 January 1939, in *Collected Essays*, I, 380–81.
8. George Orwell, "The Romantic Case," *Observer* (London), 23 July 1944.
9. Orwell, "Toward European Unity," IV, 374.
10. George Orwell, "Culture and the Classes," *Observer* (London), 28 November 1948, in *Collected Essays*, IV, 456.
11. George Orwell, *Nineteen Eighty-Four* (New York: Harcourt, Brace and Co., 1949), p. 17.
12. Ibid., p. 300.
13. Orwell, "Impenetrable Mystery," I, 334.
14. Orwell, Review of *Mein Kampf*, II, 14.
15. Orwell, *Nineteen Eighty-Four*, p. 300.
16. T. R. Fyvel, "Wingate, Orwell, and the 'Jewish Question,'" *Commentary* 11 (February 1951), p. 142.
17. Orwell, *Road to Wigan Pier*, p. 212.
18. Orwell, "Red, White and Brown," II, 26.
19. Orwell, *Nineteen Eighty-Four*, pp. 15–16.
20. Ibid., p. 271.
21. George Orwell, "England Your England," in *Collected Essays*, II, 61–62.
22. George Woodcock, *The Crystal Spirit: A Study of George Orwell* (Boston: Little, Brown and Co., 1966), p. 60.
23. Orwell, *Nineteen Eighty-Four*, p. 289.
24. Alexander Weissberg, *Conspiracy of Silence* (London: Hamish Hamilton, 1952), p. 195.
25. Orwell, *Road to Wigan Pier*, p. 183.
26. George Orwell, *Homage to Catalonia* (Boston: Beacon Press, 1952), p. 83.
27. Orwell, *Nineteen Eighty-Four*, p. 61.
28. George Orwell, "War-time Diary," 30 June 1940, in *Collected Essays*, II, 360.
29. Eugene Lyons, *Assignment in Utopia* (New York: Harcourt, Brace and Co., 1937), pp. 379–80.
30. Malcolm Muggeridge, *The Thirties* (London: Hamish Hamilton, 1940), p. 208 n.

CHAPTER XIV

1. For a detailed and interesting discussion of these issues, see George Kateb, "The Road to *1984*," *Political Science Quarterly* 81 (December 1966), 564–80.

2. Richard Rees, *George Orwell: Fugitive from the Camp of Victory* (London: Secker and Warburg, 1961), p. 97.

3. Stephen Spender, *The Creative Element* (New York: British Book Center, 1954), p. 129.

4. Rees, *George Orwell*, pp. 24–25.

5. George Woodcock, *The Crystal Spirit: A Study of George Orwell* (Boston: Little, Brown and Co., 1966), p. 26.

6. Beverley Nichols, *The Sweet and Twenties* (London: Weidenfeld and Nicolson, 1958), p. 32.

7. George Orwell, "England Your England," in *Collected Essays*, II, 68.

8. Cyril Connolly, *Enemies of Promise* (rev. ed.; New York: Macmillan Co., 1948), p. 207.

9. Isaac Deutscher, *Russia in Transition* (rev. ed.; New York: Grove Press, 1960), p. 263, n. 2. Despite a diligent search I have been unable to find the "column in *Tribune*" to which Deutscher refers in his note.

10. T. R. Fyvel, "Wingate, Orwell, and the 'Jewish Question,'" *Commentary* 11 (February 1951), 142–43.

11. Peter de Mendelssohn, *The Age of Churchill*, Vol. I: 1874–1911 (London: Thames and Hudson, 1961), pp. 378–79.

12. Connolly, *Enemies of Promise*, p. 164.

13. Anthony West, "Hidden Damage," *New Yorker*, 28 January 1956, p. 103. For comment on West's thesis, see Kingsley Amis, "The Road to Airstrip One," *Spectator* (London), 31 August 1956, pp. 292–93; and T. R. Fyvel, "Letter to the Editor," *Spectator*, 14 September 1956, p. 351.

14. Deutscher, *Russia in Transition*, p. 260.

15. George Orwell, "Impenetrable Mystery," *Collected Essays*, I, 332–33.

16. George Orwell, Letter to Roger Senhouse, 26 December 1948, in *Collected Essays*, IV, 460.

17. George Orwell, "Letter to the Editor," *Life*, 25 July 1949. With minor variations this letter appears also in *Collected Essays*, IV, 502.

18. Christopher Hollis, *A Study of George Orwell: The Man and His Works* (London: Hollis and Carter, 1956), p. 17. See also Deutscher, *Russia in Transition*, p. 264.

19. Richard J. Voorhees, *The Paradox of George Orwell*, Purdue University Studies (Humanities Series), 1961, p. 88.

20. Philip Rahv, "The Unfuture of Utopia," *Partisan Review* 16 (July 1949), 746.

21. Woodcock, *Crystal Spirit*, p. 330.
22. Deutscher, *Russia in Transition*, p. 261.
23. James Burnham, *The Managerial Revolution: What Is Happening in the World* (New York: John Day Co., 1941), p. 232 n.
24. Arthur Koestler, *The Invisible Writing* (New York: Macmillan Co., 1954), pp. 197–98.
25. Ibid., p. 199.
26. Edmund Wilson, *To the Finland Station* (New York: Doubleday and Co., 1940), p. 431.
27. George Orwell, "War-time Diary," 23 August 1940, in *Collected Essays*, II, 368.
28. George Orwell, *Nineteen Eighty-Four* (New York: Harcourt, Brace and Co., 1949), p. 79.
29. Ibid., p. 266.
30. George Orwell, "Why Machiavellis of Today Fall Down," *Manchester Evening News*, 20 January 1944.
31. George Orwell, "As I Please," *Tribune* (London), 21 July 1944, in *Collected Essays*, III, 189.
32. Orwell, "As I Please," *Tribune* (London), 29 November 1946, in *Collected Essays*, IV, 249.

CHAPTER XV

1. George Orwell, Review of *Power: A New Social Analysis* by Bertrand Russell, *Adelphi*, January 1939, in *Collected Essays*, I, 375.
2. Alan Bullock, *Hitler: A Study in Tyranny* (rev. ed.; New York: Harper and Row, 1962), p. 382.
3. Hermann Rauschning, *The Revolution of Nihilism* (New York: Alliance Book Corporation, Longmans, Green and Co., 1939), p. 31.
4. Ibid., p. 183.
5. Malcolm Muggeridge, *The Thirties* (London: Hamish Hamilton, 1940), p. 31.
6. Ibid., pp. 207–8.
7. Alexander Weissberg, *Conspiracy of Silence* (London: Hamish Hamilton, 1952), p. 499.
8. George Orwell, *Nineteen Eighty-Four* (New York: Harcourt, Brace and Co., 1949), pp. 259–60.
9. John Strachey, *The Strangled Cry* (London: Bodley Head, 1962), p. 31.
10. Hannah Arendt, *The Origins of Totalitarianism* (Cleveland: World Publishing Co., Meridian Books, 1958), p. 451. This relation to *1984* has also been noted by Irving Howe.
11. Orwell, *Nineteen Eighty-Four*, p. 46.
12. Arendt, *Origins of Totalitarianism*, p. 451.
13. Orwell, *Nineteen Eighty-Four*, pp. 257–58.
14. Ibid., p. 289.

15. Ibid., pp. 274, 275. See also Orwell's letter to F. J. Warburg, 22 October 1948, in *Collected Essays*, IV, 448.
16. Arendt, *Origins of Totalitarianism*, p. 456.
17. William L. Shirer, *The Rise and Fall of the Third Reich: A History of Nazi Germany* (New York: Simon and Schuster, 1959), p. 1070.
18. Arendt, *Origins of Totalitarianism*, pp. 457–58.
19. Arthur Koestler, *The Invisible Writing* (New York: Macmillan Co., 1954), p. 158. See Michael Polanyi, *Beyond Nihilism* (Cambridge: Cambridge University Press, 1960), pp. 19–20, for a more abstract statement of this argument.
20. Arendt, *Origins of Totalitarianism*, p. 458.
21. See David Rousset, *A World Apart*, trans. by Yvonne Moyse and Roger Senhouse (London: Secker and Warburg, 1951).
22. Orwell, *Nineteen Eighty-Four*, p. 258.
23. Deutscher argued that *1984* showed Orwell's "dark disillusionment not only with Stalinism but with every form and shade of Socialism." Isaac Deutscher, *Russia in Transition* (rev. ed.; New York: Grove Press, 1960), p. 259.
24. George Orwell, *Down and Out in Paris and London* (Garden City, N.Y.: Doubleday and Co., Permabooks, 1954), p. 134.
25. George Orwell, *Keep the Aspidistra Flying* (New York: Harcourt, Brace and Co., 1956), p. 43.
26. George Orwell, *The Road to Wigan Pier* (New York: Harcourt, Brace and World, 1958), p. 235.
27. Richard Rees, *George Orwell: Fugitive from the Camp of Victory* (London: Secker and Warburg, 1961), p. 153.
28. George Orwell, "Britain's Struggle for Survival—The Labor Government After Three Years," *Commentary*, 6 (October 1948), 346.
29. Ibid., 349.
30. Rees, *George Orwell*, p. 48. A slightly different version is given in Orwell, *Collected Essays*, III, 403.
31. George Orwell, "Shopkeepers at War," in *Collected Essays*, II, 83–86.
32. George Orwell, Review of *The Unquiet Grave: A Word Cycle* by "Palinurus," *Observer* (London), 14 January 1945, in *Collected Essays*, III, 320.
33. George Orwell, "Wilde's Utopia," Review of *The Soul of Man under Socialism* by Oscar Wilde, *Observer* (London), 9 May 1948, in *Collected Essays*, IV, 428.
34. George Orwell, "Burnham's View of the Contemporary World Struggle," *New Leader* (New York), 29 March 1947, in *Collected Essays*, IV, 322.

CHAPTER XVI

1. Michael Polanyi, *Beyond Nihilism* (Cambridge: Cambridge University Press, 1960), p. 21.

2. H. G. Wells, *The Shape of Things to Come* (New York: Macmillan Co., 1936), p. 332.
3. George Orwell, *Coming Up for Air* (New York: Harcourt, Brace and Co., 1950), pp. 27–28.
4. George Orwell, Review of *An Unknown Land* by Herbert Lewis Samuel, *The Listener*, 24 December 1942.
5. Ibid.
6. George Orwell, "Power House," *Observer* (London), 23 April 1944.
7. See Milovan Djilas, *The New Class: An Analysis of the Communist System* (New York: Frederick A. Praeger, 1958).
8. Richard Rees, *George Orwell: Fugitive from the Camp of Victory* (London: Secker and Warburg, 1961), pp. 87–88.
9. Stephen Spender, *World Within World* (New York: Harcourt, Brace and Co., 1948), pp. 172–73.
10. George Orwell, "James Burnham and the Managerial Revolution," *Collected Essays*, IV, 179. This essay was originally called "Second Thoughts on James Burnham."

SELECTED BIBLIOGRAPHY

WORKS BY GEORGE ORWELL

Down and Out in Paris and London. New York: Harper and Bros., 1933.
Burmese Days. New York: Harper and Bros., 1934.
A Clergyman's Daughter. New York: Harper and Bros., 1936.
Talking to India: A Selection of English Language Broadcasts to India. Edited with an introduction by George Orwell. London: George Allen and Unwin, 1943.
Animal Farm. New York: Harcourt, Brace and Co., 1946.
The English People. London: Collins, 1947.
Nineteen Eighty-Four. New York: Harcourt, Brace and Co., 1949.
Coming Up for Air. New York: Harcourt, Brace and Co., 1950.
Homage to Catalonia. Introduction by Lionel Trilling. Boston: Beacon Press, 1952.
The Road to Wigan Pier. New York: Harcourt, Brace and World, 1958.
Keep the Aspidistra Flying. New York: Harcourt, Brace and Co., 1956.
The Collected Essays, Journalism and Letters of George Orwell. Edited by Sonia Orwell and Ian Angus. Vol. I. *An Age Like This 1920–1940.* Vol. II. *My Country Right or Left 1940–1943.* Vol. III. *As I Please 1943–1945.* Vol. IV. *In Front of Your Nose 1945–1950.* London: Secker and Warburg, 1968.
"Kitchener." Published under the name of E. A. Blair. *Henley and South Oxfordshire Standard,* July 21, 1916.
"Awake! Young Men of England." Published under the name of Eric Blair. *Henley and South Oxfordshire Standard,* Oct. 2, 1914.
"Eye-Witness in Barcelona." *Controversy,* I (Aug. 1937), 85–88.
"Letter to the Editor." *The Times* (London) *Literary Supplement,* May 14, 1938.
"Letter to the Editor." *The Times* (London) *Literary Supplement,* May 28, 1938.
"A Catholic Confronts Communism." *Peace News,* Jan. 27, 1939, p. 8.
"Fascism and Democracy" and "Patriots and Revolutionaries." *The Betrayal of the Left.* Edited by Victor Gollancz. London: Gollancz, 1941.
"Will Freedom Die with Capitalism?" *Left News,* Apr. 1941, pp. 1682–85.

"English Writing in Total War." *New Republic*, July 14, 1941, pp. 57–58.
"Our Opportunity." *Left News*, Jan. 1941, pp. 1608–12.
"Socialists Answer Our Questions on the War." *Left*, Nov. 1941, pp. 241–46.
"Culture and Democracy." *Victory Or Vested Interest?* by G. D. H. Cole, George Orwell, and others. London: Routledge, 1942.
Review of *An Unknown Land* by Viscount Samuel. *Listener*, Dec. 24, 1942.
"World Affairs, 1945." *Junior*, I (1945), 79–88.
"The Right to Free Expression." By Randall Swingler with marginal commentary by George Orwell. *Polemic*, V (Sept.–Oct. 1946), 45–53.
Introduction to *Love of Life* by Jack London. London: Paul Elek, 1946.
"Britain's Left-Wing Press." *Progressive* (Madison, Wis.), June 1948, pp. 17–19.
"Britain's Struggle for Survival: The Labor Government After Three Years." *Commentary*, Oct. 1948, pp. 343–49.
Review of *Scott-King's Modern Europe* by Evelyn Waugh. *New York Times*, Feb. 20, 1949.
"A Critic Views a Statesman." *New Leader*, May 14, 1949, p. 10.
"Letter to the Editor." *Life*, July 25, 1949, pp. 4, 6.
"Freedom of the Press." *The Times* (London) *Literary Supplement*, Sept. 15, 1972.

OTHER WORKS

Aldington, Richard. *Death of a Hero*. London: Chatto and Windus, 1929.
Amis, Kingsley. *New Maps of Hell*. New York: Harcourt, Brace and World, 1960.
———. "The Road to Airstrip One." *Spectator*, Aug. 31, 1956, pp. 292–93.
Angell, Norman. *After All*. London: Hamish Hamilton, 1951.
Arendt, Hannah. *The Origins of Totalitarianism*. New York: Harcourt, Brace and Co., 1958.
Aron, Raymond. *The Opium of the Intellectuals*. New York: W. W. Norton and Co., 1962.
Ashe, Geoffrey. "The Servile State in Fact and Fiction." *The Month*, July 1950, pp. 48–59.
———. "Second Thoughts on *Nineteen Eighty-Four*." *The Month*, Nov. 1950, pp. 285–300.
———. "A Note on George Orwell." *Commonweal*, June 1, 1951, pp. 191–93.
Atkins, John. *George Orwell: A Literary Study*. London: John Calder, 1954.
Auden, W. H., and Isherwood, Christopher. *Journey to a War*. New York: Random House, 1939.

Barr, Donald. "The Answer to George Orwell." *Saturday Review*, March 30, 1957, pp. 30–32.
Bazelon, David. *Nothing But a Fine Tooth Comb*. New York: Simon and Schuster, 1969.
de Beausobre, Julia. *The Woman Who Could Not Die*. London: Chatto and Windus, 1938.
Beker, Miroslav. "The Duality of George Orwell." *Geste*, Oct. 27, 1960, unpaginated.
Belloc, Hilaire. *The Servile State*. London: T. N. Foulis, 1912.
Benney, Mark. *Almost a Gentleman*. London: Peter Davies, 1966.
Birrell, T. A. "Is Integrity Enough?" *Dublin Review*, Fall 1950, pp. 49–65.
Blythe, Ronald. *The Age of Illusion: England in the Twenties and Thirties 1919–1940*. London: Hamish Hamilton, 1963.
Bolloten, Burnett. *The Grand Camouflage: The Communist Conspiracy in the Spanish Civil War*. New York: Frederick A. Praeger, 1961.
Borkenau, Franz. *World Communism: A History of the Communist International*. New York: W. W. Norton and Co., 1939.
———. *European Communism*. New York: Harper and Bros., 1953.
Boye, Karin. *Kallocain*. Translated from the Swedish by Gustaf Lannestock. Madison, Wis.: University of Wisconsin Press, 1966.
Bramah, Ernest. *What Might Have Been: The Story of a Social War* (The Secret of the League). London: John Murray, 1907.
Brander, Laurence. *George Orwell*. London: Longmans, Green and Co., 1954.
Braybrooke, Neville. "The Two Poverties: Léon Bloy and George Orwell." *Commonweal*, Aug. 14, 1953, pp. 459–61.
Brockway, Fenner. *Inside the Left*. London: George Allen and Unwin, 1942.
———. *Outside the Right*. London: George Allen and Unwin, 1963.
Brombert, Victor. *The Intellectual Hero: Studies in the French Novel 1880–1955*. Philadelphia: J. B. Lippincott Co., 1960.
Brown, Ivor. *Summer in Scotland*. London: Collins, 1952.
Brown, Spencer. "Strange Doings at Animal Farm." *Commentary*, Feb. 1955, pp. 155–61.
Buber-Neumann, Margarete. *Under Two Dictators*. Translated by Edward Fitzgerald. New York: Dodd, Mead and Co. [1950].
Bullock, Alan. *The Life and Times of Ernest Bevin: Trade Union Leader 1881–1940*. London: Heinemann, 1960.
———. *Hitler: A Study in Tyranny*. Rev. ed. New York: Harper and Row, 1962.
Burnham, James. *The Managerial Revolution: What Is Happening in the World*. New York: John Day Co., 1941.
———. *The Machiavellians*. New York: John Day Co., 1943.
———. *The Struggle for the World*. New York: John Day Co. [1947].

Calder, Jenni. *Chronicles of Conscience: A Study of George Orwell and Arthur Koestler*. London: Secker and Warburg, 1968.

Calder-Marshall, Arthur. "The Case of Comrade Orwell and Mr. Blair." *Reynolds News* (London), June 12, 1949.

Caute, David. *Communism and the French Intellectuals 1914–1960*. London: Andre Deutsch, 1964.

Chesterton, G. K. *The Napoleon of Notting Hill*. London: John Lane, Bodley Head, 1904.

———. *The Man Who Was Thursday: A Nightmare*. New York: Modern Library [1917].

Cockburn, Claud. *In Time of Trouble*. London: Rupert Hart-Davis, 1956.

Coe, Richard N. "*Nineteen Eighty-Four* and the Anti-Utopian Tradition." *Geste*, Oct. 27, 1960, unpaginated.

Connolly, Cyril. *The Rock Pool*. New York: Charles Scribner's Sons, 1936.

———. *Enemies of Promise*. Rev. ed. New York: Macmillan Co., 1948.

———. *Previous Convictions*. London: Hamish Hamilton, 1963.

———. "A London Diary." *New Statesman and Nation*, Jan. 16, 1937, pp. 73–74.

———. "A Spanish Diary." *New Statesman and Nation*, Feb. 20, 1937, pp. 278–79.

———. "Year Nine." *The Condemned Playground; Essays: 1927–1944*. New York: Macmillan Co., 1946. Reprinted from *New Statesman and Nation*, Jan. 29, 1938.

———. "This Gale-swept Chip." *Encounter*, Summer 1963, pp. 92–95.

Corke, Hilary. "A Literary Essay." *Encounter*, Apr. 1958, pp. 78–80.

Coser, Lewis A. *Men of Ideas: A Sociologist's View*. New York: Free Press, 1965.

Cosman, Max. "George Orwell and the Autonomous Individual." *Pacific Spectator*, Winter 1955, pp. 74–84.

Crick, Bernard. "How the Essay ['Freedom of the Press'] Came to Be Written." *The Times* (London) *Literary Supplement*, Sept. 15, 1972.

Crossman, Richard, ed. *The God That Failed*. New York: Harper and Bros., 1950.

Crowcroft, Peter. "Politics and Writing: The Orwell Analysis." *New Republic*, Jan. 3, 1955, pp. 17–18.

Cunningham, Adrian. Review of *Down and Out in Paris and London*. *Granta* (Cambridge University literary magazine), Feb. 15, 1964, pp. 24–25.

Dalton, Hugh. *Call Back Yesterday*. London: Frederick Muller, 1953.

Day-Lewis, Cecil. *Starting Point*. New York: Harper and Bros., 1938.

Deutscher, Isaac. "'1984'—The Mysticism of Cruelty." *Russia in Transition*. Rev. ed. New York: Grove Press, 1960.

Djilas, Milovan. *The New Class: An Analysis of the Communist System*. New York: Frederick A. Praeger, 1958.

Dooley, D. J. "The Limitations of George Orwell." *University of Toronto Quarterly*, XXVIII (Apr. 1959), 291–300.

Dostoevsky, Fyodor. *Notes from Underground and The Grand Inquisitor.* Translated and with an introduction by Ralph E. Matlaw. New York: E. P. Dutton and Co., 1960.

Driberg, Tom. *Guy Burgess.* London: Weidenfeld and Nicolson, 1956.

Driver, Christopher. *The Disarmers: A Study in Protest.* London: Hodder and Stoughton, 1964.

Dukes, Sir Paul. *An Epic of the Gestapo.* London: Cassell and Co., 1940.

Dunham, Vera S. "Sex: From Free Love to Puritanism." *Soviet Society: A Book of Readings.* Edited by Alex Lukeles and Kent Geiger. London: Constable and Co., 1961.

Dunn, Avril. "My Brother, George Orwell." *Twentieth Century*, March 1961, pp. 255–61.

Dyson, A. E. *The Crazy Fabric: Essays in Irony.* London: Macmillan Co., 1965.

Eliot, T. S. Preface to *The Dark Side of the Moon.* Charles Scribner's Sons, 1947.

Eliot, Mrs. T. S. [Valerie]. Letter to the Editor, "T. S. Eliot and 'Animal Farm': Reasons for Rejection." *The Times* (London), Jan. 6, 1969.

Elliott, George P. "A Failed Prophet." *Hudson Review*, X (Spring 1957), 149–54.

Empson, William. *The Gathering Storm.* London: Faber and Faber, 1940.

Fen, Elizaveta. "George Orwell's First Wife." *Twentieth Century*, Aug. 1960, pp. 115–26.

Fink, Howard. "Letter to the Editor." *Granta* (Cambridge University literary magazine), Apr. 1964, p. 23.

Fischer, Louis. *Men and Politics.* New York: Duell, Sloan and Pearce, 1941.

FitzGibbon, Constantine. *Random Thoughts of a Fascist Hyena.* London: Cassell and Co., 1963.

———. *Through the Minefield: An Autobiography.* London: Bodley Head, 1967.

Fixler, Michael. "George Orwell and the Instrument of Language." *Iowa English Yearbook*, Fall 1964, pp. 46–54.

Foot, Michael. *Aneurin Bevan*, Vol. 1: *1897–1945.* London: MacGibbon and Kee, 1962.

Forster, E. M. "George Orwell." *Two Cheers for Democracy.* London: Edward Arnold and Co. [1951].

France, Anatole. *Les Dieux Ont Soif.* Paris: Calmann-Lévy, 1912.

Fromm, Erich. "Afterword." *1984* by George Orwell. New York: New American Library, 1954.

Fyvel, T. R. "The Real Ilya Ehrenburg." *Tribune*, August 11, 1950, p. 16.

———. "Wingate, Orwell, and the 'Jewish Question.'" *Commentary*, Feb. 1951, pp. 137–44.

———. "George Orwell and Eric Blair: Glimpses of a Dual Life." *Encounter,* July 1959, pp. 60–65.

Geering, R. G. " 'Darkness at Noon' and '1984': A Comparative Study." *Australian Quarterly,* XXX (Sept. 1958), 90–96.

George, Daniel. "Approach and Arrival." *Observer* (London), Feb. 17, 1946.

George, W. L. *A Bed of Roses.* New York: Modern Library, 1919.

———. *Caliban.* London: Methuen and Co., 1920.

Gide, André. *Retour de l' U.R.S.S.* Paris: Gallimard, 1936.

Gissing, George. *Demos.* London: John Murray, 1908.

———. *New Grub Street.* New York: Modern Library, 1926.

Gleckner, Robert F. "1984 or 1948?" *College English,* XVIII (Nov. 1956), 95–99.

Glicksberg, Charles I. "The Literary Contribution of George Orwell." *Arizona Quarterly,* X (Autumn 1954), 234–45.

Goebbels, Joseph. *The Goebbels Diaries: 1942–1943.* Translated and edited by Louis P. Lochner. New York: Doubleday and Co., 1948.

Goldring, Douglas. *Marching With the Times: 1931–1946.* London: Nicholson and Watson [1947].

Green, John. "The Tyranny of an Idea: George Orwell's 'Nineteen-Eighty-Four.' " *Sixty one* (University of Leeds), V (Oct. 1964), 11–16.

Greenblatt, Stephen Jay. *Three Modern Satirists: Waugh, Orwell,* and *Huxley.* New Haven, Conn.: Yale University Press, 1965.

Greenwood, Walter. *Love on the Dole: A Tale of the Two Cities.* London: Jonathan Cape, Florin Edition, 1935.

Grigson, Geoffrey. *The Crest on the Silver.* London: Cresset Press, 1950.

Haldane, Charlotte. *Truth Will Out.* New York: Vanguard Press, 1950.

Hamilton, Kenneth M. "G. K. Chesterton and George Orwell: A Contrast in Prophecy." *Dalhousie Review,* XXXI (Autumn 1951), 198–205.

d'Harcourt, Pierre. *The Real Enemy.* London: Longmans, 1967.

Harris, Harold J. "Orwell's Essays and *1984.*" *Twentieth Century Literature,* IV (Jan. 1959), 154–61.

Hartley, Anthony. *A State of England.* New York: Harcourt, Brace and World, 1963.

Hartley, L. P. *Facial Justice.* London: Hamish Hamilton, 1960.

Heppenstall, Rayner. *Four Absentees.* London: Barrie and Rockliff, 1960.

———. *The Fourfold Tradition.* London: Barrie and Rockliff, 1961.

———. "The Shooting Stick." *Twentieth Century,* Apr. 1955, pp. 367–73.

Hicks, Granville. *Where We Came Out.* New York: Viking Press, 1954.

Highet, Gilbert. *A Clerk of Oxenford.* New York: Oxford University Press, 1954.

Hoellering, Franz. *The Defenders.* Boston: Little, Brown and Co., 1940.

Hoffer, Eric. *The Ordeal of Change.* New York: Harper and Row, 1963.

Hollis, Christopher. *A Study of George Orwell: The Man and His Works.* London: Hollis and Carter, 1956.

Hopkinson, Tom. *George Orwell*. Writers and their Work, no. 39. London: Longmans, Green and Co. for the British Council and the National Book League, 1953.

Horrabin, Winifred. "Where's George?" *The Plebs* (London), Apr. 1941, pp. 64–65.

Howe, Irving. *Orwell's* Nineteen Eighty-Four: *Text, Sources, Criticism*. New York: Harcourt, Brace and World, 1963.

———. "Orwell: History as Nightmare." *American Scholar*, XXV (Spring 1956), 193–207.

———. "The Fiction of Anti-Utopia." *New Republic*, Apr. 23, 1962.

———. "The Life of Trotsky." *New Republic*, March 21, 1964.

———. "The Culture of Modernism." *Commentary*, Nov. 1967, pp. 48–59.

Howe, Irving, and Coser, Lewis. *The American Communist Party*. New York: Frederick A. Praeger, 1962.

Hubbard, T. L. W. "Les Book-Clubs en Angleterre." *Mercure de France*, March 1939, pp. 346–55.

Hughes, Emrys. *Keir Hardie*. London: George Allen and Unwin, 1956.

de Huszar, George B. *The Intellectuals*. Glencoe, Ill.: Free Press, 1960.

Huxley, Aldous. *Antic Hay*. New York: George H. Doran Co., 1923.

———. *Brave New World*. New York: Harper and Bros. [1946].

———. *The World of Aldous Huxley*. Edited by Charles J. Rolo. New York: Grosset's Universal Library, 1947.

———. *Ape and Essence*. London: Chatto and Windus, 1951.

———. *Brave New World Revisited*. London: Chatto and Windus, 1959.

Hyams, Edward. *The New Statesman: The History of the First Fifty Years 1913–1963*. London: Longmans, Green and Co., 1963.

Hyde, Douglas. *I Believed*. London: William Heinemann, 1951.

Isherwood, Christopher. *Lions and Shadows: An Education in the Twenties*. Norfolk, Conn.: New Directions, 1947.

Joll, James. *Three Intellectuals in Politics*. New York: Pantheon Books, 1960.

Jones, Joseph. "Utopias as Dirge." *American Quarterly*, II (Fall 1950), 214–26.

Kateb, George. "The Road to *1984*." *Political Science Quarterly*, LXXXI (Dec. 1966), 564–80.

Kegel, Charles H. " 'Nineteen Eighty-Four': A Century of Ingsoc." *Notes and Queries*, X (Apr. 1963), 151–52.

Kendall, Walter. "David and Goliath." *Geste*, Oct. 27, 1960, unpaginated.

Keynes, J. M. "Letter to the Editor." *New Statesman and Nation*, Oct. 14, 1939.

King, Carlyle. "The Politics of George Orwell." *University of Toronto Quarterly*, XXVI (Oct. 1956), 79–91.

Kingsmill, Hugh. *The Poisoned Crown*. London: Eyre and Spottiswoode, 1944.

———. *The Dawn's Delay*. London: Eyre and Spottiswoode, 1948.

Kipling, Rudyard. *The Day's Work*. New York: Doubleday and McClure Co., 1898.

———. *A Diversity of Creatures*. London: Macmillan Co., 1917.

———. *Stalky & Co.* London: Macmillan Co., 1927.

———. *Something of Myself*. London: Macmillan Co., 1937.

Koestler, Arthur. *Spanish Testament*. London: Victor Gollancz, 1937.

———. *Scum of the Earth*. New York: Macmillan Co., 1941.

———. *Darkness at Noon*. Translated by Daphne Hardy. New York: Macmillan Co., 1941.

———. *The Yogi and the Commissar*. New York: Macmillan Co., 1945.

———. *Thieves in the Night*. New York: Macmillan Co., 1947.

———. *Arrow in the Blue*. New York: Macmillan Co., 1952.

———. *The Invisible Writing*. New York: Macmillan Co., 1954.

———. *The Trail of the Dinosaur and Other Essays*. London: Collins, 1955.

———. *The Lotus and the Robot*. New York: Macmillan Co., 1961.

———. "The Intelligentsia." *Partisan Review*, Summer 1944, pp. 265–77.

———. "London Letter." *Partisan Review*, July–Aug. 1947, pp. 341–45.

Kravchenko, Victor. *I Chose Freedom*. New York: Scribner's, 1946.

Kristol, Irving. "American Intellectuals and Foreign Policy." *Foreign Affairs*, XLV (July 1967), 594–609.

Krivitsky, Walter G. *In Stalin's Secret Service*. New York: Harper and Bros., 1939.

Krutch, Joseph Wood. "Way of the Modern." *Saturday Review*, Apr. 25, 1953.

Laski, Harold. "The Road to Wigan Pier." *Left News*, March 1937, 275–76.

———. "Pamphlets." *New Statesman and Nation*, Dec. 25, 1948, p. 573.

Leavis, Q. D. "The Literary Life Respectable: Mr. George Orwell." *Scrutiny*, IX (Sept. 1940), 173–76.

Lee, Robert A. *Orwell's Fiction*. Notre Dame, Ind.: University of Notre Dame Press, 1969.

Lehmann, John. *New Writing in England*. New York: Critics Group Press, 1939.

———. *The Whispering Gallery*. New York: Harcourt, Brace and Co., 1954.

———. *I Am My Brother*. New York: Reynal and Co., 1960.

———. *The Ample Proposition*. London: Eyre and Spottiswoode, 1966.

Lermontov, Mikhail. *A Hero of Our Time*. Moscow: Foreign Languages Publishing House, 1957.

LeRoy, Gaylord C. "A. F. 632 to 1984." *College English*, XII (Dec. 1950), 135–38.

Lewis, C. S. *Surprised by Joy*. New York: Harcourt, Brace and Co., 1955.

———. "Notes on the Way: George Orwell." *Time and Tide*, Jan. 8, 1955, 43–44.

Lewis, Wyndham. *The Writer and the Absolute*. London: Methuen and Co., 1952.

Lias, Godfrey. *I Survived*. London: Evans Bros., 1954.

Lief, Ruth Ann. *Homage to Oceania: The Prophetic Vision of George Orwell*. Columbus, Ohio: Ohio State University Press, 1969.

Lindbergh, Anne Morrow. *The Wave of the Future: A Confession of Faith*. New York: Harcourt, Brace and Co., 1940.

Lipset, Seymour. "American Intellectuals: Their Politics and Status." *Daedalus*, Summer 1959, pp. 460–86.

Locke, William J. *The Red Planet*. New York: John Lane and Co., 1917.

Lockhart, Robert H. B. *Retreat from Glory*. New York: G. P. Putnam's Sons, 1934.

London, Jack. *The People of the Abyss*. New York: Macmillan Co., 1903.

———. *The Iron Heel*. New York: Grayson Publishing Corp., 1948.

Lutman, Stephen. "Orwell's Patriotism." *Journal of Contemporary History*, II (Apr. 1967), 149–58.

Lyons, Eugene. *Assignment in Utopia*. New York: Harcourt, Brace and Co., 1937.

Lyons, John O. "George Orwell's Opaque Glass in *1984*." *Wisconsin Studies in Contemporary Literature*, II (Fall 1961), 39–46.

Macartney, W. F. R. *Walls Have Mouths*. London: Victor Gollancz, 1936.

Macdonald, Dwight. *Henry Wallace: The Man and the Myth*. New York: Vanguard Press, 1948.

———. "The British Genius." *Partisan Review*, March–Apr. 1942, pp. 166–69.

———. "Russomania in England." *Politics*, Nov. 1944, p. 295.

———. "Varieties of Political Experience." *New Yorker*, March 28, 1959, pp. 132–47.

Macdonell, A. G. *England, Their England*. London: Macmillan Co., 1957.

McDowell, M. Jennifer. "George Orwell: Bibliographical Addenda." *Bulletin of Bibliography*, XXIII (Jan.–Apr. 1963), 224–29; XXIV (May–Aug. 1963), 19–24; XXIV (Sept.–Dec. 1963), 36–40.

———. "1984 and Soviet Reality." University of California Graduate Journal, I (Fall 1962), 12–19.

McNair, John. "George Orwell." *Socialist Leader*, Jan. 28, 1950, p. 3.

Maddison, Michael. "At the Crossroads of Ideology." *Geste*, Oct. 27, 1960, unpaginated.

———. "1984: A Burnhamite Fantasy." *Political Quarterly*, XXXII (Jan.–March 1961), 71–79.

Mair, John. *Never Come Back*. London: Victor Gollancz, 1941.

Malia, Martin. "What Is the Intelligentsia?" *Daedalus*, Summer 1960, pp. 441–58.

Mander, John. *The Writer and Commitment*. London: Secker and Warburg, 1961.

———. *Great Britain or Little England*. London: Penguin Books, 1963.

————. "George Orwell's Politics." *Contemporary Review*, Jan. 1960, pp. 32–36; Feb. 1960, pp. 113–19.

Mann, Erika. *The Lights Go Down*. London: Secker and Warburg, 1940.

Martin, Kingsley. *Harold Laski*. London: Victor Gollancz, 1953.

————. *Father Figures*. London: Hutchinson and Co., 1966.

————. *Editor: A Second Volume of Autobiography*. London: Hutchinson of London, 1968.

————. "Russia in Uniform." *New Statesman and Nation*, May 1, 1937, pp. 739–40.

————. "Soviet Satire." *New Statesman and Nation*, Sept. 8, 1945, pp. 165–66.

————. "Morals and Politics." *New Statesman and Nation*, June 15, 1946, p. 423.

Matthews, Herbert. "Homage to Orwell." *Nation*, Dec. 27, 1952, pp. 597–99.

Maugham, Robin. *The 1946 Ms.* London: War Facts Press, 1943.

Meisel, James H. *Counterrevolution: How Revolutions Die*. New York: Atherton Press, 1966.

de Mendelssohn, Peter. *The Age of Churchill:* Vol. I: *1874–1911*. London: Thames and Hudson, 1961.

Miles, Hamish. "Coal and Caste." *New Statesman and Nation*, May 1, 1937, pp. 724, 726.

Miller, Cecil. "Orwell and Literature." *American Scholar*, XXVI (Winter 1956–57), 128.

Miller, Henry. "The Art of Fiction." *Paris Review*, VII (Summer–Fall 1962), 129–59.

Miller, Walter M., Jr. *A Canticle for Leibowitz*. Philadelphia: J. B. Lippincott Co., 1960.

Mirsky, Dmitri. *The Intelligentsia of Great Britain*. Translated by Alec Brown. New York: Covici Friede, 1935.

Mirsky, Vera T. *The Cup of Astonishment*. London: Cresset Press, 1944.

Mitford, Jessica. *Hons and Rebels*. London: Victor Gollancz, 1960.

Moorehead, Alan. *The Russian Revolution*. New York: Harper and Bros., 1958.

Morgenthau, Hans. *Dilemmas of Politics*. Chicago: University of Chicago Press, 1958.

————. "Truth and Power." *New Republic*, Nov. 26, 1966, pp. 8–14.

Morris, John. "Some Are More Equal Than Others: A note on George Orwell." *Pleasures of New Writing*. Edited by John Lehmann. London: John Lehmann [1952].

Morris, William. *News from Nowhere*. New York: Random House, Nonesuch Press, 1934.

Morrison, Herbert. *Autobiography*. London: Odhams Press, 1960.

Morton, A. L. *The English Utopia*. London: Lawrence and Wishart, 1952.

Muggeridge, Malcolm. *The Thirties*. London: Hamish Hamilton, 1940.

Munro, H. H. (Saki). *When William Came: A Story of London Under the Hohenzollerns.* London: John Lane, 1914.

Murry, John Middleton. "Orwell and Connolly." *Adelphi,* July–Sept. 1946, pp. 165–71.

Murry, Mary M. *To Keep Faith.* London: Constable and Co., 1959.

Nichols, Beverley. *The Sweet and Twenties.* London: Weidenfeld and Nicolson, 1958.

Nicolson, Harold. "Marginal Comment." *Spectator,* Aug. 29, 1947, p. 268.

Nisbet, Robert A. "What Is an Intellectual?" *Commentary,* Dec. 1965, pp. 93–101.

Nott, Kathleen. "Orwell's *Nineteen Eighty Four.*" *Listener,* Oct. 31, 1963, pp. 687–88.

O'Brien, Conor Cruise. *Writers and Politics.* New York: Random House, Pantheon Books, 1964.

O'Casey, Sean. *Sunset and Evening Star.* New York: Macmillan Co., 1954.

Ogden, C. K. *The System of Basic English.* New York: Harcourt, Brace and Co., 1934.

Opie, Iona and Peter. *The Oxford Book of Nursery Rhymes.* Oxford: Clarendon Press, 1969.

Panter-Downs, Mollie. "Letter from London." *New Yorker,* Feb. 19, 1955, p. 84.

Paul, Leslie. *Angry Young Man.* London: Faber and Faber, 1951.

Payne, Robert. *The Rise and Fall of Stalin.* New York: Simon and Schuster, 1965.

Pelling, Henry. *America and the British Left.* London: Adam and Charles Black, 1956.

———. *The British Communist Party.* New York: Macmillan Co., 1958.

———. *Modern Britain: 1885–1955.* Edinburgh: Thomas Nelson and Sons [1960].

Peters, R. H. "Did You Hear That?" *Listener,* Sept. 22, 1955, p. 453.

Phelan, Jim. *Jail Journey.* London: Secker and Warburg, 1940.

Pitter, Ruth. "Memories of George Orwell." B.B.C. broadcast script, 1956. Orwell Archive, University College, London.

Polanyi, Michael. *Beyond Nihilism.* Cambridge: Cambridge University Press, 1960.

Porteus, Hugh Gordon. "Nights Out in the Thirties." *Spectator,* Sept. 2, 1960, pp. 342–44.

Postgate, Raymond. *The Life of George Lansbury.* London: Longmans, Green and Co., 1951.

———. "A Book to Make You Sick." *Tribune,* March 14, 1941, pp. 14–15.

Potts, Paul. *Dante Called You Beatrice.* London: Eyre and Spottiswoode, 1960.

Powell, Anthony. "George Orwell: A Memoir." *Atlantic Monthly,* Oct. 1967, pp. 62–68.

Prescott, Orville. *In My Opinion.* New York: Bobbs-Merrill Co., 1952.

Pritchett, V. S. "The Spanish Tragedy." *New Statesman and Nation,* Apr. 30, 1938, pp. 734, 736.

———. "Books in General." *New Statesman and Nation,* March 1, 1941, p. 216.

———. "George Orwell." *New Statesman and Nation,* Jan. 28, 1950, p. 96.

———. "A Pamphleteer." *New Statesman and Nation,* Oct. 28, 1950, p. 388.

Prittie, Terence. *Germans Against Hitler.* London: Hutchinson and Co., 1964.

R[?], V. "Orwell—The Humanist." *Freedom,* Feb. 4, 1950, pp. 2–3.

Rahv, Philip. "The Unfuture of Utopia." *Partisan Review,* July, 1949, pp. 743–49.

Rauschning, Hermann. *The Revolution of Nihilism.* New York: Alliance Book Corp., Longmans, Green and Co., 1939.

Raymond, John, ed. *The Baldwin Age.* London: Eyre and Spottiswoode, 1960.

Reade, Winwood. *The Martyrdom of Man.* New York: E. P. Dutton, 1923.

Rees, Goronwy. *A Bundle of Sensations.* London: Chatto and Windus, 1960.

Rees, Richard. *George Orwell: Fugitive from the Camp of Victory.* London: Secker and Warburg, 1961.

———. *A Theory of My Time.* London: Secker and Warburg, 1963.

———. "George Orwell." Scots Chronicle [Burns Chronicle and Club Directory], [XXVI] (1951), 7–14.

Rice, Elmer. *A Voyage to Purilia.* New York: Cosmopolitan Book Corp., 1930.

Richards, D. "Four Utopias." *Slavonic and East European Review,* XL (1961–62), 220–28.

Richter, Eugene. *Pictures of the Socialistic Future.* Translated by Henry Wright. London: Swan Sonnenschein and Co., 1907.

Rieff, Philip. "George Orwell and the Post-Liberal Imagination." *Kenyon Review,* Winter 1954, pp. 49–70.

Rogers, Daniel. "'Look Back in Anger' to George Orwell." *Notes and Queries,* Aug. 1962, pp. 310–11.

Rosenfeld, Isaac. *An Age of Enormity.* Cleveland: World Publishing Co., 1962.

Rousset, David. *L'Univers concentrat'onnaire.* Paris: Edition du Pavois, 1946. Published in English as *A World Apart.* Translated by Yvonne Moyse and Roger Senhouse. London: Secker and Warburg, 1951.

Rowse, A. L. *All Souls and Appeasement.* London: Macmillan Co., 1961.

Russell, Bertrand. *Freedom and Organization.* New York: W. W. Norton and Co., 1934.

———. *Power: A New Social Analysis.* New York: W. W. Norton and Co., 1938.

———. *Portraits from Memory.* London: George Allen and Unwin, 1956.

Russian Institute, Columbia University, ed. *The Anti-Stalin Campaign and International Communism.* New York: Columbia University Press, 1956.

Samuel, Herbert Lewis (Viscount). *An Unknown Land.* London: George Allen and Unwin, 1942.

Samuels, Stuart. "The Left Book Club." *Journal of Contemporary History,* I (n.d. 1966), 65–86.

Sassoon, Siegfried. *The Memoirs of George Sherston.* New York: Literary Guild of America, 1937.

Schlesinger, Arthur. "Orwell's Strange World of *1984.*" *Life,* July 25, 1949.

Schwarzschild, Leopold. *World in Trance.* New York: L. B. Fischer Publishing Corp., 1942.

Serge, Victor. *Mémoires d'un Révolutionnaire de 1901 à 1940.* Paris: Editions du Seuil, 1951.

Shils, Edward. "The Intellectuals: I. Great Britain." *Encounter,* Apr. 1955, pp. 5–16.

Shirer, William L. *The Rise and Fall of the Third Reich: A History of Nazi Germany.* New York: Simon and Schuster, 1959.

Shute, Nerina. *We Mixed Our Drinks: The Story of a Generation.* London: Jarrolds, 1946.

Sillen, Samuel. "Maggot of the Month." *Masses and Mainstream,* II (Aug. 1949), 8.

Silone, Ignazio. *The School for Dictators.* Translated from the Italian by William Weaver. New York: Atheneum, 1963.

Sissons, Michael, and French, Philip. *Age of Austerity.* London: Hodder and Stoughton, 1963.

Slater, Humphrey. *The Heretics.* New York: Harcourt, Brace and Co., 1947.

Slater, Joseph. "The Fictional Values of *1984.*" *Essays in Literary History Presented to Milton French.* Edited by Rudolph Kirk and C. F. Main. New Brunswick, N.J.: Rutgers University Press [1960], pp. 249–64.

Smith, Stevie. *The Holiday.* London: Chapman and Hall, 1949.

Souvarine, Boris. "Cauchemar en U.R.S.S." *Revue de Paris,* July 1, 1937, pp. 137–70.

Spender, Stephen. *The Backward Son.* London: Hogarth Press, 1940.

———. *World Within World.* New York: Harcourt, Brace and Co., 1948.

———. *The Creative Element.* New York; British Book Center, 1954.

Stansky, Peter, and Abrahams, William. *Journey to the Frontier: Two Roads to the Spanish Civil War.* Boston: Little, Brown and Co., 1966.

———. *The Unknown Orwell.* London: Constable and Co., 1972.

Strachey, John. *The Coming Struggle for Power.* New York: Modern Library, 1935.

———. *The Frontiers.* New York: Random House, 1952.

———. *The Strangled Cry.* London: The Bodley Head, 1962.

Swingler, Randall. "The Right to Free Expression (Annotated by George Orwell)." *Polemic*, V (Sept.–Oct. 1946), 45–53.

Symons, Julian. *The Thirties*. London: Cresset Press, 1960.

———. "George Orwell." *Tribune*, Jan. 27, 1950, p. 23.

———. "Orwell, a Reminiscence." *London Magazine*, Sept. 1963, pp. 35–49.

Thale, Jerome. "Orwell's Modest Proposal." *Critical Quarterly*, IV (Winter 1962), 367–68.

Thomas, Edward M. *Orwell*. London: Oliver and Boyd, 1965.

Thompson, Edward P., ed. *Out of Apathy*. London: Stevens and Sons, 1960.

Thompson, Frank H., Jr. "Orwell's Image of the Man of Good Will." *College English*, XXII (Jan. 1961), 235–40.

The Times (London). "German Atrocities in Russia," Dec. 17, 1943.

The Times (London) *Literary Supplement*. "Power and Corruption," June 10, 1949.

———. "The Eccentric Idealist." Aug. 31, 1956.

de la Torre, Lillian. "Let's Hope It's an Illusion." *New Republic*, Oct. 1, 1962, p. 21.

Toynbee, Philip. *Friends Apart*. London: MacGibbon and Kee, 1954.

———. "Passionate Sanity." *Observer* (London), Dec. 3, 1950.

———. "Common Sense." *Observer* (London), Sept. 2, 1956.

Trilling, Lionel. *The Middle of the Journey*. London: Penguin Books, 1963.

———. "Orwell on the Future." *New Yorker*, June 18, 1949, p. 78.

———. "Was Orwell Shrewd. . . ." *Nation*, Jan. 24, 1952, pp. 597–99.

Trotsky, Leon. *The Revolution Betrayed*. Translated by Max Eastman. Garden City, N.Y.: Doubleday, Doran and Co., 1937.

Upward, Edward. *In the Thirties*. London: Heinemann, 1962.

Urofsky, Melvin J. "Truth and Power: A Rejoinder to Hans Morgenthau." *New Republic*, Dec. 17, 1966, p. 15.

Vanocur, Sander. "George Orwell, a Cricketer's Christian." *Reporter*, Jan. 24, 1957, pp. 43–46.

Viereck, Peter. *Shame and Glory of the Intellectuals: Babbitt, Jr. Vs. the Rediscovery of Values*. Boston: Beacon Press, 1953.

Voorhees, Richard J. *The Paradox of George Orwell*. Purdue University Studies (Humanities Series). West Lafayette, Ind., 1961.

———. "Orwell as Critic." *Prairie Schooner*, XXVIII (Summer 1954), 105–12.

———. "George Orwell: Rebellion and Responsibility." *South Atlantic Quarterly*, LIII (Oct. 1954), 556–65.

———. "Nineteen Eighty-Four: No Failure of Nerve." *College English*, XVIII (Nov., 1956), 101–2.

Wadsworth, Frank. "Orwell as a Novelist: The Early Work." *University of Kansas City Review*, XXII (Winter 1955), 93–99.

———. "Orwell as a Novelist: The Middle Period." *University of Kansas City Review,* XXII (Spring 1956), 189–94.

———. "Orwell's Later Work." *University of Kansas City Review,* XXII (Summer 1956), 285–90.

Wain, John. *Sprightly Running.* London: Macmillan Co., 1962.

———. "The Last of George Orwell." *Twentieth Century,* Jan. 1954, pp. 71–78.

———. "Orwell in Perspective." *New World Writing,* Twelfth Mentor Selections. New York: New American Library, 1957, pp. 84–96.

Walsh, Chad. *From Utopia to Nightmare.* New York: Harper and Row, 1962.

Walsh, James. "George Orwell." *The Marxist Quarterly,* III (Jan. 1956).

Walter, Nicolas. "George Orwell: an Accident in Society." *Anarchy 8* (London), Oct., 1961, pp. 246–55.

Warburg, Frederic. *An Occupation for Gentlemen.* London: Hutchinson, 1959.

Warburg, F[rederic] J. "George Orwell." *The Bookseller* (London), Feb. 11, 1950, p. 200.

Waugh, Evelyn. *Love Among the Ruins.* London: Chapman and Hall, 1953.

Webb, Beatrice. *Diaries: 1912–1924.* Edited by Margaret I. Cole. London: Longmans, Green and Co., 1952.

Weintraub, Stanley. *The Last Great Cause: The Intellectuals and the Spanish Civil War.* New York: Weybright and Talley, 1968.

Weissberg, Alexander. *Conspiracy of Silence.* Translated by Edward Fitzgerald. London: Hamish Hamilton, 1952.

Wells, H. G. *The Island of Dr. Moreau.* Garden City, N.Y.: Garden City Publishing Co., 1896.

———. *When the Sleeper Wakes.* New York: Harper and Bros., 1899.

———. *Tono-Bungay.* London: Macmillan Co., 1909.

———. *The New Machiavelli.* New York: Duffield and Co., 1910.

———. *Men Like Gods.* London: Cassell and Co., 1923.

———. *The Dream.* London: Jonathan Cape, 1924.

———. *The Shape of Things to Come.* New York: Macmillan, 1936.

———. *The New World Order.* New York: Alfred Knopf, 1940.

Werth, Alexander. *France in Ferment.* New York: Harper and Bros. [1935].

West, Anthony. "Hidden Damage." *New Yorker,* Jan. 28, 1956, pp. 98–104.

Wheeler-Bennett, John W. *King George VI: His Life and Reign.* New York: St. Martin's Press, 1958.

Wicker, Brian. "An Analysis of Newspeak." *Blackfriars,* June 1962, pp. 272–85.

Williams, Raymond. *Culture and Society.* London: Chatto and Windus, 1958.

———. *George Orwell.* New York: Viking Press, 1971.

Willison, Ian. "Orwell's Bad Good Books." *Twentieth Century,* Apr. 1955, pp. 354–66.

Wilson, Edmund. *To the Finland Station.* New York: Doubleday and Co., 1940.

———. "Animal Farm." *New Yorker,* Sept. 7, 1946, p. 97.

Wollheim, Richard. "Orwell Reconsidered." *Partisan Review,* Winter 1960, pp. 82–97.

Wood, Neal. *Communism and British Intellectuals.* New York: Columbia University Press, 1959.

Woodcock, George. *The Writer and Politics.* London: Porcupine Press, 1948.

———. *Anarchism: A History of Libertarian Ideas and Movements.* Cleveland: Meridian Books, 1962.

———. *The Crystal Spirit: A Study of George Orwell.* Boston: Little, Brown and Co., 1966.

———. "Five Who Fear the Future." *New Republic,* Apr. 16, 1956, pp. 17–19.

———. "Utopias in Negative." *Sewanee Review,* LXIV (Winter 1956), 81–97.

Woodhouse, C. M. "Animal Farm." *The Times* (London) *Literary Supplement,* Aug. 6, 1954, pp. xxx–xxxi.

Woolf, Leonard. *Hunting the Highbrow.* London: Hogarth Press, 1927.

———. *Sowing.* London: Hogarth Press, 1960.

Woolf, Virginia. *A Letter to a Young Poet.* Hogarth Letters No. 8. London: Hogarth Press, 1932.

———. "The Leaning Tower." *Folios of New Writing* (London), Autumn 1940, pp. 11–33.

Yorks, Samuel. "George Orwell: Seer Over His Shoulder." *Bucknell Review,* IX (March 1960), 32–45.

Young, G. M. *Stanley Baldwin.* London: Rupert Hart-Davis, 1952.

Zamiatin, Eugene. *We.* Translated by Gregory Zilboorg. New York: E. P. Dutton and Co., 1959.

Zeke, Zoltan G., and White, William. "George Orwell: A Selected Bibliography." *Bulletin of Bibliography,* XXIII (May–Aug. 1961), 110–14.

———. "Orwelliana." *Bulletin of Bibliography,* XXIII (Sept.–Dec. 1961), 140–44; XXIII (Jan.–Apr. 1962), 166–68.

INDEX

Steinhoff

George Orwell and the
origins of 1984